TRANSCENDING BLACKNESS

TRANSCENDING
BLACKNESS

≡

From the New Millennium Mulatta

to the Exceptional Multiracial

RALINA L. JOSEPH

DUKE UNIVERSITY PRESS

DURHAM AND LONDON   2013

© 2013 Duke University Press

All rights reserved

Printed in the United States of America on acid-free paper ∞

Designed by Heather Hensley

Typeset in Whitman by Tseng Information Systems, Inc.

Library of Congress Cataloging-in-Publication Data appear
on the last printed page of this book.

FOR JJ, TJ, AND NV

CONTENTS

FROM BIRACIAL TO MULTIRACIAL TO MIXED-RACE TO CRITICAL MIXED-RACE STUDIES

In the autumn of 1992, I arrived at the oldest dorm on Brown University's campus, a stately, crumbling edifice complete with ivy-covered walls and cinder-block lined rooms that rebelled against my efforts to tack up my leftie political posters and batik-print tapestry. I was a nervous kid outfitted in meticulously ripped jeans, tan Birkenstocks, and a lingering fear that an admissions officer was going to pop out at any moment and announce that there had been a big mistake: I, the daughter of a secretary and a mechanic, really was not allowed into this hallowed Ivy League institution. Class and race, and my exhausting efforts to avoid talking about both, structured my life. While class remained a more-easily submergible entity in neobohemian, grunge-accented Providence of the early 1990s, the changing signs and signals of race glowed and blinked like my own personal fluorescent sign. I worried that my racially ambiguous but clearly nonwhite looks made me hypervisible, and before going to college I bobbed and weaved the ubiquitous "what are you?" questions, to save myself from having to reveal what I shrugged off as my race story.

My efforts to remain race neutral were supported by my utter lack of language to begin to chip away at the race question. Before college I had never uttered "multiracial." "Mixed" was the term we used inside my suburban Virginia house and "biracial" seemed popular with outsiders referring to me. But even within the confines of my immediate family, those terms were not my own: they were monoracially applied descriptors that did not quite match up with my interior racialized self. At Brown I found myself embraced by the vibrant community of students of color and given the language to understand that my unique racialization was not all that special, a revelation that was a complete and total relief. I soon learned of the term *multiracial* as an "us" term, one applied by mixed-race people in the process of self-identification. To me it quickly meant community; it meant not having to define myself further; it meant having a safe space to collectively articulate my frustration with the outside world's confusion about my phenotype. As a first-semester first-year confronted with the new-to-me term "multiracial," I embraced it immediately. At seventeen, I could not have imagined that that word would enter my daily, even hourly, vocabulary over the next four years at college. In the United States during the twenty-first century, racialized labels are just as multiple, contentious, and slippery as they were during the twentieth century, but for me, that new word, "multiracial," and that alone, felt just perfect. Just as Stuart Hall became black in Jamaica of the 1960s with the advent of Black Nationalism in the United States, I became multiracial in New England of the 1990s with the advent of the multiracial student movement on my liberal college campus.[1] I was privately mixed for the first seventeen years of my life until I publically came out as multiracial.

My initiation into the world of multiraciality came about at the Third World Center (TWC) whose moniker bore its 1960s activist roots. There I learned of the Brown Organization of Multiracial and Biracial Students (BOMBS), a group that some student leaders had started two years earlier. When Brown's paradigm-shifting minority student orientation, the Third World Transition Program (TWTP), asked participants to break out into racial affinity group sessions, a number of multiracial first-years had felt split about where to go. So they created their own multiracial affinity group, which eventually became BOMBS. When I was first introduced to the group I remember immediately loving the implied destruction in the group's name, which was so counter to the other blandly multicultural student group names I would come to be familiar with, such as, "prism" or "mosaic." As my coming into a multiracial consciousness did nothing less than explode my earlier attempts at racial neutrality, BOMBS resonated with my mixed-racial epistemology.

We modeled our organization after the university's existing racial support and advocacy student groups, such as the Organization of United African Peoples (OUAP), the Asian American Students Association (AASA), and the Latin-American Students Organization (LASO), which modeled themselves after traditional civil rights groups. BOMBS meetings took place in the warm embrace of the TWC, in community with other students-of-color groups. In order to populate our meetings in those early pre-email days, BOMBS members rounded up recruits by official means, including posting fliers for the group around the campus cafeterias and unofficially by slyly approaching the racially ambiguous dormmate down the hall. In September of 1991, a year before I arrived at Brown, BOMBS put out its first flier:[2]

BOMBS!
Brown Organization of Multi- and Biracial Students

This is an organization especially designed for any and all persons who have ever felt left out or marginalized by members of groups to which they partly or wholly belong. Our organization is intended as a support group for bi/multiracial or multicultural people who have in the past been forced to "choose" between the different races and cultures that are parts of their identities.

In the past, we have been ignored and treated as though we were invisible, solely because we have always been defined in terms of OTHER people. NO MORE. The reason why our people have been ignored throughout history is because there has never been any sort of political base or forum from which to make our voices heard and to raise society's awareness of our existence. Presently, organizations like ours have been springing up at college campuses NATIONWIDE. Why? Because our numbers are growing. With the absence of anti-miscegenation laws since 1967, and the consequences thereof, THERE ARE MORE OF US THAN EVER BEFORE. Even the U.S. government has been forced to sit up and take notice of us, as they are being pressured to include us as a separate category on the year 2000 census forms.

Why do we say "our people"? Because, like members of other recognized racial groups in this country, our people DO have a common experience from which to draw unity and solidarity. Not only do we feel the same racism from the white majority as do our other Third World brothers and sisters, but we get it from them as well. We refuse to sit by and be ignored any longer. We are the invisible minority within a minority, but this is about to CHANGE.

WE EXIST. WE ARE HERE AMONG YOU.

WE ARE A POLITICAL PRESSURE COOKER ABOUT TO EXPLODE.

join us.

1st ORGANIZATIONAL MEETING:

SUNDAY, SEPTEMBER 22, 7:00 PM

1ST FLOOR OF THE TWC.

SEE YOU THERE.

The "we," the "us," the "our," the all caps were intoxicating to me, and to my cohort, a newly formed group of multiracial subjects. Both idealism and budding militancy were apparent. When I showed the flier from September 1991 to BOMBS members in 2009, they told me that its dramatic "old-school" style sounded markedly different from their own less politicized rhetoric. We were a first-generation movement and, as such, we were emphatic about defining ourselves with each other and against "whole" race, or monoracially identified people. We used what was even then old-fashioned language of oppositionality to stake a claim of victim status. We believed our multiracial identification was new, radical, and incendiary. Later I learned that various multiracial peoples had indeed collaborated, and colluded, in other places and times. For example, elite mixed-race people, deemed variously "black," "mulatto," or "colored" by white society, helped cement African American color and class distinctions by creating a "beige-ocracy," to use the word of the founding multiracial studies historian Paul Spickard.[3]

But this type of a privileged legacy was not apparent to us, those born in the early 1970s to race-traitor parents just a handful of years after the *Loving v. Virginia* decision decriminalized interracial marriage in 1967. BOMBS's first newsletter bears evidence of this particular history and our sense that we were pioneers:

> If a multiracial organization gets off the ground, it has the potential to be very powerful. We know that there are a lot of us out there, but the problem has always been that we have never identified ourselves as a separate group. We have always been either in limbo or forced to choose sides. Hasn't it always been hard for you, multiracial friend, to define your own identity because others felt obligated to choose it for

you? No more. This organization is important because it will allow us to have a separate space for multiracials, where we can define ourselves in terms of ourselves, and not in terms of other groups. What we need are committed people willing to stick together and carve a niche for ourselves at this university so that our voices can be heard. Previous attempts at starting and maintaining similar organizations in the past have failed, but only because of lack of support or commitment. But we know that you're all out there (we've seen you). Don't just wish us luck. Come join, bond—unite!

Reading these words so many years later, I can see how this racially provocative organization spoke so eloquently to kids like me, the multiracially awkward soul wading through late adolescence in the early 1990s. One phrase that particularly jumps out to me is "we've seen you." I wonder now: Is it an observation? A lure? A threat? A wink from one insider to another? The writers assumed that we racial outsiders shared multiracial pain and exclusion and the concomitant desire to become visible, a desire to become racially legible, named, and claimed. To exchange status as "them" for "us." Their rhetoric asserted that group identity alone would create a space for our support and resistance.

These two documents from the 1991–92 school year represent the very beginning of BOMBS. They were the founding documents that I pored over as a first-year. I joined and began attending weekly meetings, later planning those meetings and leading the organization forward. As multiracial student activists, we were struck by the sense that we were doing something new and different in the very old world of race. In BOMBS I found a community of fellow self-described racial outsiders. Regulars tended to be people like my late-teenage self, whose self-identity was bound up in those three little words, not a romantic "I love you," but an incredulous "what are you?" Through conversations at BOMBS I understood that I didn't have to answer that question the way the asker intended. That I could turn the question around on my interrogator: why do you want to know? That I could identify in an unsatisfyingly nebulous way. Although I never personally described myself as "human" or "American" as some of my fellow BOMBS members defiantly did, I gave annoyingly nebulous answers such as "woman of color" that allowed me to provide a politicized response and yet avoid laying bare my personal history. I relished being able to resist "what are you?," which to me was akin to avoiding opening a vein to the genealogy that might logically explain my oddly racialized looks. Nestled within the protective cocoon of the TWC, BOMBS allowed me the space to resist racialization by performing a multiracial identity.

Resist and perform I did! Multiracialism simply obsessed me at Brown. I read, discussed, wrote about, and challenged everything and anything having to do with mixed-raciality. In my sophomore year, I became one of the second sets of co-chairs of BOMBS. I hosted forums such as "Hair Issues," a deliberation for women of color on the relationship between gender, racial authenticity, and hair. Not to be outdone by traditional student race groups, we began Multiracial Heritage Week. We brought mixed-race speakers, professionally multiracial folks, such as the journalist Lisa Jones, the author and the daughter of the African American writer and activist Amiri Barka (Leroi Jones), and the white, Jewish writer Hettie Jones; academics, such as the philosopher Naomi Zack; and comedians, such as Amy Hill. Intrigued by the vast number of mixed-race women at Brown who did not necessarily identify with the term *multiracial* or even each other, I worked with Sachi Cunningham, my friend and one of the founders of BOMBS, to create *Mixed Girls*, a documentary that examined mixed-race women's perceptions of and reactions to their own multiraciality.[4] I became the undergraduate teaching assistant for an anthropology course called "Growing Up Ethnic and Multicultural" and co-designed the curriculum for a Group Independent Study Project, "Multiraciality in the United States," where we examined the "multiracial movement's" founding texts from the late 1980s to early 1990s.

While in the early days of BOMBS we took our political cues from civil rights and racial nationalist groups, we took our naming and identity cues from authors in the emerging multiracial movement, many of whom identified as mixed-race, and all of whom distanced themselves from past work pathologizing interracial relationships and multiracial people. In the early 1990s, we read the historians Paul Spickard's *Mixed Blood* (1989) and F. James Davis's *Who Is Black?* (1991), the psychologist Maria Root's anthology *Racially Mixed People in America* (1992), and the philosopher Naomi Zack's *Race and Mixed Race* (1994). The most influential of these scholars to the multiracial movement was Root, who has argued vehemently that mixed-race people have a nearly constitutional right to self-identify and even deserve their own bill of rights.[5] With a new body of work in multiracial studies came the choice of terminology not frequently in circulation before: "multiracial," and then, following a similar movement of scholarship in the United Kingdom, "mixed-race." As a first- and second-year college student, I found these books thrilling because they defended, named, and historicized my own existence.

Mixed-race was the object of my personal, political, and academic study—a full-blown preoccupation. I learned as much as I could about the history, literature, and racialization of mixed-race folks. Through BOMBS, my haven of the TWC, TWTP, all of the various programs supporting students of color, and my coursework in American civilization, then Afro American (now Africana) studies, semiotics, literature history, and sociology. I also learned about larger questions of race, class, gender, sexuality, and, most importantly, power. I learned that racialized choice, a key value of the multiracial movement, was not an option for most, while racialized conscription, which we special mixies fought against, was. I learned about structural racism and how to explore the lived realities of race, from differential rates of homeownership, healthcare, and high school graduation rates, among other measures. Consequently, I soon found that questions of power were largely absent from early multiracial movement literature. I found myself questioning: what happened after we created our own terms? Outside of fulfilling one's own self-identity desires or sating the curiosities of onlookers, what does a term that provides an "accurate" account of "what mixes?" or "what percentages?" reveal? What happens after the missing story is told, or the incorrect story is righted? What happens after we join the table? And most importantly, were we reinforcing the racial order rather than blowing it up?

These budding questions converged in my senior year at Brown when I wrote a thesis on the representations of a cross-section of mixed-race women in magazine advertisements, a study that drew on the multiracial, interdisciplinary track I had been pursuing. I identified two dialectics of representation, "crossover/spice" and "beauty/beast" and argued that these advertisements overwhelmingly sought to categorize and exoticize mixed-race women, demonstrating discomfort with miscegenation and multiracials themselves. Even though my study, in retrospect, was overly ambitious, methodologically questionable, and incoherently written in places (in my attempt to sound similar to the theory I fought to comprehend), researching and writing in a new scholarly area was so exciting that I realized that I wanted to make a career out of my questioning. I wanted to be an academic who studied multiraciality.

Over the course of my four years at Brown I learned that the "what are you?" question that so plagued me and that I initially identified as solely the lot of multiracial folks like me, was actually the lot of all people who did not appear to belong, whether through race, gender, sexuality, or ability status. This idea has percolated more over the years, as has the notion of cross-identity, or perhaps more specifically to use the words of Stuart Hall, "cross-identification connections."[6] I've been traveling from the questions "who is mixed-race?" to "what does mixed-race mean?" to "how do people use mixed-race?" to "why is it important to name, understand, and unpack mixed race?" These questions led to the topic that became a central concern of this book: the attempted silencing and demeaning of the blackness in mixed-race blackness, a pernicious dynamic that did not appear to pollute all representations of the nonwhite aspects of multiracial Asian Americans, Latinos, and American Indians.

In my final year as an undergraduate I became disillusioned with the utopian promises of multiracial studies and activism. They seemed so focused solely on naming and claiming a multiracial identity, and that was no longer enough for me. Things just seemed more complicated than that. One moment of revelation came to me while chatting with a white woman who attended a BOMBS public event: I was alarmed to hear that she came to learn how to obtain a nonblack identity for her mixed-race African American preschool-aged daughter. I was even more alarmed later to learn that she was not alone; the political scientist Kim Williams investigated mothers just like this on the nationwide scale. Williams found that the leaders and participants of multiracial advocacy groups were overwhelmingly white women married to black men. The most famous of these women is Susan Graham, founder of Project RACE (Reclassify All Children Equally), who led the fight for the multiracial category on the census, and even had her young son testify before Congress, so that he did not have to identify as black.[7]

Graham and other well-known spokespeople in the multiracial moment identified multiracialness as the only possible form of racial identification, which simultaneously pathologized blackness, apparently unrepentantly. From this type of multiracial activism, and not from the type of minority-based community articulated by BOMBS, sprang the so-called 1990s-era multiracial agenda, with the first item being the establishment of a new census category. Arguments for color blindness and against race-based measures such as affirmative action, which began to be dismantled across the country immediately after I graduated from college, accompanied this embrace of "the multiracial cause."[8] For example, in the mid-to-late 1990s, Newt Gingrich, the former Republican Speaker of the House, aligned himself with a so-called multiracial cause, and supported such measures as the addition of a "multiracial" category on the 2000 U.S. Census, which was, much to the chagrin of multiracial activists, defeated in lieu of a "mark one or more" option. Because of these strange collaborations I began questioning the politicians', the media's, and even my own embrace of multiracialism. Was love of mixed-race people really love, or was it a disguised hatred of monoracial African Americans, a form of coded antiblack racism?

The antiblack racism in the multiracial movement from the 1990s did not fit with my multiracial college activism, and yet it stuck with me. It unsettled me to understand how politicians and the media manipulated multiracialism into an alignment of "my people" with the politics of the Far Right. Understanding the split dividing national multiracial advocacy groups from college-based activists helped me see why some of my closest friends around the country, who were mixed black and white and who grew up with close ties to African American communities, didn't want anything to do with this multiracial thing. Why weren't their stories a part of the burgeoning narrative of mixed-race? Other questions loomed for me: In our celebrations of mixed-race, were we excluding or dismissing the experiences, histories, and racializations of other minoritized communities? How could multiracialism work to dismantle and not fortify the privileges of whiteness? How could we articulate our agenda in a way that might forge cross-racial coalitions, instead of separations?

After I left college I began to answer many of my questions on the utility of mixed-race through the writings of the essayist Lisa Jones in her book *Bulletproof Diva* (1994). I had read Jones's essays initially in her column in the *Village Voice*, and I thought about them time and again as I developed my own multiracial research agenda. Jones captured the "what are you?" question—the variety of ways in which mixed-race people are often questioned because of their "racially ambiguous looks"—better than anyone had managed to do:

> Who are you, what are you, where are you from, no, where are you really from, where are your parents from, are your grandparents Americans? Are you from here, what's your background, what's your nationality, where do you live? Are you black, are you white, do you speak

Spanish? Are you really white, are you really black? Are you Puerto Rican, are you half and half, are you biracial, multiracial, interracial, transracial, racially unknown, race neutral, colorless, colorblind, down with the rat race and the human race? Who are you? Where are you coming from? Who are your people?

She helped me understand that the "what are you?" question and all its permutations mark mixed-race people as either pathological or extraordinary, the object-like "what" or exotic and desirous "who."

At another level, I would encounter popular representations of multiracial people in memoirs, novels, television shows, and films that were equally dim about who and what multiracial people might be. Like most people, I instinctively read texts against lived experiences, and in the case of multiracial African Americans, the representations do not reflect the true complexity of lives. For years, from teaching high school English in Miami to studying ethnic studies in graduate school in San Diego to teaching difference and communication courses in Seattle, I have struggled to accept the limitations of representations of multiracial African Americans. I have wanted to find resistant counternarratives that echoed the rich diversity of experiences and racialized identifications that multiracial people have, from identifying with one monoracial identity, to two or more monoracial identities, to a race not in his or her own background, to "multiracial" as a category, to all of the above. But what I've come back to over and over for the case of mixed-race blackness is the failure of the representative landscape to meet the experiential one.

The experiential landscape is what has inspired *Transcending Blackness*. My readings in this book wouldn't be possible without all of the experiences I have enjoyed with a vibrant community of organic and trained intellectuals and activists. Because this project began with BOMBS, I must begin by thanking the people who powered BOMBS, especially Sachi Cunningham, Mike Hurt, Dean Karen McLaurin, and Jason Sperber, and who powered me through BOMBS, including Praveen Fernandes, Jeffery Mingo, Heather Reid, and Jim Wallace. My BOMBS critique was crying out for a frame, and at the University of California, San Diego, my professors Jane Rhodes, Daphne Brooks, Yen Espiritu, Nicole King, Ross Frank, and George Lipsitz opened up new worlds of ethnic and cultural studies to frame my ideas. Cherise Smith, Sarita Cannon and Lisa Ze Winters — members of the East Bay dissertation-writing group — beautifully modeled ethical, positive scholarship and provided the support necessary for me to finish my dissertation—and they along with Allison, Mike, Alonzo, and Ava Marie Smith keep me longing for Oakland. At the University of Washington, WIRED (Women Investigating Race, Ethnicity, and Difference) has bolstered me through many a long, gray day, and I want to thank all the members of our collective for making Seattle an intellectually and personally productive space; my WIRED writing group, LeiLani Nishime, Habiba Ibrahim, and Tyina Steptoe for validating and pushing my work; and Luis Fraga for his support of WIRED. My students, including Manoucheka Celeste, Madhavi Murty, Elizabeth Cortez, Anjali Vats, Kate Bell, Kris Mroczek, Jennifer McClearen, Tabitha Bronsma, Jamie Moshin, Vanessa Au, Monique Lacoste, Camille Elmore-Trummer, Desireé Boyd, Michelé Prince, Juana Reid, and the Barbados crew, helped this work to come alive in the classroom. My colleagues Crispin Thurlow, Christine Harold, Leah Ceccarelli, Valerie Manusov, Jerry Baldasty, David Domke, Michelle Habell-Pallan, Sonnet Retman, Angela Ginorio, Judy Howard, Andrea Griggs, and Lea Vaughn warmly welcomed me into the UW fold. A special thanks for the pedis and pep talks with my Seattle sisters, Janine Jones, Alexes Harris, and Joy Williamson-Lott; raucous laughter with Wadiya Udell; coffee shop work dates with Jen Neighbors; and family fun with the Kalbach-Udells, LaBordes, Fabers, Joneses, Bonney-Retmans, Espanias, and Wu-Floyds. A variety of fellowships provided me with the time and space to think, including the American Association of University Women, the University of California President's Fellowship, the Ford Foundation, and the Woodrow Wilson Career Enhancement Fellowship. When my faith in this project waned, the advice, support, and critique of Daphne Brooks, Matt Jacobson, Laura Helper-Ferris, Ken Wissoker, and my two anonymous reviewers rocketed me through my revisions. Thank you to Shosanna Weinberger for allowing her incredible image to grace the cover of the book. I will be forever grateful to the University of Washington's Whiteley Center for providing me with the most beautiful space in the world to think and write. Much love to my families the Landwehrs, Captains, D'Souzas, Whites, and Scanlans. My utmost appreciation to the people who encouraged me to ask too many questions: my parents, Richard and Irene Landwehr, and Grandpi, Jesse Meeks.

Most of all, I thank James, TJ, and Naima Joseph for endlessly embracing their spacey partner and mama. We live this book every day. Questions, comments, compliments, complaints, and jokes about multiraciality are an integral part of our everyday lives. I am a multiracial woman, partnered with a multiracial man, and together we have two multigenerationally mixed-race children. Our children are racialized quite differently from each other: our caramel-complexioned son is read as "minority" (although racially ambiguous to many), while our ringleted, olive-skinned daughter is read, for the most part, as white. When I registered my son for kindergarten in the Seattle public school system, the older African American woman who took my registration forms (none of which, surprisingly, asked for race) looked at me and at the required picture of him that I presented along with his birth certificate and entered "black" for our boy. Our girl has been racialized by the system as well: after she became ill at her preschool, a paramedic filling out his routine paperwork noted her as "white." But what would have happened if either of these events had occurred after a beach-heavy July in San Diego instead of a house-heavy February in Seattle? Our "race" switches with the seasons and with geography. We, as a family, work to normalize and concretize our discussions of race and mixed-race that have made their way into every page here. This book is dedicated to them, my own race-conscious, race-shifting, racially plural family, who are my inspiration, support, and favorite distraction.

READING MIXED-RACE AFRICAN AMERICAN
REPRESENTATIONS IN THE NEW MILLENNIUM

I have never been at home in my body. Not in its color, not in its size
or shape. Not in its strange, unique conglomeration of organic forms
and wavy lines. . . . There's an awkwardness to my body, a lack of grace,
as if the racial mix, the two sides coming together in my body have yet
to reconcile.
—**Rebecca Walker,** *Black, White, and Jewish*

For a young man of mixed race, without firm anchor in any community,
without even a father's steadying hand, the essential American ideal —
that our destinies are not written before we are born, that in America
we can travel as far as our energy and talents will take us — has defined
my life. With a mother from Kansas and a father from Kenya, I know
that stories like mine can happen only in the United States of America.
—**Barack Obama, "What Is Patriotism?"**

Representations of multiracial Americans, especially those
with a black parent and a white parent, appear everywhere
in the twenty-first-century United States, from the memoirs
of celebrity children to the reality shows of supermodels to
the speeches of presidential candidates. Some representations
equate mixed-race with pain: the multiracial individual is
mired in the confusion and problems imagined to be inherent
in the racial mixture of black and white. These images, such

as the ones Rebecca Walker conjures in her memoir, feature a twenty-first-century twist on the old stereotype of the "tragic mulatto," a phrase coined by the poet and literary scholar Sterling Brown in 1933 to connote the character who represents the problem of race mixing, and who is inevitably ruined because she or he is a person "without a race."[1] Other representations equate multiraciality with progress: the mixed-race person functions as a bridge between estranged communities, a healing facilitator of an imagined racial utopia, even the embodiment of that utopia. These images, such as the one Barack Obama's team cultivated during his first presidential election campaign, feature a special, sometimes messianic mixed-race character who has moved beyond the assumed confines of his or her African American heritage, and whose very existence portends racial liberation. In both positive and negative modes, despite their many differences, blackness operates as metaphoric tether. Further, blackness is presented as an internal, secret attribute of the multiracial individual, something to be struggled with or repressed in private.

This book examines the legacy of the problem-special dichotomy. Blackness remains pathological in both typological iterations. In the former it is the root cause for the multiracial African American woman's emotionally and sexually unbalanced behavior; in the latter the multiracial African American subject's metaphorical sloughing off of blackness is the root cause of her success. Multiracial nationalist advocacy for a "multiracial" category on the 2000 U.S. Census used this dual trope: multiracials need self-identification because they are troubled by confusing choices and are a special people. The texts I examine in *Transcending Blackness* largely advance the idea that mixed-race identity formation, characteristically marked by struggle, takes place in isolation; such individual and personal experiences are thought to be antithetical to a larger group or community sentiment.[2] In general, monoracial characters in the texts that I analyze do not question the permeability of racial borders.

Without question, racist laws are at the root of the mandate that multiracial African Americans identify as black: the one-drop rule, more technically called hypodescent, dictated that anyone with any degree of black "blood" was considered black, and biologically based chattel slavery and Jim Crow racism in the United States helped confirm that blackness was inferior. Nevertheless, one unintentional result of racist law and action has been the growth and strength of multiracial African Americans through membership in black communities; in the words of Valerie Smith, "these 'rules' were internalized by African Americans who converted them from mere signifiers of shame to markers of pride."[3] Representations of blackness as something to be transcended fly in the face of the historic embrace of multiracial African Americans in African American communities. Such flat representations of mixed-race African Americans belie the complexity of real-life experiences of such subjects, who live simultaneously as black and mixed-race, in a messy multiplicity that is rarely contained in any racialized nomenclature.

Racialized expression, including nomenclature, is not a foregone conclusion but a form of representation, which Stuart Hall describes as "an essential part of the process by which meaning is produced and exchanged between members of a culture."[4] Representations are vehicles that drive controlling and alternative images of race, gender, class, and sexuality, the social forces that govern our society. Popular cultural representations are fertile areas of study because they allow us to analyze the myths of our culture, or as Hall puts it, "popular culture . . . is where we discover and play with the identifications of ourselves, where we are imagined, where we are represented."[5] In other words, popular representations, where identity is imagined as both a site of social domination and agency, transform seeming fictions of racialization and sexualization into something close to reality. Evelynn Hammonds argues that visual representation, in particular, is a fundamental scholarly site because "in the U.S. race has always been dependent upon the visual."[6]

But such representations do not simply create meaning in a one-way process. As Hall and the Open University scholars illustrate in their famous circuit of culture, because of the interplay of audiences and texts, culture reflects, critiques, and creates changing ideologies.[7] Just as culture is perpetually mutating, so are racial meanings. Michael Omi and Howard Winant explain that race is not an essence, but "an unstable and 'decentered' complex of social meanings constantly being transformed by political struggle," a process that works to apply racial meanings, which they deem racialization.[8] Because both culture in general and racial representations more specifically are dynamic, it might seem that shifts in culture keep up with quick transformations in racialization. Racialization works by means of cultural representations, and representations actualize racialization; put another way, lived experiences of race inform representational ones, and representational race informs experience.[9] Changes in culture and racialization do not, however, immediately translate to changes in material life in such areas as state and public policies.[10] And most representations of mixed-race African Americans do not reveal the reciprocal complexity produced through this exchange. The script of multiracial blackness is stuck in a circuit of controlling, anti-black images.

In this "mulatto millennium,"[11] to use the author Danzy Senna's phrase, images of multiracial blackness largely do not illuminate the benefits of identifying as black. Instead of showing Americans embracing blackness in messy, hybridized, multiracial forms, the unspoken dictate in contemporary representations of multiracial Americans is that blackness must be risen above, surpassed, or truly transcended. In order to avoid being the "new millennium mulatta" who is always divided, alone, and uncomfortable, as exemplified in the first epigraph, popular images suggest that one must become the "exceptional multiracial" who is the unifying, post-racial, U.S. ideal, as exemplified in the second epigraph. To be more specific about the terms of this binary, on the one hand, multiracial blackness is *disdained* for its imagined primordially raced nature, with its tragic-mulatta lineage. On the other hand, multiracial blackness is *desired* for its imagined transcendent quality, where it is ahistorically divorced from racism and sexism in the United States with its troubling history of chattel slavery, Jim Crow racism, and entrenched misogyny. Because the popular conception that race means black, the end of race must mean the end of blackness. Whiteness, imaged as pure, invisible, and promise-laden, remains prized as the savior for multiracial African American figures from blackness, presented as sullied, hypervisible, and tragedy filled.

The new millennium-mulatta image is not supplanting the exceptional multiracial but is functioning in tandem with it, with both modes operating simultaneously in a dialectic. As dialectical stereotypes, the two images are, in the words of Yuko Kawai, "ambivalent as they contain contradictory messages simultaneously."[12] The condemnation of blackness is either implicit, where blackness is stigmatized through the presentation of tragic-mulatta inevitability, or explicit, where throwing off the yoke of blackness means arriving at a safely post-racial state. The struggle with black transcendence occurs through not only racialized but gendered and sexualized performances. Gender is not a floating additive characteristic in the representations I examine; it is an essential intersectional category that structures and restructures race, as well as other imbricated categories, such as class and sexuality.[13] In the representations I examine, gendered identity helps racialized identity become operative, and vice versa. Indeed, this book is concerned with images of mixed-race African American women who before the popularity of Obama were the most prevalent signifier of mixed-race blackness. The stereotype of the tragic mulatto has, in actuality, been the tragic mulatta, whose excessive sexual appetites necessitate her use and abuse by white men.

Mixed-race African American representations from 1998 to 2008 have crystallized the two-sided stereotype of the new millennium mulatta and the exceptional multiracial. These are watershed years for understanding a new era of race politics in the United States, and the politics of multiracial U.S. blackness in particular. The time from 1998 to 2008 comes in the aftermath of the passionate debates surrounding mixed-race identification and the census.[14] Part of the politics of the census, the major political issue surrounding mixed-race in the late 1990s and early 2000s, concerned citizens choosing a high-prestige group and disidentifying with a lower one.[15] Spanning the end of Bill Clinton's presidency, all of George W. Bush's years in office, and the election of Barack Obama, these years illustrate a moment when the so-called color-blind politics of the Bush era (with its much heralded "diverse" cabinet) vehemently erased the Clinton era's nonthreatening and cursory nod to multiculturalism. The Obama era came in at the tail end with a new breed of multiculturalism cum color-blind post-racialism.

In this time period, neoliberal citizenship has been perfectly and discursively embodied by such "naturally" post-racial citizens as mixed-race African Americans, whose very existence, the literal fusion of historically bifurcated black-and-white America, portends the end of racism and identity politics in the United States. In 1997, as Kimberly McClain DaCosta notes, "the Office of Management and Budget (OMB) officials were deciding the future of [multiracial people and] census classifications," and, as Habiba Ibrahim explains, the "celebrity and self-naming of Tiger Woods" proclaimed the multiracially unique term "Cablinasian." And in 1998, the mainstream news media exploded over the newly imagined multiracial subject.[16] At the other end of the decade, 2008 remains a landmark year in racial and mixed-racial history, the year the nation's first multiracial African American president was elected. Obama's ascension to the highest executive office of the United States makes him, and the exceptional multiracial, the ultimate sign of mixed-race blackness in the beginning of the twenty-first century.[17]

In these ten years, coded anti-black sentiments operated in a variety of illustrative and representative mixed-race African American cultural sites. After exhaustive research I believe that the overwhelming majority of mainstream images of mixed-race blackness fall into categories of the "new millennium mulatta" or the "exceptional multiracial," and *Transcending Blackness* includes the representations that illustrate this dialectic in the clearest possible manner. Instead of focusing each chapter on a selection of representations (drawing upon the substantive database of multiracial African American representations that I have amassed over the years), I have chosen here to dive deep into a single, representative text per chapter; this depth versus breadth approach allows me to more fully examine the textual nuances that construct the new millennium mulatta and the exceptional multiracial. I present the representations as operating along a nonchronological spectrum from the new millennium mulatta, the exceedingly tragic and mixed-racial, to the exceptional multiracial, the strikingly successful and post-racial. In part I, "New Millennium Mulattas," I explore contemporary performances of the self-reflexive, tragic mulatta as "the bad race girl" in Jennifer Beals's portrayal of Bette Porter on the cable television drama *The L Word* (2004–8) and as "the sad race girl" in Danzy Senna's novel *Caucasia* (1998). In part II, "Exceptional Multiracials," I interrogate representations that develop the character of the racial-transforming mixed-race figure in Alison Swan's independent film *Mixing Nia* (1998) and racial-switching mixed-race figure on an episode of Tyra Banks's reality television show *America's Next Top Model* (2005).

While the first half of the book shows how blackness is cause and effect of sadness and pain for the multiracial African American figure, the second half of the book shows that blackness is an irrelevant entity for the multiracial African American figure. The representations' reliance upon the trope of black transcendence reveals the idea that we live in a post-racial society, that the civil rights movement did its job in eliminating inequality and in enabling "all of us" to compete on a level playing field. At the same time, paradoxically, these late-twentieth- and early-twenty-first-century images of multiracial African Americans are also bound by the perception that blackness must be surpassed in order for the mixed-race subject to arrive at a state of health or success. In a post–civil rights era where race, much less racism, cannot be mentioned without public outcry, anti-black racism remains prevalent yet coded.[18] Contemporary black-white representations do not go beyond the binary of the new millennium mulatta and the exceptional multiracial; instead they operate within the umbrella metaphor of black transcendence. The trope of black transcendence that circulates within representations of mixed-race African Americans illustrates the flourishing of anti-black racism, despite the continued desire for "black cool," and despite the existence of the first (multiracial) (black) president. Ultimately, mixed-race African American representations—and by extension the subjectivities of multiracial African American individuals—continue to be delimited by the racist notion that blackness is a deficit that black and multiracial people must overcome. The very language that Americans use to name these figures, and the painful legacies of racial debates from abolition through the civil rights movement, shape my analysis of the exceptional multiracial millennium mulatta.

Naming the Multiracial African American Figure

The etymologies of the terms applied to those with one black and one white parent illuminate the processes of their racialization. With the swell of interest in issues of mixed-race comes a concomitant concern about multiracial terminology. The notion of "mixed-race" and "monoracial" as separate categories to describe certain African Americans can seem almost nonsensical and voluntary, and yet representations of mixed-race blackness do just this. Contrary to much popular discourse on mixed-race, the fact of mixing does not automatically disprove racial categories because the terms themselves include race: the names for mixed-race people signal their grounding in race itself. Indeed, the very ability to "mix" races rests upon the premise that race is a stable and singular entity. Reflecting this complicated history, we lack a pithy, neutral term for mixed-race African Americans that is not irreparably damaged by its troubling past. "Mulatto" is not a viable candidate. Despite the fact that a *New York Times* cover story in 2011 announced that young multiracial Americans are reclaiming "mulatto," I have not personally encountered a widespread reclamation of the term.[19]

In the anthology *Interracialism*, Werner Sollers illustrates the troubled history of "mulatto" by including the *Oxford English Dictionary*'s tracing of the term from its Spanish and Portuguese etymology of animalism ("*mulato* young mule, hence one of mixed race") to its use as a descriptor of sickness like "mulatto jack," meaning "a term for yellow fever," to a "mulatto complexion" generally described as unfortunately "tawny" in color. However, the term's history is far from simply negative. The privileged materiality of mixed-race blackness is evident in historic ties between "mulatto" and the "mulatto elite," which attempted to garner power by disassociating with blackness through practices like post–Civil War Blue Vein societies and even slaveholding.[20] Because of this history, scholars such as P. Gabrielle Foreman and Caroline Streeter meet "mulatto" with considerable skepticism.[21] This term, far from being a neutral descriptor, has long been seen by many as divisive, troublesome, and antiquated.

Nevertheless, in popular culture "mulatto" remains popular, often dropped to prompt a laugh. For example, on an episode of the sitcom *Will and Grace* in 2004, a one-episode character who we are told is despicable for his wide variety of offensive views, laments the existence of his "bastard mulatto grandson"; the anachronistic term cements the character's laughably in-the-past understanding of race that is ostensibly at odds with the urbane, white, liberal, gay and gay-friendly New Yorkers on the show. As the character's grandson is never actually shown, he remains a convenient comedic ploy through racialized allusion, and not an uncomfortable and dramatic insertion of embodied racialized difference. In a second example, on an episode of the sitcom *Scrubs*, also from 2004, the goofy white protagonist J. D. is enticed, as if by trance, by black-and-white Milano cookies, which he lovingly and mistakenly calls "mulattoes" before being corrected and reprimanded by his black best friend, Turk, and Turk's Dominican American wife, Carla. In this case the mere existence of African American and Afro Latina supporting players allows the show to spin the term's deployment as nothing more than an endearingly naive (mis)understanding of contemporary race and racialized nomenclature.

In a third example, in a bit at the White House Correspondents' Association's annual dinner in May of 2009, the African American comedienne Wanda Sykes cracked to President Obama, "This is amazing. The first black president. I know you're biracial, but the first black president. You're proud to be able to say that. That's unless you screw up. Then it's going to be, what's up with the half-white guy? Who voted for the mulatto? What the hell?"[22] The punch line for Sykes's joke is simply the weird word "mulatto." In the joke's setup, Sykes initially claims Obama as family. She then playfully pushes him away with this anachronistic word, which signifies the authenticity politics that dogged Obama from the beginning of his presidential election campaign until he became the target of racism by the Clintons and their supporters.[23] As Michael Tesler and David Sears note, "The most pressing racial issue of 2007 seemed to be whether Barack Obama was actually 'black enough.'"[24] As an out black lesbian with a French wife and white twin daughters, Sykes's playing with the tropes of black essentialism remains innocuous: she too can be read as inauthentically black by the imagined "black authenticity police," so she has license to make such a joke.[25] As the camera cuts to Obama's laughing, open face, the joke is shown to be lighthearted ribbing and not nasty indictment. All three examples show how "mulatto" variously produces disgust, desire, and playful rejection of the imagined and embodied multiracial African American body.

Why is "mulatto" fodder for mainstream comedy? Like "Negro," it is an anachronistic term clearly cemented to a past historical moment. However, "Negro" is not generally deployed within comedic settings meant to appeal to a broad swath of the country, such as network sitcoms and presidential roasts. Nor is "Negro" acceptably used by white people in mainstream comedy, as in the first two examples. In a world in which liberals and conservatives lament, genuinely and not, the so-called PC police and a subsequent surveillance of the correct use of racialized language, does "mulatto" remain funny and popular because it is an ostensibly harmless race joke about a seemingly post-racial group that is, by its very definition, safely passed oppression?[26]

The history of the term makes it impossible for me to use "mulatto" as contemporary racialized nomenclature. Nevertheless, we do not have a short and noncontentious term for mixed-race African Americans, as the term "hapa" is for many multiracial Asian Americans.[27] When specificity is the goal, alternative terminology such as "black/white" is simply confusing. The self-described multiracial movement of the 1990s chose as its major political issue the creation of a "multiracial" category on state and federal forms, an institutional and national opportunity movement of self-definition and self-naming. This activism stemmed in part from the introduction of new terminology, such as "multiracial" from the United States–based movement of scholarship and activism and "mixed-race" from a similar set of scholarship and activism in the United Kingdom.[28] These two terms were popularized in the explosion of scholarship following the psychologist Maria Root's anthology *Racially Mixed People in America* (1992). However, in the United States during the twenty-first century, racialized labels, even relatively new ones, continue to be contentious and slippery. Because of the very real possibility that using terms such as "mixed-race" or "multiracial," without including black or African American, are a way to run from blackness, I am left with cumbersome but inclusive terms.

In *Transcending Blackness*, when I am speaking historically, or of images that conjure historic stereotypes, I use "mulattoes" and "mulattas." When referring to new-millennium imagery, I sometimes use the more specific term "black-white," but I more frequently use "mixed-race" or "multiracial." "Mixed-race" and "multiracial" are adjectives modifying "black" or "African American," and I use them interchangeably, following the lead of the representations I investigate. I prefer these two terms to "biracial," a term that highlights the so-called graphic division between black and white. "Multiracial/mixed-race African American" also names the positive alliances that multiracial people forge in and as part of black communities. Even though I am analyzing representations of black-white individuals, I do not use "multiracial white" as a phrase: I acknowledge that by doing so I am, in a sense, following the logic of the one-drop rule, where any degree of black heritage connotes blackness, even when talking about multiracial identities. I fully acknowledge that all racialized terminology is inherently encumbered by its history and roots in biologically based racism, and that race is, as Michael Omi and Howard Winant have illustrated, a material reality and a social construction.[29] However, as I am examining popular cultural representations and not postulating about other (non)racialized possibilities, I necessarily use racialized terms.

Finally, I heed the black feminist media scholar Jacqueline Bobo's warning in *Black Women as Cultural Readers*: "Although it is patently evident [that] the representations of black women in mainstream media have been persistently negative, scholarship by black women should not limit itself to a hunt for negative imagery. This can be self-defeating in that it diminishes any hope for change. As a critical practice the hunt for and dissection of negative imagery also centers and makes concrete the thought of black women as being something other than human."[30] In the representations I examine, I leave open possibilities for counterhegemonic readings, and for the progressive possibilities that can come with imagining racial fluidity.

The Genealogy of the New Millennium Mulatta

The history of mixed-race African American representations is inseparable from the history of race itself; part of the anxiety over mixed-race is the anxiety over race. In order to lay the groundwork for the contemporary representations I analyze in this book, I provide a mostly chronological genealogy that illustrates the pain and anxiety of race actualized in the figure of the new millennium mulatta. This genealogy, starting with condemnation of mixing in the colonies and ending with the end of U.S. antimiscegenation laws, only becomes fully evident by examining the history, social scientific research, literary and film representations, and criticism that together produce the new millennium mulatta. The new millennium mulatta figure that composes half of the representational landscape of contemporary multiracial African Americans is indelibly marked by the stereotype of the tragic mulatta. As part I of *Transcending Blackness* illustrates, the new millennium mulatta is a "race girl": a self-reflexive character who is knowledgeable, angry, or sad about and self-conscious of her tragic destiny. Nevertheless, despite her many efforts to the contrary, she is unable to perform outside the confines of the tragic mulatta and ends up inevitably living up to the stereotype. Where are the tragic mulatta's roots in the United States?

The first answer lies in the parent cause of multiracialism. Interracial unions, as representations of mixed-race African Americans are inextricably entangled with the history of U.S. antimiscegenation law.[31] In 1661 the colony of Maryland enforced the first antimiscegenation law in what was to become the United States by prohibiting marriage among whites and blacks and Native Americans. Following suit, for more than three hundred years, thirty-eight states established and enforced antimiscegenation laws between whites and people of color.[32] Such racialized boundaries worked to actually create race; the story goes that race precedes mixed-race, but the history of antimiscegenation laws illustrates that the opposite is true. As early as the 1600s, white North American settlers called mulattoes a "spurious issue" and an "abominable mixture," demonstrating, in the words of Thomas Gossett, a desire "to keep the races separate"; mixed-race is therefore taboo from the moment of conquest.[33]

However, powerful white forces consolidated their rule through the use of mixed-race black bodies; their creation in slavery was encouraged through interracial sex and procreation, although their legitimacy was disallowed through bans on interracial marriage. Eugene Genovese explains how "self-serving slaveholders" created and perpetuated stereotypes about slaves' lusty sexual appetites in order to justify their own sexual violence against black women.[34] Scholars such as Lisa Ze Winters illustrate that most relationships between black women and white men actually consisted of forced sexual relations and rape as "the economy of interracial concubinage is neither liberating nor romantic, but rather entrenched in the brutal violence of slavery."[35] Indeed, the U.S. institution of slavery depended on interracial sex for the reproduction of slave bodies. Ruth Frankenberg puts it plainly: white men's "sexual intercourse with enslaved women—in the context of matrilineal descent laws for enslaved people—produced more slaves."[36] This reproductive labor of black women has been at the heart of the symbolic history of interracial sex in the United States; Patricia Hill Collins notes that during slavery "efforts to control black women's reproduction were important to the maintenance of the race, class, and gender inequality characterizing the slave order."[37] This mixing has thus also helped constitute core American notions of race and sex.

Mulattas were associated with an image of a jezebel, a woman who, in Deborah Gray White's words, "was the counterimage of the mid-nineteenth-century ideal of the Victorian lady. She did not lead men and children to God; piety was foreign to her. She saw no advantage in prudery, indeed domesticity paled in importance before matters of the flesh."[38] The sexualized figure of the tragic mulatto or mulatta featured prominently in slavery-era "fancy girl" (prostitution) markets where, Genovese notes, "girls young, shapely, and usually light in color, went as house servants with special services required."[39] Slave stories and songs frequently featured, according to Genovese, "'yaller gals' as dangerous temptresses while making clear their sexual desirability; but when not more in fun than in hostility, these songs and stories suggest criticism of the sexual irregularity that marked the girls' origins."[40] Mulattas, like other black women, were not therefore deemed worthy of protection from sexual abuse; "yaller gals" were labeled, says E. Frances White, so "unrespectable" that regular "sexual assaults on black women [were] perpetrated by white men."[41] Thus, images of African American multiraciality have been bound up for hundreds of years in ideas of mixed-race female hypersexuality, as the mulatta was both the imagined product of and partner in illicit sex, the very projection of white men's sexual freedom.

Slavery tamed the sexually marked mulatta, whose value arose from her sexual submission to white men. F. James Davis notes, "keeping mulatto concubines became a luxury of many white men in Southern cities during slavery."[42] Part of white men's desire for the mulatta body was a celebration of the taboo union of whiteness and blackness: the mulatta mythically embodied dark sexual deviance and white acceptability.[43] Some white men highly prized American mulattas for their sexual desirability, and yet simultaneously and paradoxically, in order to discourage race mixing, early theoreticians condemned multiracials as having a sickly countenance stemming from psychological dysfunction.[44]

The body of a mulatto or mulatta has inspired considerable scientific debate over the course of American history. Discussions around the beginning of the nineteenth century highlighted the "hybrid-degeneracy theory" where "mulattoes — like mules — tend to be barren," because "no species of animals in the natural world was known to have developed from the union of two separate species."[45] In the mid-1800s scholars studied mulattoes to discern the biological distance or proximity between blacks and whites. John Mencke writes that, particularly in the realm of manumission, "although mulattoes were generally classed as Negroes in the United States, distinctions were drawn between mulattoes and blacks during the ante-bellum period."[46] An extensive series of anthropometric studies during the U.S. Civil War measured virtually every body part of soldiers and concluded that "full-blood" blacks were physiologically inferior to whites, and mulattoes were inferior to both "parent" groups.[47] After the death of this debate, mulattoes were still seen as different and often "superior" by virtue of their white blood, but were "classed" with "full-blood" blacks.[48] Foregrounding social and not biological degeneracy, in 1871 Darwin shot through the biological debate in his own racist way, arguing, "the seemingly low fertility rate of mulattos resulted from the degraded and anomalous position of their class; their absorption into the black race; and, of course, the assumed profligacy of mulatto women."[49] These debates, which were in effect in earnest until approximately 1910, were informed by biological determinism, or scientific research that sought to explain how different "races" were, in fact, different "species."[50]

After the abolition of slavery, the U.S. Census distinguished between mulattoes and Negroes from 1870, when it first fully counted black citizens as human beings, to 1920, when it deemed that census workers' practice of eyeballing citizens to determine racial ancestry had become impossible and estimated that 75 percent of the black population had some degree of white or Native American heritage.[51] In the realm of spatial segregation, the case of *Plessy v. Ferguson* (1896) put an end to questions about legal difference between Negroes and mulattoes. Creating the "separate but equal" doctrine, the U.S. Supreme Court ruled that Homer Plessy, a light-skinned "octoroon" from Louisiana, could not ride in a white railway car.[52] With this the U.S. government sanctioned the one-drop rule of hypodescent because an image of a mixed-race body expressed fear of black infringement upon white space.[53] From *Plessy* came the ratification of spatial segregation through the legal enforcement of Jim Crow laws, which ensured that, as James Grossman writes, "regardless of how interdependent the races might be in the South, they would not inhabit the same public spaces."[54] Again, this reflects whites' fears of, in Rachel Moran's words, "interracial intimacy," which helped keep interracial marriages illegal in a number of states until the last third of the twentieth century.[55] To keep white purity intact, miscegenation—and its product, the mulatto—had to be perceived as an immediate threat.

As part of a larger critique launched against racist representations of blacks, a number of African American scholars, including W. E. B. Du Bois, were vocal in expressing their disgust with popular denigration of "the mulatto."[56] Speaking against the origin-of-the-species debate, Du Bois states: "it [is] impossible to draw a color line between black and other races, [and] in all physical characteristics the Negro race cannot be set off by itself as absolutely different."[57] In order to prove this idea, Du Bois presents photographs of African American men and women of various proportions of white, black, and Native American ancestry. These photographs demonstrated how those who contain mostly "black blood" can easily "look white," as well as how those with a majority of "white blood" can easily "look black." Du Bois critiques easy and erroneous connections between looks and race. In 1906, African American novelists devoted significant space to the mulatto; Suzanne Bost points out, "the canon of turn-of-the-century African-American literature is mulatta literature, and the most studied authors of this period contribute to mulatta mythology."[58] For example, Alain Locke documents how "the Negro has been shunted from one stereotype into the other," and how one of the earliest stereotypes was "the mulatto house servant concubine and her children."[59]

The Birth of a Nation (1915) is a prime example of the texts that African American scholars and critics identified as racist depictions of mixed-race people. The film portrays the major mixed-race female character as performing her racialization through the confines of a singular iteration of her sexuality. This trope would persist through the twentieth century in books and films such as *Imitation of Life*. *The Birth of a Nation*, the earliest influential cinematic portrayal of mixed-race womanhood, demonstrates such an indelible filmic attachment of mixed-race to sex, which cannot be escaped during a nearly century-long translation to the new millennium mulatta. This landmark film spins a tale of the romanticized glory days of the pre–Civil War South, the unnecessary U.S. Civil War, the unlawful, desegregated South of the Reconstruction period, and the final triumphant rise of white supremacy and control.[60]

D. W. Griffith's film *The Birth of a Nation* was based on Thomas Dixon's novels *The Clansman* (1905) and *The Leopard's Spots: A Romance of the White Man's Burden, 1865–1900* (1902),[61] and it was also inspired by President Wilson's unquestionably racist *History of the American People* (1902). The film was thus informed by nostalgic white male Southerners living in the North around the beginning of the nineteenth century. In *The Birth of a Nation*, brute sexuality informs white fear of newly freed slaves desirous of miscegenation. The storylines include tales of an attempted rape of a young white girl by Gus, an animalistic black "buck," and a ventured marriage between Silas Lynch, a shameless, rabble-rousing mulatto, and Elsie Stoneman, a pure and prominent white woman. In addition, *The Birth of a Nation* features Lydia Brown (played by the white actress Mary Alden), a passionate, calculating, and slightly insane mulatta who is having two affairs: one with a powerful white abolitionist carpetbagger and the other with a mulatto insurrectionist. Like all of the principal "black" actors, Lydia's character performed in blackface (brownface).

In the mulattoes' characterization, while both Silas and Lydia are shown as sexually driven and keenly intelligent, Silas organizes large numbers of Southern blacks while Lydia schemes crazily in back rooms. Silas's mixed biology allows him to think logically, "like a white man," but lust after white women, "like a black man," whereas Lydia's mixed biology appears to drive her insane. Lydia's invisible whiteness allows her to be intelligent and attractive and her visible blackness forces her to be conniving and hypersexual. The unstable mix creates her insanity and lust for power. Griffith portrays the mulatta character of Lydia as ruled by the entwined forces of sexual desire, mental instability, and a need for power. Lydia's clothes always appear to be falling off her body, denoting the uncontrollable combination of unbridled sexual energy and unstable mental condition. Lydia's disheveled appearance can also reference the rape of her mother in Lydia's own conception. Her mixed-race female body is unquestionably outside of true womanhood, which is coded as white, domestic, and middle class and is represented in the film by young, blond Lillian Gish, who plays Elsie.[62] While one could assert that Lydia acquires power through her sexuality, she never directs this power outward, and it instead thrashes within her body. Superfluous sexuality defines the hyper-feminized tragic mulatta, rendering her useless outside the imagined bedroom.

The film's pathologization of the mixed-race body helped a so-called white nation define itself against the mulatto, or helps define itself as pure.[63] The film scholar Daniel Bernardi writes, "as propaganda, *The Birth of a Nation* accomplished the significant feat of transposing the national myth of the South into terms congruent with the mythology of white American nationalism."[64] The film's final scenes ultimately allay the fears created by Lydia's mixed-race body as the Ku Klux Klan saves the South, and reconfirms white power. During the time the film was released, science and popular culture in the United States were shifting from a discourse of "radical racism" to, in historian John Mencke's words, "the more respectable doctrine of eugenics." Whereas the former was demonstrated in polemics against uncivilized, brutish, and even cannibalistic blacks, the latter was a more genteel, but perhaps even more virulent form of scientific racism.[65]

Popular culture in the United States illustrated that mulattoes such as Lydia had greater mental capabilities than full-bloods, but at the same time they were denigrated for their "physical degeneracy and moral weaknesses."[66] As products of imagined sexual impropriety, they were naturally prone to sexual wantonness, and as scientific ideas of animal hybrids at the time dictated, they were physically lesser than pure breeds (also an explanation for their mental instability). A mixed-race character such as Lydia serves as a vehicle to both express and explore relations between blacks and whites. Lydia warns against the dangers of miscegenation because she results from such pairings. She also demonstrates how the looming power of miscegenation can disrupt the nation's racial boundaries if it is not contained by white violence, symbolized here by the Ku Klux Klan. Griffith's representation of licentious, conniving, and uncontrolled black bodies circulated contemporary popular, political, and scientific myths about the danger contained within African Americans. In particular, his representation of the tragic mulatta Lydia warned the public of the danger of miscegenation and multiracial black women. Despite, or perhaps because of, the imagined instability of Lydia's boiling bloods, Griffith has her question her racial alliance as "just black" by seeking partnership with a white man.

The filmic image of the tragic mulatta bore so much power because of its echoing in additional cultural spaces. Just three years after *The Birth of a Nation*'s release, Edward Reuter published *The Mulatto in the United States* (1918), one of the earliest and most comprehensive social scientific takes on the tragic-mulatto myth: "Psychologically the mulatto is an unstable type [because] between these two groups, one admiring and the other despising, stand the mixed bloods. . . . They are uncertain of their own worth; conscious of their superiority to the native they are nowhere sure of their equality with the superior group."[67] Reuter's denigration of the "uncertain" and "self-conscious" mulatto is symptomatic of a palpable fear of white-appearing mixed-race bodies infiltrating white America. Where the hybrid-degeneracy theory expressed just twenty years earlier highlighted a biological pathology, Reuter's narrative of tragedy focused upon psychological dysfunction.[68]

The other landmark social scientific mulatto book-length study, Everett Stonequist's *The Marginal Man* (1937), uses the sociologist Robert Park's theory of the taxonomically in-between "marginal man," originally devised for Jews and other white ethnics, and extends it to "racially hybridized people."[69] But while Park celebrated his marginal man as a more modern creation whose cosmopolitan nature allowed him to move between identity categories, Stonequist asserts that the mixed-blood's liminal position, being "torn between two courses of action," results in psychological dysfunction characterized by a "nervous strain," self-absorption, hypersensitivity, "racial disharmony," a "clash of blood," and an "unstable genetic constitution."[70] The biological, and hence unchangeable, nature of this description is particularly salient. With their theories of hybrid degeneracy and the marginal man, Stonequist's and Reuter's books have been regularly referenced in scholarship from their historical moment until today, demonstrating the indelible mark of tragedy on the bodies of mixed-race African Americans.[71] While Reuter and Stonequist focus their sociological studies on men and women, the representational subject of mixed-race popular culture was always overwhelmingly a woman.

The multitextual narrative *Imitation of Life* further defined the myth of the tragic mulatta. *Imitation of Life*, initially a novel published in 1933 by Fannie Hurst, was turned into two melodrama "weepies," a film by John Stahl in 1934 and another one by Douglas Sirk in 1959. I focus on the more widely seen version, the 1959 film, at that time Universal Pictures's biggest moneymaker ever.[72] This version continues to be rerun on television today, exposing new generations of viewers, for example, me as a channel-surfing elementary school kid of the 1980s, to the late-1950s version of the tragic mulatta. *Imitation of Life* can be situated during the New Deal era when the novel was written, the post-war time when the story opens, and the civil rights movement when the film's narrative ends and it was released. Perhaps most significant among the many historical changes over these years, the end of the war in 1945 also marked the beginning of the civil rights movement. But *Imitation of Life* deploys mixed-race as a filmic device and not as a gaze into the real-life racism, acts of resistance, or political activism of the day. Instead, issues of artifice run through nearly every facet of the film as the plot revolves around acting as both profession and lifestyle. The constant performances put into question the existence of any "real" racialized or sexualized body; as new millennium mulatta representations of multiraciality itself, all is mimicry and none is original.

Imitation of Life features Lana Turner as Lora, a self-interested white actress and the mother of naive and neglected Susie, played by Sandra Dee, a teenager who at the time earned the distinction of being the highest-paid teen model for her image of the all-American girl. The sweetly submissive African American maid Annie, played by Juanita Moore, and the fiercely sexual tragic mulatta Sara Jane, played by Susan Kohner, parallel the white mother and daughter team. Sara Jane is portrayed as perpetually angry, precocious, violent, and mean. She hurls her emotions mercilessly at her long-suffering mother: Sara Jane longs to be white and blames Annie for imbuing her with an imagined stain of blackness, instead of, as Lauren Berlant points out, lambasting the state or the law.[73] She finds an escape from this stain through a sexualized flaunting of her body: she dates white boys and performs at a white burlesque club. Berlant also describes how Sara Jane "chooses a style of racial passing that negates her mother's 'servile' mentality and manner, featuring instead libidinous, assertive physicality."[74] However, Sara Jane is punished for this racial transgression when her escape to whiteness causes her mother to die of a broken heart. Nevertheless, as Judith Butler argues, with this punishment Sara Jane also receives her long-desired whiteness: "Sara Jane takes her place next to [Susie] as one of Lana's girls, suggesting that she finally achieves the great white mother she has always sought."[75] She is finally freed from her mother, the visible burden of her blackness. In Butler's reading, the tragic mulatta is brutally utilitarian and cruelly ambitious as she uses the occasion of her mother's death to move up in social status and race.

Susan Kohner, the daughter of a white American film agent and a Mexican film star and who plays the character of Sara Jane, was described consistently as "white" by the film studio's press materials. She was cast in the movie in the aftermath of the Hollywood Motion Picture Production Code, or the Hays Code, which functioned as Hollywood's own version of an antimiscegenation law. In effect from 1929 to 1952, representations of miscegenation were banned in Hollywood along with, in Linda Williams's words, "the very existence of a mixed-race character on the screen . . . [because he or she demonstrated] problematic proof of the prior 'crime' of miscegenation."[76] Exemplifying the multiple levels of imitation or performance seen throughout *Imitation of Life*, Kohner is a so-called white actress performing the role of a black woman who imitates a white woman. However, there are clear limits to the boundaries pushed in these portrayals; the film is only an imitation of border breaking, or, as Sirk put it, of "social criticism." Indeed, Sirk fell short of his stated desire to make "social criticism," and instead he ended up producing an identity film, devoid of the racialized political economy of the New Deal, World War II, and civil rights periods.[77] But these issues are not absent from the film: instead of placing his action and all of his characters in the midst of these struggles, Sirk makes the tragic-mulatta character Sara Jane the film's sole bearer of social consciousness. In the end, the 1950s-era mulatta cannot be anything but tragic because to empower her would be to celebrate miscegenation.

In pop culture and scholarship, the multiracial African American scripted as the tragic mulatta largely fell out of vogue in the civil rights era. Discussions about antimiscegenation laws were often attached to issues of civil rights. However, it is important to point out that interracial marriage and not interracial sex was made illegal. While the institution of marriage dictates the handing down of appreciable commodities, the act of sex denotes no legal legitimacy. In 1945 the sociologists Horace Cayton and St. Clair Drake discerned this, writing, "many whites will continue to exploit the fear of intermarriage as a means of retaining economic dominance."[78] More recent scholars contend that in addition to the protection of white womanhood and the prevention of the miscegenated body, the root of fears regarding interracial marriage also lay in the guardianship of white capital.[79] In other words, not all miscegenation simply elicits an emotional or moral response. Instead, the legal union of interracial marriage had been a major threat to an institution that denotes inheritance and property. Property is the clear benefit of whiteness: an asset that appreciates in value.[80]

The civil rights movement did not articulate antimiscegenation as a primary issue, because leaders did not want it to appear as though the true aim of civil rights was for black men to marry white women.[81] Nonetheless, the Supreme Court case of *Loving v. Virginia* (1967) knocked down centuries of antimiscegenation laws by citing civil rights advances, arguing that "antimiscegenation laws unconstitutionally discriminated on the basis of race in violation of equal protection and that they interfered with the fundamental right to marry under the due process clause."[82] In that same time period, the discourse of black threat flourished throughout U.S. culture; perhaps most pervasively, the anthropologist Oscar Lewis's "culture of poverty" thesis resonated even into liberal policy in the Moynihan Report in 1965, blaming African American inequality on faulty culture instead of racist institutions.

The tragic-mulatta genealogy dictates the new millennium mulatta's iteration of angry and sad race girl. The works I examine in the first part of *Transcending Blackness* channel the history of the tragic mulatta by demonstrating how mixed-race blackness functions in the throes of a racialized identity crisis (the result of extreme uncertainty and self-consciousness regarding race) spurred on by a cultural context dictating that one must choose a singular identity category. To different degrees all the representations in *Transcending Blackness* feature protagonists who struggle to define themselves in any one category and remain there for a permanent amount of time. Indeed, the exceptional multiracial figures fight so much with their racialization that the texts have them metaphorically transform races in order to escape blackness.

The Genealogy of the Exceptional Multiracial

While the genealogy of the new millennium mulatta began with white racist condemnation of colonial-era mixing, the genealogy of the exceptional multiracial begins with white racist "defense" of black bodies through abolitionism. Arguments for abolitionism flourished in popular culture, putting forward an exceptional multiracial as the other face of the tragic mulatta. While the failure of the mixed-race black body constitutes a significant portion of the image of the multiracial African American body, the exceptional multiracial, the focus of part II of this book, is the other half of the historic image of mixed-race African Americans. Antislavery fiction posited that the mulatto or mulatta character is not only damned for being a product of the tragic union of the races, but he or she is also valuable for having a measure of whiteness. Although the mulatto has been demeaned throughout much of American history, there has always been a contingent of black Americans and white Americans who have celebrated multiracial exceptionalism. In the exceptional multiracial typology, prizing mixed-race blackness over "pure" blackness, just as denigrating mixed-race blackness over "pure" whiteness, serves the purpose of valuing whiteness above blackness. In short, while whites sometimes feared mulattoes because of their proximity to whiteness, they valued them for this very reason.

In abolitionist literature such as Harriet Beecher Stowe's *Uncle Tom's Cabin* (1852), mulattoes were imagined to be imbued with greater humanity than full-blood blacks. Abolitionists featured mulatto bodies as the key to illustrating the inhumanity of slavery,[83] and particularly beautiful (read: white-looking) young mulattas were showcased by abolitionists to gain support for their cause. For example, beginning in 1848, the white preacher from New York City and brother of Harriet Beecher Stowe, Henry Ward Beecher, held so-called antislavery auctions where he would parade young, near-white-looking female slaves around his congregation in order to raise the money required to buy their freedom.[84] Throughout the years of these auctions, "the girls (all of them Christian and attractive) grew whiter and whiter, until in 1856 Beecher found and 'auctioned' one slave who was completely indistinguishable from one of his parishioner's fairest daughters."[85]

As passer slaves on display for abolitionists, exceptional multiracials are more valuable than monoracial African Americans because they are akin to these "beautiful," safe girls. The cause of the new millennium is not putting an end to chattel slavery (without significant change to racialized inequalities) but rather putting an end to the idea of race (again, without significant change to racialized inequalities).[86] Jules Zanger notes that the tragic-mulatto character also took the guise of a passer who was often referred to as the "'tragic octoroon[,]' . . . a beautiful young girl who possesses only the slightest evidences of Negro blood."[87] Her beauty is central to her portrayal and her ability to garner sympathy from whites. Thus, the mixed-race African American figure continues to almost always be gendered as female in cultural representations.[88]

The exceptional multiracial, a figure who, unlike the new millennium mulatta, is not simply a rollout of an old controlling image, has roots in progressive African American critiques of essentialism, despite the neoconservative ideologies that arise from her contemporary representation. Such critiques came not just from Du Bois but also from other scholars, including early black feminist scholars like Anna Julia Cooper. In an essay from 1892 Cooper critiqued a black male novelist for his misrepresentations and singular notions of *the* black community. She recoiled at "the intimation that there is a 'black voice,' a black character, easy, irresponsible and fond of what is soft and pleasant, a black ideal of art and a black barbaric taste in color, a black affinity."[89] Almost one hundred years later, Stuart Hall describes "black" as a "politically and culturally *constructed* category." As such, the category should recognize "the extraordinary diversity of subjective positions, social experiences, and cultural identities."[90] The legacy of the exceptional multiracial is also of this critique. However, the exceptional multiracial goes to the far extreme of the critique of authenticity. The exceptional multiracial figure is scripted to dismiss "the black voice" so much that it erases blackness entirely.

The exceptional multiracial is most clearly rooted in the hope promised through the decriminalization of interracial marriage in *Loving v. Virginia*. The plaintiffs in the case—Mildred Loving (née Jeter), an African American woman, and Richard Loving, a white man—married in Washington, D.C., in 1958, where interracial marriage was legal. The Lovings were arrested when they returned to their home state of Virginia, where they were charged with "cohabiting as man and wife, against the peace and dignity of the Commonwealth." With the help of the ACLU, the Lovings fought—and defeated—the ban on interracial marriage. In a unanimous vote of the Supreme Court, led by Chief Justice Warren, Virginia's Racial Integrity Act of 1924 was overturned. To commemorate the decision, every June 12 various groups around the country celebrate multiracial individuals and interracial couples through the Loving Day Celebration.[91] At the *Loving* moment, representations of multiracial bodies transitioned from discursively maligned intolerable creations to celebrated future bridges to a color-blind utopia.[92] Catherine Squires describes this change as the movement from "hybrid degenerates" to "multiracial families."[93] Although repercussions of three hundred years of marking interracial relationships as illicit did not vanish overnight, *Loving* signifies a turning point in American attitudes toward images of mixed-race people and in the numbers of those people.

Civil rights legislation also helped transform mixed-race images into a multiracial "hope."[94] The Southern historian Joel Williamson's *New People: Miscegenation and Mulattoes in the United States* (1980), taking its name from a phrase in the novelist Charles Chesnutt's *House behind the Cedars* (1900), demonstrates such civil rights–era optimism. In refuting the hybrid-degeneracy theory, Williamson romanticizes mixed-race, stating that multiracials will heal America's still-festering race wound. Assuming a black-white paradigm, Williamson describes mixed-race people as "the first fully evolved, smoothly functioning model of a people who have transcended both an exclusive whiteness and an exclusive blackness and moved into a world in which they accept and value themselves for themselves alone — as new and unique, as indeed, a new people in the human universe."[95] As representations of so-called new people, the images I examine both express and critique much of this optimism, longing for and lamenting the time when mixed-race individuals will be "just people" and not "just black."

But in the 1980s, civil rights gains spurred a conservative backlash. Interestingly, instead of multiracial subjects feeling the conservative wrath along with other people of color, they found that conservatives "celebrated and politically recognized" them as model-minority figures. This political atmosphere of mixed-race exceptionalism, which helped elect Barack Obama in 2008, persists. In the post–civil rights era, celebratory mixed-race images abound as multiracial people experience a new racialization in the United States. Mixed-race African Americans, as a new model of an imagined-to-be deracialized population, have been envisioned as racial bridges to a new United States. They are the sum of all races and, therefore, no race at all. Neoconservative and neoliberal Americans deploy images of mixed-race saviors to soothe white fears of allocating equal authority to people of color. And yet, as Michael Omi suggests, "despite legal guarantees of formal equality and access, race continues to be a fundamental organizing principle of individual identity and collective action."[96] In other words, the American racialized power dynamic has not changed with a so-called positive shift in images of mixed-race people.

For the first time, most of the authors writing on multiraciality from the early 1990s onward explicitly identified themselves in their texts as mixed-race or monoracial and interracially coupled. A proliferation of the first generation of multiracial studies scholarship advanced the idea of multiracials as special people. Some related their scholarship to their personal histories and staked a separate space for multiracial people as they spoke back to prior constructions of the hybrid degenerate and the marginal man. The most influential of these is Maria Root's *Racially Mixed People in America* (1992), which the sociologist David Brunsma sums up as articulating "a burgeoning movement arguing *against* the essentialism and inheritability of race . . . while at the same time *reinscribing* essentialism and immutability onto multiraciality itself."[97] First-generation multiracial scholarship and activism largely embraced an additive race model, where mixed-race functioned as another valid category to tack on, instead of a way to deconstruct race or complicate currently existing racialized categories.

In the 1990s the academic side of the multiracial movement was frequently intertwined with activism.[98] While these early works broke out of the black-white model to include mixed-race people of various backgrounds, many of the authors tended to essentialize racial identification, proclaiming that all mixed-race people should identify under the new racial rubric of "multiracial." This divorcing of racialized identity from economic and social contexts, or what Brunsma calls "the reinscribing of essentialism . . . onto multiraciality," ignored the fact that, in the words of Siobhan Somerville, "the discursive constructions of race are inseparable from the material status of bodies."[99] Such divorcing resonated uncomfortably with this era of neoconservatism and neoliberalism, both of which arguably sought to keep racial borders intact through multicultural policies that acknowledged diversity without examining relations of power.

The exceptional figure is part of a color-blind discourse, a painful, negative downside to the hope that the civil rights movement might have won. The change in multiracial imagery, then, accompanies a politicized rationale that race no longer matters, even in material arenas, as the races are now mixed together. A multiracial agenda has also, at times, been embraced by neoconservative and neoliberal figures who appear to see the popularity of the issue of mixed-race as an opportunity to argue for color blindness and against race-based measures.[100] For example, Kim M. Williams writes that in the mid to late 1990s, Newt Gingrich, former Republican Speaker of the House, aligned himself with a so-called multiracial cause, supporting such measures as the addition of a "multiracial" category on the 2000 U.S. Census (this was defeated in lieu of a "mark one or more" option).[101] Neoconservatives in the post–civil rights era of the 1990s aligned themselves closely with "the multiracial cause," which somehow gave them license to deploy the language of the civil rights movement in a manner counter to the movement's progressive politics. Various reactionary, anti–affirmative action organizations use civil rights language, including The Campaign for Color Blind America Legal Defense and Educational Foundation and The American Civil Rights Coalition.[102] In their very titles, these organizations co-opt contemporary calls for diversity, multiculturalism, and color blindness.[103]

Arguments against applying race-based measures such as affirmative action surface in what the sociologist Eduardo Bonilla-Silva describes as "color-blind racism" where discourses of race ignorance effectively work to reinscribe racialized discrimination and safely insulate racists from allegations of racism.[104] Some celebrations of mixed-race, for example, in the exceptional multiracial formulation, constitute a type of color-blind racism where multiraciality is used to mean "no race" despite the persistence of structural racialized inequalities. This connection is illuminated by Catherine Squires in the mass media arena: "In most mainstream media accounts, multiracial identity is yet another vehicle for denying the social import of race and reinforcing the dominant notion that race is a matter of individual tastes and psychology, not structural inequalities."[105]

In a stark example of Squires's statement, Ward Connerly, the neoconservative ideologue, former University of California regent, and author of California's Proposition 209 (the anti–affirmative action measure in California from 1996), now cloned around the country, uses images of rapidly increasing numbers of mixed-race people as the example of why race no longer matters. Such an assumption is based on the notion that interracial marriage and multiracial personhood void the issue of race in both private and public spheres. Connerly argues that race should be made opaque through bills such as the proposed and failed Racial Privacy Initiative of 2003, where racial and ethnic data would have been prohibited from inclusion on state forms. However, many critics of these efforts have pointed out that racialized inequalities and not race itself are obscured through erasures of race-based measures.[106] In other words, ignoring race fails to remove it from its intrinsic tie to the economic, social, cultural, and historic fabric of the United States. As part of this effort, multiracial people are exalted in popular culture as the new model minority, the example of people who can mythically transcend race.[107] They heroically eschew the crutch of race or never play the so-called race card. The subtext is that other black and brown people who cannot get over their racialization are lazily choosing not to. *Transcending Blackness* contests the political tide in which mixed-race African Americans are used as a deracialized excuse, deployed against other people of color as the solution to the problem of race.[108]

Proponents of color blindness, an ideology linked to mixed-race by the idea that mixing races makes them disappear, proclaim that they fail to see race. Ruth Frankenberg breaks through the veneer of color blindness to link it to essentialist racism, describing them as "a double move towards 'color evasiveness' and 'power evasiveness'"; both ideologies are complicit with structural and institutional racism.[109] Color blindness is a convenient bait-and-switch trick where a utopian notion, embodied in the figure of the exceptional multiracial, is used as the bait and is switched for the perpetuation of institutional racism against people of color. Some of the exceptional multiracial's primary characteristics are that he or she is smarter, more attractive, and generally more redeemable because of the residue of whiteness. Mixedness thus enables black transcendence. In the post–civil rights era, politicians and pundits celebrate an image of the mixed-race individual, like Obama, as the bridge to future racial utopia. As the imagined "sum of all races," the mixed-race African American has somehow magically transcended race; the logical extension of this idea is that race no longer matters. This change has at least partially occurred because of anger and resentment over minority gains in the civil rights movement. Celebrating mixed-race is a way to value whiteness over blackness and still safely engage with people of color. Therefore, the exceptional multiracial is an utterly transformable being who moves from old-school passing to a twenty-first-century racial masquerade. Mixed-race African American subjects as the exceptional multiracial are represented in late-twentieth- and early-twenty-first-century popular culture as flexible racialized bodies, the ultimate "floating signifiers," to use the words of Claude Lévi-Strauss and Stuart Hall,[110] or empty vessels who can conveniently be filled with any desired racialized image from hyperraced or starkly racist (like the figure of the tragic mulatta) to de-raced or e-raced (like the figure of the post-racial healer).[111]

The term that denotes an imagined time after racism and racialized identities themselves is "post-race," which stems from the ideology of color blindness.[112] Similarly, another "post," post-feminism, is contingent upon the assumption that the second wave feminist movement eradicated sexism to the extent that it no longer exists, so issues of patriarchy and gender discrimination are simply moot.[113] Just as race and gender intersect in the stereotypes under consideration here, the gambits of post-race and post-feminism inform each other.

Susan Koshy writes that post-race is a metaphoric expression of the "future perfect tense," something that will magically happen if simply described as coming to fruition.[114] Post-race equates the power of people of color's racialization with white racialization. Mary Waters notes that whites see their ethnicity as "optional," a voluntary label. For many whites, according to Waters, "ethnicity is increasingly a personal choice of whether to be ethnic at all, and, for an increasing majority of people, of which ethnicity to be. An ethnic identity is something that does not affect much in everyday life."[115] This philosophy becomes dangerous when people of color are assumed to have this same flexibility, or the same ability to throw off forces of racialized ascription. The philosophy of "optional ethnicity" can lead to "neo-racism," in the words of philosopher Etienne Balibar, which is a "racism without races," produced through a variety of sophisticated practices, discourses, and representations.[116] Images of the exceptional multiracial can stand in as politically correct neoracism, a celebration of whiteness and denigration of blackness. The best evidence about the anti-black racism that constitutes the exceptional multiracial figure is the way in which a conjuring of the exceptional multiracial frequently accompanies political moves such as erasures of race-based initiatives like affirmative action.

Because racialized discourses are undeniably gendered, and gendered discourses are undeniably raced, *Transcending Blackness* works to present an imbricated critique of race and gender, which in the case of the exceptional multiracial is also a critique of post-race and post-feminism. Post-feminism capitalizes upon the feminist idea of choice. Post-feminism dictates that the United States in the twenty-first century no longer needs the antiquated ideals of 1970s-era feminism because we have reached a state of gender equity. Susan J. Douglas traces the term "post-feminism" to a *New York Times Magazine* article from October 1982, "Voices from the Post-Feminist Generation."[117] Post-feminism was popularized in the 1990s by such white female critics as Naomi Wolf, Camille Paglia, and

Katie Roiphe.[118] According to Wolf, post-feminism is a move away from "victim feminism," which she claims "casts women as sexually pure and mystically nurturing, and stresses the evil done to these 'good' women as a way to petition for their rights" and toward "power feminism," which "sees women as human beings—sexual [and] individual."[119] Women under this ideal use performances of femininity to take responsibility for themselves and gain liberal subjecthood. Post-feminism denotes a period of time that comes after "traditional" second wave feminism.[120] Post-feminism claims that the source of women's power is their sexuality. The paradoxical images of post-feminism are most evident in popular culture where, for example, young women might wear skin-tight, midriff-bearing "Girl Power" T-shirts. Post-feminism has also been characterized by critics, such as Ginia Bellafante, as "fashion spectacle, paparazzi-jammed galas, [and] mindless sex talk" and emblematic of "a popular culture insistent on offering images of grown single women as frazzled, self-absorbed girls."[121] These images serve to erase issues of power and privilege, and the very real social and economic situations that affect women's rights.

The ideology of post-race, most evident in the figure of the exceptional multiracial, is facilitated through performances of post-feminism. In other words, movement beyond race occurs by deploying certain racialized performances of femininity. Premising a shared cultural value of "equality," both ideologies of post-race and post-feminism focus more on individual (or micro) experiences as opposed to institutional (or macro) analyses. Like the ideology of post-race, the ideology of post-feminism largely ignores structural or historical boundaries. Post-race and post-feminism are dangerous political ideologies because they provide an excuse for those empowered in society to celebrate and not challenge their privilege. They are individualist philosophies where hard work earns gains, laziness merits loss, and structural inequalities simply do not exist. With these two blinding ideologies, empowered individuals feel justified in their continued oppression of others.

Why Mixed-Race and Why Mixed-Race Blackness?

We are in the midst of what scholars and critics have dubbed the "biracial baby boom."[122] The swell in multiracial births has been well documented by scholars, activists, and federal and state governments.[123] Since the 1990s the topic of multiraciality in the United States exploded in a variety of realms, including social science and humanities scholarship and films, fiction, and television. Mixed-race is a topic of interest in political arenas as well. From the early 1990s until the announcement in 1997 of the "check one or more" category on the 2000 U.S. Census, public debates on mixed-race centered on the counting and identification of multiracial people.

Despite their overrepresentation in popular culture, multiracial African Americans are not the largest or fastest-growing of all multiracial groups. In her analysis of the 2000 U.S. Census, Ann Morning reports that only 5 percent of all African American respondents marked two or more races, while, by comparison, 14 percent of Asian Americans did.[124] By historical comparison, in 1918, when white male enumerators and not individuals accounted for racialized labels, government officials estimated that approximately 75 percent of all African Americans had some non-black ancestry. Comparing the 1918 and the 2000 figures, we can also surmise that people who claim multiracial blackness are usually first generation; a person with one black parent and one parent of another race would be more likely to "mark one or more" than an African American person who might be multigenerationally mixed-race (e.g., someone who has two multiracial parents).

Rising mixed-race numbers, while dramatic, do not, in themselves, reveal any new truths about how race operates. Such numbers, produced today through self-identification, are far from scientific and do not necessarily reflect the numbers of multiply raced people within the U.S. population. In addition, the question of how scholars arrive at these numbers, of checking boxes and counting races, is highly contested. Census statistics are hypervalued in scholarly and popular realms because they reveal the changing demographics of the country. However, in the public sphere, debate rarely moves beyond excitement or trepidation over the mixing of America to truly question what such changes mean for life chances. The constant, differential rates of poverty, by comparison, are shown far less frequently, and the dramatic spike in income inequality is not fair game. Indeed, our new millennium is also marked by the persistence of racialized inequality. Despite this evidence, some cultural workers promote the twenty-first-century solution to the problem of the color line, to tweak Du Bois's famous phrase, as race mixing.[125]

The census is essentially another representation. Scholars who analyze the multiracial numbers from the 2000 U.S. Census contend that debates on mixed-race are really about multiracial African Americans, even though they do not constitute the largest number of mixed-race Americans.[126] The sociologist Nathan Glazer argues that while other mixtures can frequently be dismissed as nonissues, the "divide" between black and white lives on in the contestations of multiracial black Americans' identification as mixed-race and not exclusively African American.[127] Indeed, according to the popular press, the loudest complaints against including a multiracial category in the 2000 U.S. Census came from African American civil rights organizations who interpreted the inclusion of a "check one or more" option as leading inevitably to a decline in their memberships.[128]

While individual events, such as 9/11 or the immigration "crisis," might temporarily reorder the racial hierarchy, the social distance between African Americans and white Americans remains significant and ostensibly unsurpassable. This divide has traditionally given individuals who are racially mixed black and white an air of "impossibility," to quote the literary scholar Jennifer Brody.[129] In the new millennium United States, nearly 150 years after the end of chattel slavery and more than fifty years after the end of de jure racial segregation, the black-white divide continues to bear real and symbolic weight. From birth weight to life expectancy to home ownership to tenuring rates, white Americans outpace African Americans,[130] and a divide rooted in structural, institutional, and material inequality is obscured while African Americans are blamed for so-called faulty culture, spending habits, or work ethics. This obfuscation is reflected in a wide range of representational spaces. Multiracial African American representations in the late-twentieth- and early-twenty-first-century United States both reflect and inform the material and the social; they influence the ways in which census numbers are read and defined. While dramatic numbers might illustrate that mixed-race is a viable area of research, I am interested in understanding not the remarkable multiracial population increase but the discursive meanings behind one effect of such an increase: popular representations of African American mixed-race.

Questions of anti-black racism get more muddled after *Loving*, as issues of racial fluidity enter the picture. The question becomes: would the new millennium mulatta or exceptional multiracial find herself in the same predicaments as the tragic mulatta? Now that multiracial people are doing the creating, by writing, acting, directing, and exercising greater creative control, might there be a chance that representations will come closer to lived experience? The answer to this question lies in the scripting of the quintessential post–civil rights subject, personified most dramatically in the figure of Obama, as often mixed-race. Hybridity and border crossing, two qualities underscored as ideals in the post–civil rights United States, are constitutive to the interracial family and the interracial body, for whom navigating multiple identities is an everyday means of existence. But this quality does not make multiracials exceptional. Trey Ellis and other authors assert that contemporary monoracial African American artists embody a hybridized "New Black Aesthetic . . . [that] shamelessly borrows and reassembles across both race and class lines." These artists, deemed "cultural mulattoes" by Ellis, "grew up feeling misunderstood by both the black worlds and the white."[131] Mixed-race representations illuminate how race is a construction, and, at the same time, how the forces of racialization and the historic one-drop rule of hypodescent, temper elements of personal volition.

The mixed-race African American representations from 1998 to 2008 engage issues of multiracial black racialization and sexualization, tragedy, and privilege. I chose the particular works examined in the book because they feature fictional and nonfictional mixed-race African Americans self-consciously engaging with racialized, gendered, class, sexuality, and color performances and, often, crises. These particular works are representative of this particular time period and particular subgenre of multiracial African American representations. Not surprisingly, identity is very much at the core of these popularly consumed works and many of the representations are both about and by "us," and not "them." In part I, "The New Millennium Mulatta," I investigate late-twentieth- and early-twenty-first-century representations of the reimagined tragic mulatta, a self-reflexive, highly sexualized, and, to varying degrees, ultimately angry and sad figure whose salvation would come about through black transcendence. In chapter 1 I analyze Jennifer Beals's portrayal of Bette Porter on the popular television drama *The L Word*. I contend that Beals's performance of the angry race girl Bette is mired in tragic-mulatta misfortune; haughty, beautiful, arrogant, and emotionally volatile Bette is continuously punished, just like the historic trope of the tragic mulatta. Bette stands out because of the paucity of images of multiracial black women on television. The few representations of mixed-race African American and white women exist primarily in black ensemble casts, such as the sitcoms *The Jeffersons*, *A Different World*, and *Girlfriends*.[132] Television studies scholars note that televisual representations are influential in the creation of self.[133] Televisual representations also function as powerful means of control.[134]

In chapter 2 I investigate the way in which the novelist Danzy Senna reformulates the passing narrative and reinterprets the tragic-mulatta heroine in her production of a new millennium mulatta representation in *Caucasia*. This text has quickly become a popular and scholarly darling; it populates reading lists from high school English classes to college courses on mixed-race. Scholars have also already begun to write extensively about the novel, and Senna herself has been investigated as a type of twenty-first-century multiracial spokesperson. Scholarship and cultural productions on racial passing illustrate that race is far from stable and monolithic, as the mixed-race body can move from a "black race" to a "white race." Amy Robinson argues that the "most rudimentary lesson of passing [is that] the visible is never easily or simply a guarantor of truth."[135] The reality of mixed-race bodies encompassing many races in their (invisible) blood demonstrates just this. To differing degrees, a search for "racial truths" plagues all the mixed-race African American representations that I examine in *Transcending Blackness*; the characters are shown to suffer through racial and sexual performance anxieties. Although Senna's character Birdie, as the sad race girl, bears traces of the old tragic-mulatta characters, as a new millennium mulatta she also functions as a vehicle to critique the tragic mulatto and mulatta and the exceptional multiracial, post-racial, post-feminist ideology. Senna's Birdie also has echoes of the antiracism that scholars such as Ann duCille point out is always central in portrayals of tragic mulattas; duCille writes that for African American writers like Pauline Hopkins and Frances Harper, "the use of the mulatta figure was both a rhetorical device and a political strategy . . . [that] . . . allowed black writers to explore the proscribed social and sexual relations between the races."[136]

In part II, I deconstruct the figure of the mixed-race transformer. In chapter 3 I analyze the independent film *Mixing Nia*. The exceptional multiracial Nia experiences an identity crisis akin to the new millennium mulatta, but her escape from blackness produces her moment of liberation. Chapter 4 investigates an episode of the popular reality television show *America's Next Top Model* in which the contestants are given the dictate "switch ethnicities" to sell a product. While a mixed-race African American character's black-transcending (race-switching) photograph is the lead up to her subsequent victory for the season, all of the contestants engage in the exceptional multiracial masquerade by trading races. My reading reveals the clear corporate forces colluding to sell post-race, post-feminism, and black transcendence. Notably, these representations also reflect 1990s-era ideas of identity fluidity taken to incredible extreme. For example, Stuart Hall writes that while it might be surprising to some, "the representative modern experience" is actually one of being "dispersed and fragmented."[137] Hall argues that identities are not "armor-plated against other identities" and are "not tied to fixed, permanent, unalterable oppositions." He thus proposes choosing "identifications" over "identity" because "once you've got identification, you can decide which identities are working *this* week."[138] However, and importantly, exceptional multiracial representations do not illustrate another vital part of Hall's arguments about identity: while they might be fluid, they are also "historically specific" and a "set of practices."

Whether in the guise of the new millennium mulatta or the exceptional multiracial, the mixed-race African American body is still tied to an imagined, excessive sexuality. As post–civil rights subjects, the characters I examine receive some of this history, but both the new millennium mulatta and the exceptional multiracial figures resist, to different extents, the wholesale marking of their bodies as illicit and illegal. At the same time, mixed-race African Americans bear the marks of a certain degree of prestige because they have historically embodied *the* beauty standard within African American communities. The figures I examine are represented as battling with the forces of both prestige and ostracism. Sometimes their perceived mixed-race desirability grants privileges and sometimes this privilege prevents them from understanding themselves outside of sexual relationships. The characters' explicit racial border crossing demonstrates how racialization is indeed quite malleable: in a number of cases the characters are presented as trying on different racial and sexual personae by altering hair, speech, partners, and manner of dress.[139]

Such identity play illustrates that ideologies are not absolute; they are not sutured shut. I strive to write in the slippages in *Transcending Blackness*. For the new millennium mulatta, and to a certain extent for the exceptional multiracial, the problem of performing "authentic" race is solely the purview of the mixed-race African American character: within a given text, the mixed-race character is the only one questioning racial alliances or attempting to perform authentic racialized identities. Questions of authenticity are thus at the forefront of this book. The texts I examine are not isolated representations of mixed-race African Americans; they are representative texts that showcase contemporary American tropes of the tragic mulatta, multiracial exceptionalism, and black transcendence. The representations in this book are thoroughly imbricated with the social and political landscape of race, gender, class, color, and sexuality in the twenty-first-century United States as well as with the demographic reality of a burgeoning multiracial population, and a multiracial African American president. And yet they miss the complexities of lived mixed-race black American experiences.

The multiracial African American subjects, as new model minorities, are envisioned to be quintessential "new Americans" because, in theory, they coalesce the two poles of ethnicity that have historically divided the United States: they are proof that civil rights succeeded. At the same time their representations are unmistakably tied to historic stereotypes of "mulattoes": they are proof that the races should stay apart. Structuring these representations are the new millennium ideologies of post-race, an imagined time after racialized inequality, and, indeed, race itself, and post-feminism, a fantasized moment after gender discrimination; both ignore the reality that race and gender still dictate life chances in the twenty-first-century United States. Blackness is not seen as a positive part of a multiracial identity or as providing access to community or cultural support. Representations of black-white mixed-race, communicating that black heritage dooms the mixed-race figure to tragedy and that black transcendence sets up the mixed-race character for success, proclaim that racism and sexism are antiquated notions in our new millennium and that blackness must be transcended.

PART I

THE NEW MILLENNIUM MULATTA

CHAPTER ONE

TELEVISING THE BAD RACE GIRL

Jennifer Beals on *The L Word*,

the Race Card, and the Punishment

of Mixed-Race Blackness

From 2004 to 2009, the premium cable channel Showtime aired a groundbreaking nighttime television program, a "lesbian soap opera" that featured a cast of beautiful, and almost exclusively white, young women, whose love, friendship, family, and work lives provided much (melo)dramatic fodder for the show's many loyal fans.[1] At *The L Word*'s inception, its two bankable, big-name stars were women of color both famous for earlier cult-classic films: Jennifer Beals, most notable for her breakout "racially ambiguous" welder/dancer Alex in *Flashdance* (1983), and Pam Grier, celebrated for her "sassy supermama" roles in the Blaxploitation films *Coffy* (1973) and *Foxy Brown* (1974).[2] For a certain segment of viewers hungry to see mixed-race actresses and images in popular culture, extratextual information conveniently provided by press coverage about how Beals "really" is mixed-race (the daughter of an African American man and a white woman) paved the way for her multiracial iconicity. From her first film role to *The L Word*, Beals's race(s) can be seen multiply according to the viewer's differential readings of race; she becomes variously white or racially ambiguous in the films *The Bride* (1985), *Vampire's Kiss* (1988), *Troubled Waters* (2006), and *The Book of Eli* (2010), but she is singularly multiracial and African American in the film *Devil in a Blue Dress* (1995), the television movie *A House Divided* (2000), and the miniseries *The Feast of All Saints* (2001).[3] With this multiply racialized representational past, Beals entered *The L Word* as the feisty "power lesbian" Bette Porter,[4] a role the writers made mixed-race at Beals's request.

The best way to understand *The L Word*'s depiction of Bette is to enter into one of her characteristic scenes. In season 2, as in every season of the show, Bette endures emotional punishment. In this particular episode, Bette transitions from scenes of personal strife to workplace strife. She works at a starkly white, modern, and metal-infused museum as a curator. Light-brown-skinned Bette sits at a board meeting, with her dark hair long, loose, and curly. Her white, tailored pinstriped shirt, replete with silver and black cufflinks, peeks out from her snug brown pinstriped vest; she stands out among the gray-haired, pink-skinned, suit-and-tie-wearing men (see fig. 1).[5] In this scene the only people shown talking are Bette and the man seated directly across the table from her, her boss Franklin, the straight white chair of the board. Franklin makes the mistake of casually describing a lesbian museum associate as "one of your people." Bette immediately understands that Franklin is talking about the associate's sexuality, but as she has already endured a punishing day and as her explosive personality has been written, she dives headfirst into conflict. Her eyes flash with anger and her voice quivers just slightly as she questions, "What are you referring to? What, is she a Yale graduate? Is she an art history major? Is she a mulatto gal? Is that what you're trying to say?" (2.3).

The movement in Bette's questions is telling: her descriptors traverse from two elite markers, an Ivy League degree and a prestigious college major, to a racialized identity of the past. "Mulatto" is an antiquated and, to many, derogatory term. It is not neutral. Paired with "gal," a demeaning and antebellum South–sounding way of describing black women, it seems racist and frozen in the past. Bette's twenty-first-century deployment of the phrase "mulatto gal" in a Los Angeles–area art gallery board meeting is so out of place with "Ivy League" and "art history major" that any discussion of her race is exposed as inappropriate, incongruous, and even laughable. Sexual orientation remains the structuring force in Bette's questions, so large and present that she does not have to name it. Bette constantly and explicitly highlights her sexuality, gender, and class (the

FIGURE 1 Bette in a board meeting.

show manages to drop the phrase "Ivy League" into a surprising number of episodes), so her lesbian identity, womanhood, and privileged status are understood to be integral, constitutive parts of herself. But by dismissing mixed-race blackness as outdated, *The L Word* makes any racialized identity inappropriate for Bette to apply to herself. By inserting race talk through the phrase "mulatto gal" into the show's progressive, post-racial ideological space, the character of Bette uncomfortably "plays the race card," or, through the erroneous and post-racial logic of the phrase, drops racialized meaning into a situation where race supposedly does not exist. By her actions, Bette, a primary signifier for multiracial African American women on television, constantly oversteps her bounds. She is the "bad race girl," the volatile new millennium mulatta who uses race, or, more specifically, uses blackness, when she needs it. The message remains: if Bette would just silence all references to her mixed-race African Americanness, that is, metaphorically transcend her blackness, the entire show would become more functional (and, admittedly, for some viewers, less deliciously dramatic).

Through six seasons of *The L Word*, Bette is written as a character whose multiple, intersectional identities are celebrated in all of their complexity, except when race surfaces. While the show presents Bette's identities of gender, sexuality, and class as imbricated, it compartmentalizes race as a separate, nonintersectional, and ultimately damaging add-on. The treatment of race as a single-axis distraction produces an anti-intersectional "elision of difference," in the words of the critical race theorist Kimberlé

Crenshaw.[6] This scene showcases a persistent narrative element of *The L Word*: the attempted boxing in of Bette's racialized identity and dismissing it as so trivial that it devolves into a mere quip that remains on the level of playing the race card. At times, Bette speaks back to power structures, which Franklin represents, in ways that many minoritized subjects might only fantasize about. In these moments Bette is presented as a superwoman of the type named by Michele Wallace in 1979 as "a woman of inordinate strength, with an ability for tolerating an unusual amount of misery and heavy, distasteful work. This woman does not have the same fears, weaknesses and insecurities as other women, but believes herself to be and is, in fact, stronger emotionally than most men."[7] However, she is not solely a superwoman because Bette is often punished after she speaks back.

The punishment of mixed-race African American characters is typical in representations of the historic tragic mulatta, the damned mixed-blood whose racial illegitimacy marks her as destined for tragedy. Such characters cause an emotional rupture in the text because they are, in the words of Valerie Smith, "signs of the inescapable fact of miscegenation[;] they testify to the illicit or exploitative sexual relations between black women and white men or to the historically unspeakable relations between white women and black men."[8] The difference in this twenty-first-century portrayal, or what makes Bette Porter a new millennium mulatta, is the reimagining of the tragic mulatta through the superwoman; although Bette appears destined for punishment, she refuses to accept such a lot, and, as a result, stops just short of becoming tragic. She is also a new millennium mulatta because she plays the race card. She can "play" race as a "card" because it fails to hold structural, institutional, or material weight in her life. Despite the softening of the historical stereotype of the tragic mulatta (i.e., she no longer goes insane and now has a powerful job), the new millennium mulatta is inevitably a tragic figure (i.e., she is emotionally volatile, which causes her to lose her powerful job). Just like the tragic mulatta, issues of blackness arise only in times of strife for the new millennium mulatta. While *The L Word* negotiates the intersections of upperclass, female, and queer identity through Bette, the series ultimately fails to fully contend with her mixed-race blackness, and instead it embraces a post-racial formulation to treat race as a card. Bette Porter, an emblematic multiracial African American character on television, becomes a convenient metaphor to reinscribe the centrality of whiteness and denigrate blackness.

The Race Card: A Mark of the New Millennium Mulatta

To fully uncover how "the race card" becomes a marker of the new millennium mulatta, I will contextualize the phrase. What, precisely, does "the race card" mean? What are its origins? Who is playing the race card and who is being played? Most writers appear to use the metaphor as a one-off, drop-in, attention-grabbing phrase that is meant to bring a heightened awareness to a person's, an article's, or a book's political leanings; it is a signifier for a certain type of politics rather than a clear-cut, descriptive metaphor. To be reductive for the sake of clarity, this polysemic phrase is used to mean two divergent entities:[9] (1) to an audience that acknowledges racism, it means race baiting (as cause and effect of racism) by white people (and this is the original and more historic usage of the term), and (2) to an audience that denies racism, it means (so-called) race baiting (as cause and effect) by people of color (and this is the more contemporary treatment of the term that I believe *The L Word* is using in its portrayal of Bette). In this first estimation, white people are playing the card and people of color are being played, and in this second estimation, people of color are playing the card and white people are being played. Both envision race, or more specifically, blackness, as a card to be dealt, an ultimate trump, a trick up one's sleeve that is played at a key moment to boost the odds of winning. Because power sets the terms for both sides of this so-called game, I must refute the equivalence of these two readings; the deployment of white racism is not comparable to people of color either illuminating the fact of white racism or inserting discourses of racialized difference.

An early usage of "the race card," deployed in the first formulation, was in newspaper coverage of racist 1960s-era political campaigns in the United States and United Kingdom. This is exemplified in the United Kingdom by the Tory candidate Peter Griffiths's campaign slogan "If you want a nigger for a neighbour — vote Labour" and Enoch Powell's famous "Rivers of Blood Speech."[10] Race baiting also has had much political success in the United States as part of the "Southern strategy," which journalists described as the race card.[11] Race baiting is, of course, not just a Southern phenomenon and is not rooted to some version of the racist, historic past, as illustrated by George H. W. Bush's 1988 Willie Horton ads or the ads from 2006 that targeted the African American Democratic Senate candidate Harold Ford Jr.[12] In these instances, playing the race card means race baiting perpetrated by white racists, for example, how white political campaigns garnered votes by inciting fear of minority encroachment.

The first usage of the "race card," meaning white racism, still exists in contemporary academia; some scholars analyze how racists play the race card with the end result of fomenting white racism. For example, in *Welfare Racism: Playing the Race Card against America's Poor*, the sociologists Kenneth Neubeck and Noel Cazenave call out how racially coded language results in racially stratified poverty. They write of "playing the welfare 'race card' as a strategy in rising calls for meanspirited welfare reform."[13] Similarly, in *Playing the Race Card: Exposing White Power and Privilege*, the education scholars George Dei, Leeno Karumanchery, and Nisha Karumanchery-Luik expand the field of antiracist pedagogy "to critically address and resist the foundations and machinery for racism." They want "to address how the subtleties of racism go unseen, unacknowledged and denied in the eyes and ears of privilege."[14] The phrase is used in the books' titles by antiracist scholars to mark that they are going to speak out against color blindness, or against the assumptions that the United States is now a meritocracy. Such scholars center race and racism as contemporary, structuring forces in personal and institutional ways of life. This scholarship can be used as a call to arms, a statement of praxis, or a way of integrating antiracist theory and action. This is the historic, less popular today, and therefore resistive reading of the phrase "the race card."[15]

But *The L Word* uses the second meaning of "the race card," the predominant, hegemonic one deployed by both popular audiences and academics. The legal scholar Richard Thompson Ford, in *The Race Card: How Bluffing about Bias Makes Race Relations Worse*, defines the phrase as "jumping to a conclusion not compelled by the facts" and "false or exaggerated claims of bias."[16] Interestingly, "race" is not named in Ford's definition. Today the phrase is most often used to mean that people of color unfairly use their racialized difference to their advantage. This usage surged in popularity during the O. J. Simpson trial where media critics accused the defense, and Johnnie Cochran in particular, of playing the race card or of introducing issues of race and racism as a type of bait-and-switch technique. However, in *Playing the Race Card: Melodramas of Black and White from Uncle Tom to O.J. Simpson*, the film theorist Linda Williams writes that in actuality, the prosecution's deployment of the phrase in the Simpson trial illustrates that "the metaphor of the race card attempts to discredit any racialized suffering that can be turned to advantage now that color-blindness is supposedly in effect."[17]

In this second definition, minority status becomes both beneficial and a choice, not an entity laden with economic, structural, historic, and political legacies. There is no understanding of the contemporary salience of racism and of how race structures life chances. There is no understanding of how racism today is often "inferential," to use the words of Stuart Hall, and not always "overt."[18] "Race" functions as a stand-in for minority status, or, more usually, blackness, while whiteness remains the absence of race,[19] and, by extension, the absence of bias. To clarify: in the second use of the phrase, "playing the race card" is really the moment of white racist accusation. In a sense, in crying "race card!," white racists are accusing black people of doing what they themselves are doing. But white racists also do not acknowledge that they are playing the race card as no one actually says publicly, "hey, I'm going to play the race card."

In this second use of the phrase, "the race card" functions as a cover-up for protecting white power, a narrow, ahistorical, nonreality-based understanding of people of colors' racialized identities as merely strategic choice. Even though the phrase is supposedly about minority identity, it reveals far more about whiteness and, in particular, the true material benefits of whiteness, or the "possessive investment in whiteness," to use George Lipsitz's phrase.[20] The assumption in the second use of the phrase is that people of color are winning because of or are making money off of race. The opposite is true. "Playing the race card" is a post-racial statement about the so-called utility of race, which illustrates, as Roopali Mukherjee puts it, "white 'sympathy fatigue' metastasizing to racial resentment and wrath."[21] The second use of the phrase is an outgrowth of new millennium white power, where the benefit of "whiteness as property," to cite Cheryl Harris, is ignored.[22] Race outside of (illegitimate claims to) victimhood is erased in popular understanding of the phrase, and whiteness is not seen with its concomitant material gains. It is not seen as institutional, or even real or operative, in the twenty-first century.

Inherent in the second use of the phrase is an ideology of white victimhood that dismisses racism as a mere relic of the past. This is exemplified in books such as Peter Collier and David Horowitz's *The Race Card: White Guilt, Black Resentment, and the Assault on Truth and Justice* (1997). Collier and Horowitz, a notorious provocateur, write, "Never have the prospects of black people been better in America, and yet never has there been so much talk of race and racism. Moreover, much of the talk, even at the highest intellectual levels, is disingenuous, involving rhetorical guilt trips, hidden agendas, and verbal muggings. Attempts at candor are shut down by the eternal charge of 'racism,' which has become more often a way of invoking cloture on debate rather than a description of psychological pathology."[23] The topic of the book is the race card and yet the main people the book discusses are African Americans. Thus, the first assumption is that race is something that applies solely to African Americans, as they are the ones who truly "have" race, and subsequently have racialized resentment or chips on their shoulders. Black people should be happy with "progress"—true equality, material or otherwise, shouldn't be the goal, just evolution from some unnamed, imagined moment, perhaps slavery, perhaps the Jim Crow South. "Racism" written in quotes denotes that it does not really exist, is only "psychological pathology," and not structural force. Could we turn Collier and Horowitz's sentiments around to assert that they are actually playing the race card? Are they the ones being "disingenuous" with their "hidden agendas" and "verbal muggings," as they appeal to base emotions of white fear of blackness to foment racial anger? A more honest approach would indeed consider African Americans' increased standards of living since de jure segregation, but then would go on to examine, in Michelle Alexander's words, the "New Jim Crow," how in our contemporary movement inequality is racialized structurally and institutionally and is inscribed into every aspect of our lives from infant mortality rates to incarceration to employment to education to housing.[24]

How is the race card used in *The L Word* with regards to Bette? Similar to many times the phrase is deployed in U.S. media culture in the twenty-first century, it does not appear to be about a person of color speaking a moment of truth or unveiling a racialized reality. Instead, the race card signals a moment when a person of color, in this case Bette, shuts down a conversation by unfairly inserting race. Race is thus dismissed as irrelevant, outmoded, and inconsequential, or even a tool to promote reverse discrimination. In *The L Word*, Bette's relationship to her mixed-race blackness is marked by her playing the race card. In the context of the show, whiteness is stripped of its privileged materiality because Bette only discusses race when she needs to win an argument. When a multiracial person with partial white heritage plays the race card, it is presented as even more tragic because such illegitimate subjects foster an internal whiteness, which means that they don't deserve to talk about race. In reality, as a representation, Bette exemplifies the behavior that neoliberal and neoconservative proponents of post-race claim that blacks perform. While the show does not often drop the actual phrase "the race card," it uses the ideology of the phrase in the construction of Bette.

Minoritized groups play a particularly important role in the growth of diverse characters on television in the twenty-first century. The dearth of television characters of color, as well as lesbian, gay, bisexual, and transgender characters, has been lamented by a variety of advocacy groups. One of the ways in which Showtime dealt with "diversity," and complaints of lack thereof, was to produce *The L Word*. Consequently there has been significant attention paid to how *The L Word* represents people who have historically been excluded from television, or those whom the communication scholar Larry Gross describes as "symbolically annihilated," which he defines as "ignored or denied [and] . . . when they do appear they do so in order to play a supportive role for the natural order and are thus narrowly and negatively stereotyped."[25] Some critics have celebrated *The L Word* for its incorporation of racial issues.[26] The performance studies scholar José Esteban Muñoz has defended *The L Word* in the midst of his larger critique: "in neoliberalism's gay formations, race is 'merely cultural' and therefore a kind of symbolic surplus value." Muñoz writes, "The racial particularity of Bette and her half-sister Kit seems initially to be light multicultural window dressing, although that proves not to be the case, insofar as the narrative does not try to contain or manage race."[27] However, *The L Word* has also been critiqued as a show that largely subsumes women of color to primarily focus on white women. Critics cite the paucity of women of color series regulars and the lack of sustained and complex storylines for the few women of color actresses on *The L Word*; indeed, Beals and her sister on the show, Kit Porter (Pam Grier), are the only two women of color who star in the entire series and do not simply drop in for an episode or a storyline. This type of casting and scripting reveals that Showtime is playing the race card to excuse itself from critiques of insufficient racial diversity.

Superwoman Bette

The role of Bette Porter was initially written for a white woman, but Beals was desired for the part. She requested that the writers make Bette mixed-race and African American,[28] which necessitated that the creators, producers, and writers re-envision the character as a multiracial black woman. The effect of this appears to be that in the first season, when Beals's demands were fresh, Bette's racialized identity was explicitly grappled with at a number of points. In subsequent seasons, however, Bette's racialized identity is dropped and she, in effect, passes for white within the show's storylines. However, despite the show's lack of race talk, Beals's performance of Bette is coded as new millennium mulatta (as evident in her haughty, emotional, strident personality). Such coding can be understood through Daphne Brooks's formulation of the "politics of opacity," which permits critical viewers "to read across the gaze of the normative spectator."[29] Identifying the politics of opacity that structures the representation of Bette illuminates the ways in which the character is thoughtfully developed through gender *and* class *and* sexuality, with the occasional add-on of race. In other words, reading Bette through the politics of opacity illustrates the failure of the show to fully grapple with mixed-race blackness as a component of intersectionality.

In *The L Word*, which critics have described as a space where "all the women are beautiful, all are thin, all enjoy material comfort, and all have impeccable sartorial style,"[30] Bette is the main character, the linchpin upon whom the other storylines depend. The critic Sarah Warn, founder and editor of AfterEllen.com, asserts that Bette is "so central . . . to the narrative and rhythm of the series . . . that her emotional state tends to drive the overall tone of the show. . . . [A]s Bette goes, so goes *The L Word*."[31] However, although Bette is arguably the main character of this ensemble cast, she is often absent from the group scenes, the ones described by Warn as "the best scenes . . . when the characters are simply hanging out together: bantering, arguing, advising, and teasing one another, while providing an undercurrent of support."[32] As a superwoman, Bette never has time for these gatherings, and the show positions her as alone and sanctimoniously above the other characters.

Through its representation of Bette as tragic, *The L Word* presents race as something old and biological. Additionally, through its representation of Bette as a character for whom racialized identity is an occasional add-on, the show presents race as malleable, volitional, and untouched by structure or institutions. These are clearly contradictory statements about race, which are, perhaps, merely an effect of the paradoxes of racialization itself. The sociologists Michael Omi and Howard Winant describe race as prescribed, institutional, and singular and yet also constructed, hybrid, and multiple.[33] The difference between Omi and Winant's and *The L Word*'s contradictions about race is the framing of mixed-race blackness as a race choice, an effect of the show's race-card view of race. As a superwoman, Bette has the ultimate power to make any choice she likes, including race choice.

Bette, the alpha female of the group, is a character study of intensity. In an ensemble cast where the actresses exercise whole ranges of emotions, Bette is stuck between anger, indignation, and mourning. She rarely smiles unless it's a rueful smile, which audiences come to understand will soon be followed by an enraged bark or a desolate tear. Some of this might just be Beals's particular acting style, described by one journalist as "a credible combination of hesitation and fortitude."[34] Perhaps Bette's constantly agitated persona illustrates that she is written as an angry lesbian, angry feminist, or angry black woman. Bette does not make a joke unless it will accompany a dig. She is competitive and controlling. The show suggests that Bette feels she is entitled to abuse her friends and coworkers: she is beautiful, takes advantage of her near-white-skinned privilege, and has an elite education and career. Reflecting the myth of the lusted-after tragic mulatta, Bette is also shown as highly desirable. In the brief period of time that she's uncoupled, the whole of the lesbian community in Los Angeles is presented as lusting after her (4.2).

Bette's character is written in tandem with her on-again, off-again, calm, caring, domestic white partner, Tina Kennard (played by Laurel Holloman). In many "diverse" or "multicultural" iterations of popular culture, blackness is understood through its apparent polar opposite, whiteness. As whiteness animates blackness (even the mixed-race blackness of Jennifer Beals), in this liberal, multicultural television show, Bette functions in relation to blond Tina, portrayed as white woman incarnate and celebrated as the most redeemable and most moral character on the show. The audience meets Bette and Tina in some of the very first shots of the premiere episode, because their narrative is at the center of the story. They are the metaphoric parents to the group, the oldest members, and the only consistent (if on-again, off-again) couple, whom Eve Kosofsky Sedgwick describes as "the grown ups."[35] While the show does not comment on the ages of the characters, Beals is significantly older than Laurel Holloman and the other supporting actresses, outside of Pam Grier.[36] Within the couple, Bette is clearly the one in charge: she has the high-powered job, and in the very first episode Tina reveals to a neighbor that she has quit her job "to prepare [her] body for pregnancy" (1.1). The critic Rebecca Beirne writes that Bette and Tina, as "the primary lesbian relationship" of the show, are "portrayed as being structured by visual and narrative gendered and racial difference." These differences are evident, for example, in their communicative styles as well as the characters' clothes: Bette often wears business attire while Tina is dressed in "peasant clothes and that on the rare occasions when both are wearing suits, one is in white and the other is in black."[37] Even their wardrobes announce that they are foils to be read against each other.

Despite the writers' punishment of Bette, an online community worships Bette and Tina as a couple. Dubbing themselves "Tibettans," fans have created a website, a Myspace page, and scores of YouTube video clips and video montages.[38] For viewers, Bette's demanding personality and upper-crust tastes make her an object of derision, while her alpha female personality also makes her an object of desire. *The L Word* suggests that Bette deserves her punishment, which I will examine in depth, partially because she is self-absorbed; Tina tells a friend after she and Bette have broken up and Bette has failed to notice that she is four months pregnant, "Bette's pretty wrapped up in herself. She doesn't always see what's right in front of her" (2.5). Bette expects and demands elite status and is mocked for that. However, she is also praised for going up against power structures. Thus, the majority of the show's characters, reflecting the preferred meaning of the narrative, experience a joint admiration and contempt for Bette.

Bette's disdainful nature is classed and racialized. We know that Bette is an Ivy League graduate (like Beals) and this fact is underscored throughout the show. Like the entitled tragic-mulatta passer figure, Bette expects the accoutrements of an elite lifestyle, which translates to demanding whatever she wants precisely when she wants it. Like the superwoman, her competitive nature is unparalleled in *The L Word*'s cast of characters, whether in a board meeting, basketball game, or Baby and Me gathering. In a children's music class with her six-month-old daughter, Angelica, and Tina, Bette's failure to procure a triangle for her baby results in her hissing at the triangle grabber, "asshole" (3.1). While such incidents make her seem childish and irrational, not to mention unmaternal, the show simultaneously illustrates her as a powerful figure who is able to protect her friends and family, particularly in scenes of business negotiation, such as when Bette helps her sister wrest back control of her business (5.9).

For example, Bette's almost laughable bravado is showcased when a social worker comes to her house to investigate if she is fit to legally adopt Angelica, as Tina is Angelica's biological mother. The wheelchair-equipped social worker rolls around Bette's living room, raising her eyebrows in disbelief as she picks up dangerous objects, such as a fireplace poker and a sculpture with spikes. In response to the social worker's incredulity, Bette remarks, "I don't really believe in baby proofing per se. I mean, first of all, it's ugly and I really want Angelica to develop an intrinsic sense of beauty" (3.1). The audience is meant to laugh at Bette as she snootily demeans commonly understood practices to create safe playing and learning environments in lieu of an elite, and dangerous, ideal of beauty. Bette's superwoman-like flouting of state power is simultaneously infuriating (Who does she think she is? Doesn't Bette know what could happen to her?) and empowering (She doesn't care what could happen to her!). Additionally, Bette's version of privileged multiraciality in this scene can also be read as a rejection of state intervention in the form of racialized identity and raising children without state regulation. She will, however, be punished for such behavior.

In a related vein, one of diva Bette's more emphasized personality traits is her narcissism. Bette hosts a dinner party ostensibly thrown to introduce her friends to her new deaf girlfriend, Jodi (played by Marlee Matlin); post–dinner party Bette lashes out at Jodi, complaining about how "hard" the evening was for her. Feisty Jodi, the opposite of pushover Tina, expresses no sympathy for Bette as she pointedly illustrates Bette's abuse of her class privilege even within their relationship: "You want to be in a relationship with someone who works *for* you." When Jodi amps up her critique, naming all the people whom Bette attempted to control, Bette reverts to her common response in confrontations: she curses at Jodi (4.10).[39]

The scene and the episode end with Bette practically spitting at Jodi, "I had no idea you felt so fucking persecuted. It makes me feel so fucking sad for you. I think that for one minute you should ask yourself, what am *I* experiencing? What is my fucking experience?" In delivering the second-to-last line Beals hits her own chest for emphasis on the "*I*," showing her nearly physical need to script herself perpetually into the center and her inability to accept fault or apologize. With Bette's delivery of the last line, a discordant, high-pitched metallic sound explodes, matching the discord between Bette and Jodi. Bette storms out and slams her bedroom door while a slow drumbeat leads to the credits. Bette is exposed as a dysfunctional personality who infuses anger into a variety of situations and destroys relationships.[40] Furthermore, Bette's lines sound eerily similar to reverse discrimination claims, the rhetoric produced by anti–affirmative action proponents that presumably illustrates how those in power are actually disempowered. Such rhetoric, according to Catherine Squires, "either implies or explicitly states that racism no longer exists or is not widespread enough to continue justifying affirmative action."[41] Why use this coding with Bette? The answer appears to lie in the management of Bette's on-again, off-again relationship to her mixed-race blackness. In the show's neoliberal, anti–affirmative action bias, racialized identity is something a new millennium mulatta strategically deploys for gain but does not otherwise affect one's life: it's a race card.

Race, Reproduction, and Bette

Multiracial African American identity and its representation are bound up in issues of reproduction from the legacy of hundreds of years of U.S. antimiscegenation laws. Subsequently, the majority of Bette's race scenes are related to her daughter, Angelica. A key scene to examine regarding race, reproduction, and multiraciality is when Bette is absent for central moments of the storyline, but where her very absence structures the scenes. In the premiere episode of *The L Word*, before we learn anything else about Bette and Tina, we learn that they want to have a baby, and that Tina will be the one to get pregnant. Bette surprises Tina by choosing a donor without consulting her. When introducing Tina to the idea of the donor, Bette tells her, "I know exactly what you and I are looking for and he is so perfect." Bette neglects to mention race and instead emphasizes that the donor, Marcus (played by Mark Gibson), is an artist of some renown who "has just been selected for the next Whitney Biennial." Tina is presented as having no voice in the matter. Bette is absent from the scene where Tina meets Marcus, but that absence is glaringly present as Bette is the one who holds the secret that structures the episode: Marcus is black.

When Marcus arrives at Bette and Tina's house, the camera replicates Tina's point of view and then cuts away as she opens the front door. The camera then reveals part of the mystery outside the door as it frames an expanse of blue shirt but does not show an inch of skin. It too is complicit with Bette's neglect to mention race; the camera and Bette withhold the secret of blackness, saving it up for race-card play later in the episode. From inside the door we see Tina craning her neck up and saying, incredulously, "Marcus?" as the door continues to conceal Marcus's form. After standing at the door for an awkward amount of time, Tina sputters, invites Marcus in, and leaves the room. She has no words to convey her emotions when meeting this large black man and exhibits a form of what Eduardo Bonilla-Silva calls "rhetorical incoherence," nonsensical speech filled with "digressions, long pauses, repetitions and self-corrections" that for whites "is the result of talking about race in a world that insists race does not matter."[42] In other words, Tina's awkward actions and words reveal her fear of blackness and not her eventual claims of color blindness.

As Tina leaves the room, the camera finally frames Marcus as he enters the house. He is a tall, broad, dark-skinned, bald-headed black man in a blue polo shirt, with sunglasses perched on his head, and a shoulder bag strewn over his right shoulder. Left alone, Marcus closes the door and sits back onto the sofa, chewing gum, waiting expectantly, and looking the slightest bit irritated. Meanwhile the camera cuts to show Tina sitting on her bed, head in hands, looking confused, worried, and nervous. She sums up these emotions with a curse, and then summarily attempts to hide her obvious fears of black masculinity by patting her hair and walking briskly to Marcus. In the intervening moments, Marcus has figured out what has gone on and says, "Did Bette not tell you I was black?" Tina responds, her words, double negatives and all, spilling nervously over each other, "No, not at all. But she didn't not tell me because it doesn't matter either way, right?" Marcus doesn't entertain Tina's desire to hide her racism behind color blindness and simply states, "Well, I can't answer that for you." Throughout the scene the camera emphasizes how much bigger Marcus is than Tina. Tina is shot from a high angle and looks small, while Marcus's broad frame encroaches upon the foreground of the shot. While Tina might be condemned by some viewers for her racism, I would argue that the show's preferred message is that Bette's inability to discuss race, her keeping Marcus's blackness a secret, marks her at fault for Tina's (the show's perpetual good girl) discomfort.[43]

In the follow-up scene when Tina confronts Bette about keeping Marcus's race a secret, Tina's liberal white racism goes unnamed while Bette is presented as the inconsiderate partner, forcing blackness into the body of Tina without her consultation or consent. If Bette were more vocal about her mixed-race African Americanness, would Tina's response have been quite so vehement? Bette's silence about her multiracial blackness, her use of race only as a card, allows Tina the luxury of not thinking about race, as having a mixed-race African American child is unthinkable until she is confronted by a large black man about to hand over his sperm.[44]

And this sperm does eventually produce a child whom Tina bears. The show explores the race card not only through Bette but through her proxy, her mixed-race daughter. Even before Angelica is born, she becomes a useful platform upon which *The L Word* ruminates about diversity and the race card.[45] The show plays with the notion of using diversity for gain within privileged sites. Before Tina becomes pregnant, their friend Alice opines, "You're really cutting edge now. Lesbian moms. Biracial child. Well, you're not going to have trouble getting that kid into the Center for Early Education. It's going to be like diversity poster child" (1.3). This is a prosaic statement: four seasons later Bette indeed uses Angelica's difference in their hunt for the most prestigious preschool, because Bette is as intensely ambitious for Angelica as she is for herself. To Tina's angry admonition, "I'm not going to let your overachieving, psycho dysfunction stress out our kid before she's three years old," Bette screams in reply that getting their daughter into an elite preschool is equivalent to "a fucking Ivy League education" (4.6), the class marker that informs so much of Bette's own identity. After Angelica interviews at one posh preschool, Tina, Bette, and Angelica run into their competition, a gay male couple with their adopted son. Reiterating Alice's earlier statement, Bette confidently tells their family, "Well I think we've got a pretty good shot. Biracial daughter, lesbian moms" (5.1). Both families' minoritized status is represented as a marker to exploit for entry into an elite institution. The two same-sex families are presented as competing against each other for the imagined single LGBT family slot.[46] This is particularly interesting in a post–Proposition 209 California where in the public sector affirmative action has been abolished and some see race as over. However, in the privileged private school world in which Bette and Tina hope to raise Angelica, "diversity" is assumed to be an entrance ticket into elite spaces, or, in other words, a race card.

The actual phrase "the race card" is deployed on the show surrounding custody arrangements for Angelica. In the season 3 cliffhanger, Bette kidnaps Angelica. Bette believes that she will be excised from Angelica's life by Tina and her current white boyfriend. Season 4 begins with all of the supporting characters weighing in on Bette's actions, and Kit finding Bette and Angelica hidden in a deserted cabin. Kit talks Bette into returning Angelica to Tina, but Bette and Tina meet in Bette's white lawyer's office because Bette wants sole custody of Angelica. When the lawyer, Joyce (Jane Lynch), speaking on behalf of her client, tells Tina that they are going to "play the race card" in the custody battle for Angelica, Bette interrupts Joyce and says, "It's not a card. It's something I know to be firmly and intrinsically true. Tina's not qualified to parent a biracial child." Interestingly, here Bette resists the deployment of the race card to mean that race is inconsequential: race is something real in Bette's estimation, and it's something so real that it prevents a white woman from raising a healthy, happy multiracial African American child (and with Bette's words the audience is free to imagine that damaged Bette was poorly parented by her own white mother). If this statement were presented by another character on the show with an established degree of credibility, it might hold some weight. However, iterated by irrational and vindictive Bette, it ends up being presented as a mere ploy (4.1).

Bette continues, explaining how she deserves full custody of Angelica:

> Tina may have given birth to her but really Angelica is the mirror of me. I know what she's going to experience as a biracial girl growing up in a divisive world. I mean, let's face it, when Tina goes out in public with Angelica, people automatically assume she's been adopted. But when they see me with Angelica, they see mother, daughter. I'm the one who's going to be able to give her a sense of belonging. . . . I do not want my daughter growing up in a house where she feels like an outsider because everyone else is white. . . . She's going to get that enough as it is in the world at large and I know, I know what that feels like. Angelica belongs with me. (3.11)

Bette's face fills the frame in an extreme close-up shot during this monologue. In this intimate view, Bette's emotions fluctuate between her rueful smile, quivering sadness, and pride in her conviction that she is revealing the unqualified truth. Bette is refuting race and biology: if one were to follow biological proximity, Angelica would go with Tina, her biological mother. However, Bette's objection to biology is not on the basis some might think—love matters, not race. In fact, she is arguing the opposite: *looks alone* match her to Angelica, even though, incidentally, the young actress who plays Angelica (Olivia Windbiel) could not possibly pass for white as Bette can. Even in the ostensibly safe domestic space of her house, Bette predicts Angelica's tragic lack of belonging and her inevitable search for a racial role model. Bette's monologue reveals a disdain for non-race-matching family that seems particularly troubling given her role as Angelica's nonbiological mother. Again, the writers have Bette play the race card when it is convenient for the storyline. Such cavalierly racialized storylines produce a statement about the racially flexible nature of mixed-race blackness, or how multiracial African Americans use race (or more specifically, use blackness) when they need to win but otherwise choose not to engage in racial issues.

When the show does delve deeper into racial issues, for example, by challenging notions of black essentialism, such ideas are dismissed because they are tinged with homophobia. Another race and reproduction example arises when Bette's father, Melvin, the iconic African American film actor Ossie Davis, visits during a multiepisode arc. After Tina becomes pregnant, Bette excitedly tells him, "You're going to have another grandchild!" Melvin immediately rejects the notion on the basis of biology, telling Bette and Tina in his formal, old-fashioned diction, "that is biologically impossible. . . . I cannot realistically be asked to participate in this fiction of your creation." As Tina is now shown to be 100 percent behind bearing a mixed-race African American child, her response to Melvin's dismissal is to tell him, a bit deflated but still quite eagerly, that they have chosen a black donor so that their child will reflect Bette's paternal side of the family. Melvin refutes the notion of this child as family summarily, rhetorically questioning Bette, "And because of this I'm supposed to feel closer to this child? Because all of us blacks are somehow connected? We can be traced back to some tribe in Africa where we were beating drums? That is absurd. You are an Ivy League–educated woman. How is this logical?" (1.6).

On the one hand, Melvin defines family as something purely biological and thus rejects the idea that Bette can even create a family with Tina. On the other hand, Melvin's critique can be read as a challenge to black essentialism. Bette's seemingly faulty logic and educational pedigree are called upon in Melvin's questioning. His objection clearly stems from his homophobia, linked with his disdain for the reproductive technologies used to create Bette and Tina's baby. What remains present but unexamined is that while black men are rendered unnecessary, except for their sperm, for the reproduction of (mixed-race) black children, blackness never surpasses the level of race card, or racialized metaphor.

The New Millennium Mulatta Comes Home to Whiteness

Bette is perhaps so punishable, like the tragic mulatta, because of her desire for whiteness. Despite the fact that *The L Word* has been celebrated as groundbreaking for being the first lesbian drama, it has not similarly broken ground in terms of race. Journalists have called the show "a gay 'Friends' meets 'Melrose Place,'"[47] and "a cross between a female *Queer as Folk* and *Sex and the City*."[48] All four series share overwhelmingly white casts. And whiteness also structures the narrative of *The L Word* and remains the unspoken but determining force. Whiteness also centrally defines Bette through her relationship with Tina, described by Tavia Nyong'o as "the show's archvictim [who] is victimized from first to last."[49] This is a particular iteration of white womanhood where Tina needs, and deserves, rescuing, often from Bette. In opposition, Bette has no rescuer and deserves her falls.

Bette and Tina's dynamic, and the show's celebration of Tina versus its punishment of Bette, is evident in one scene in the penultimate episode of season 2. During one of their reconciliations, Bette reclines on very pregnant Tina as she strokes Bette's hair (fig. 2). The two women are spending the evening in Bette's low-lit living room, watching her father die. From his rented hospital bed, Melvin has been fading in and out of consciousness and has become increasingly delusional. Silence dominates this scene; the primary sound is the regular beeping of Melvin's monitors. The quiet is broken when Melvin wakes briefly to comment to both women, "now that's what I like to see," and then directly to Tina, "now promise to take good care of my girl." The camera cuts between intimate medium close-up shots of Melvin and Bette and Tina. Bette beams up at Tina and Tina smiles contentedly. Melvin's gentle tone stands in stark contrast to his normal judgment of their relationship, where his homophobia prevents him from saying Tina's first name, much less referring to her affectionately. However, as soon as they relax into this glimmer of kindness from Melvin, he continues to Bette, "and you, you take good care of your mother too." As the women realize that Melvin has mistaken Tina for his former wife, Bette continues her collapse into grief, mourning the loss of her father and his misrecognition of Tina.

Ostensibly about the imminence of death and life, this scene reinforces

FIGURE 2 Bette and Tina.

the centrality of white women as objects of desire and longing. Bette cannot be seen without the specter of her white mother or white partner.
Whiteness is an unnamed but always central aspect of *The L Word*. As
Bette is understood through this celebration of whiteness, the show for-
gets about Bette's (multiracial) blackness and thus scripts her into whiteness. Perhaps a way to understand how Bette's mixed-race blackness defaults to whiteness is P. Gabrielle Foreman's notion of "passing *through*"
whiteness, which is "the concept of passing *through* whiteness rather than
passing *over* and out of the race, of temporary appropriation that stops
short of ontological identification. No one has to catch [passers] or 'get'
them 'back into their racial role' in any literal sense."[50] *The L Word*'s presentation of Bette illustrates a similar, merely temporal notion of passing.
Bette's character is so bound by whiteness that, as with Foreman's analysis of earlier mulatta characters, she does not need to be caught: she will
script herself into metaphorical whiteness, if only as a temporal stop. But
while Bette is represented through a default or unnamed whiteness, her
punishments arise from her valuing and embodying whiteness. What further solidifies *The L Word*'s focus on whiteness is Bette's ultimate longing for Tina, which defaults to longing for whiteness. Bette desires to, in
her words during one of their reconciliations, "come home" to Tina (5.9).
This is an echo of the tragic-mulatto trope: a hidden but central longing
for whiteness. Through racialized, gendered, and sexualized coding, the
power at play is one of black versus white, and home front versus work
sphere. Reflecting the show's celebration of whiteness in Bette and Tina's

relationship, their house is starkly white and sparsely furnished, so that the art on the walls, which is valuable, the audience is told multiple times, is showcased. Home becomes a sterile, beautiful, gallery-like, and very white space.

Thus, regardless of the self-conscious referencing of mixed-race blackness at certain opportune moments, multiraciality and blackness writ large remain peripheral to Bette's representation, outside of coding, such as "haughty" personality traits.[51] Bette is not shown in relation to people of color, outside of her father; sister, daughter; or a five-episode story arc about an affair with an Afro Latina carpenter (1.11–2.1). Although she has a close relationship with Kit, she is not a part of a community of color and she does not have more than a cursory relationship with the other women of color on the show. Instead, Bette is shown to engage with issues of her racialized identity when it is going to mark her as a victim, make her seem special or different, benefit her in an argument, or gain her entry into a limited-access arena. Bette is constructed as a character who does not live as a woman of color but instead uses race for personal gain.

Such framing of race, and particularly mixed-race blackness as the race card, begs the questions: We all know race is constructed, but what are the limits? Where does racialized representation end and racialized real life begin? Describing the limits of understanding blackness through pure performativity, E. Patrick Johnson depicts "lived experience" of blackness as "the inexpressible yet undeniable racial experience of black people — the ways in which the 'living of blackness' becomes a material way of knowing."[52] By eschewing Bette's "living of blackness," The L Word has her reject the epistemological iterations of blackness and instead play the race card (4.1). Volitional engagement with race thus becomes a defining characteristic of the televisual new millennium mulatta.

(Mis)Reading Multiracial Blackness

The construction of Bette Porter's identity vis-à-vis the race card and white womanhood is not simply made through strategic deployment of race, passing as a white woman, being a child of a white woman, or a partner to a white woman. Bette's characterization illustrates the show's inability to, in the words of Valerie Smith, "read simultaneity," represent a messy intersectionality full of the multiple facets, contradictions, and complications of Bette's multiple identities.[53] Bette's multiracial blackness is at times a central part of her storyline and at other times a forgotten entity. In other words, Bette's mixed-race African Americanness operates as an add-on character device, conveniently deployed when the show casts Bette as an undeserving woman claiming victimhood, as in the tragic mulatta, but it is forgotten most other times, as in superwoman Bette.

For Bette, race, and blackness in particular, remains unnamed except when she brings it to the surface in moments of conflict. Blackness is therefore bad for Bette, because it is solely about difficult moments, unless it is being stripped of all history and social import to be pumped for benefits. Blackness does, however, resonate in the show in ways that inform but are largely peripheral to Bette's character. The casting of Ozzie Davis and Pam Grier as Bette's father and sister, respectively, signals politicized modes of black representation. In season 1 the rapper Snoop Dogg plays a hip-hop artist who reveres Kit, who has a mostly ignored backstory as a funk icon from the 1970s, even as he steals the rights to her sample. While the metatextual intergenerational indebtedness applies to Bette through familial proxy, as a character, Bette is placed outside of black pop cultural resonances. Instead, Bette is presented as attempting to manage her racialization in the same way that she manages other aspects of her life: she wants to control the way in which other people see her race(s), a tricky if not impossible endeavor.

With the exception of the topic of race and reproduction, most of the discussion of Bette's racialized identity happens in asides or in quick, sporadic moments and not in more central aspects of her storyline. Perhaps this is simply a realistic representation of how racialization is managed in the life of someone who often passes for white. For example, an evangelical Christian debating with Bette on a television program gets under her skin by remarking, prior to their debate, "It must be hard for makeup people to find your color. It's so in between. I guess they'll have to mix" (1.10). The show informs us that this knowledge of Bette's mixed-race was acquired through careful homework on the part of the debate opponent's people and not by a mere reading of Bette's physicality. The speaker's comments reveal that outing Bette as "in between" or mixed-race will upset and destabilize her because the opponent has found Bette's weakness by discovering her hidden black heritage.

At the same time, at other moments when she can benefit from her racialized minority status, Bette is a character who demands to be read as a person of color in a volitional engagement with racialization. When the show engages in a self-referential show-within-a-show storyline in the fifth season, Bette is furious that the film version of her is played by a white actress. Bette rages to Tina while the actress listens with a curious expression on her face: "I am flabbergasted that [the filmmaker] cast such a white actress [to portray me]. She's white. OK, was Mary Fucking Poppins unavailable? I mean really, what the fuck can she possibly know about my life? What can she know?" Bette punctuates this sentiment by storming out of the room. Comically, as soon as Bette leaves, the actress lazily questions Tina, "Is she black?" (5.5). In this scene the audience is to understand that Bette's identity as African American is an add-on, something unreadable to most and something that she deploys at moments when she feels angry or frustrated about any number of nonracially specific issues. As her passing is noted by the actress, Bette is not seen as black by outsiders, which makes her assertion of her blackness appear to be pure fabrication (playing the race card). Bette is not attempting to pass herself off as white, but, rather, she is being passed by an observer.

Passing versus being passed is an important distinction that remains largely unexamined in the show, except for the ninth episode of season 1, which touches on intra–African American dynamics of race. Although Bette has agreed to attend group therapy with Tina, her dismissive, skeptical looks in a session show that she is closed off to the experience. When the group members are each directed to speak in turn about their greatest parenting fears, Bette is the only one who says "pass." The word "pass," with all of its variable meanings, is not an accident. She requests skipping a turn to avoid having to engage deeply with the issues, but instead receives a critique of her ostensible race passing. The other African American member of the group, a brown-skinned woman named Yolanda, criticizes Bette for vocally claiming her lesbian identity, and not letting herself pass as straight, but not claiming her black identity, and letting herself pass into whiteness. Yolanda's statements are predicated upon the idea that Bette cannot be read as black by white people, or as she puts it, "I mean [the others in our therapy group are] wondering what the hell we're talking about because they didn't even know you were a black woman."

The literary theorist Amy Robinson formulates the "triangular theater" of passing, which stars the passer, the in-group member, and the dupe. In this case Bette is the passer, Yolanda functions as an in-group member, and the rest of the characters in the scene are the dupes, with the exception of Tina.[54] Bette's passing only resonates if both an in-group member and a dupe can participate. Later in the scene Bette describes herself as "half–African American and my mother is white." In her failure to follow the rules of parallel structure, Bette neglects to name her father while she names her white mother. Whiteness informs her identity by proxy, but blackness does not figure at all. When she is pressed by Yolanda to solely claim a black identity, Bette retorts, "I would never define myself exclusively as being white any more than I would define myself exclusively as being black." She continues, "I mean really, why is it so wrong for me to move more freely in the world just because my appearance doesn't automatically announce who I am?" With these words the writers have Bette equate blackness with lack of freedom, a metaphoric shackling. Whiteness, on the other hand, denotes freedom and success. This formulation surfaces time and again for the multiracial African American figure in the twenty-first century, and we will see it again in the exceptional multiracial formulation.

Yolanda is typified as the angry black woman whose excesses are made to seem outmoded and ridiculous. Kimberly Springer points out that although the stereotype of the angry black woman is ubiquitous in twenty-first-century television, "the question rarely asked, though, is why these black women are so angry."[55] Springer speculates that the answer lies in the hegemony of post-feminist and post-racial discourses, which "erase history and claim equality as today's norm for women and people of color."[56] In her scene with Yolanda, Bette, as a different kind of (but not really) black woman, announces the unviability of black feminist thought for the contemporary multiracial African American female subject. As black womanhood is only understandable as Yolanda's angry black woman, Bette is further scripted into default whiteness, and the show illustrates its refusal to recognize intersectional feminist thought.

Furthermore, while race passing, or the intertwined logics of race and sexuality passing, receives scant attention on The L Word, there is significant attention paid to the issues of passing and sexuality. Consideration of race is largely written out of the show with regard to Bette's character, so passing translates to sexuality passing. In addition, as the group therapy session illustrates, visible versus invisible or legible versus illegible identities are driving themes in The L Word and in Bette's representation. Instead of presenting her identity categories as intertwined and intersectional, with one informing the other, Bette's race and sexuality, in particular, are often juxtaposed, with sexuality placed hierarchically above race. In the portrayal of Bette, the show appears to assume that there exists some real black identity that only occasionally applies to those who pass as white. A discussion of passing often circles around a problematic discussion of what it means to "really" look like a member of a certain group, or to authentically perform as a member of a minoritized group.

In opposition to the silencing of race talk, Bette is quite outspoken about being an out lesbian. As opposed to her often-silent acceptance of being passed as white, she vehemently refuses to pass as straight and constantly outs herself. In the pilot episode Bette is the first member of the cast to explicitly describe herself as lesbian, telling her therapist that he, a "straight male," "couldn't possibly understand a lesbian relationship" (1.1). Later in that same episode Bette balks at their fertility doctor's suggestion that she sexually arouse Tina in order to aid in their conception, spitting, "I mean, frankly I find it incredibly inappropriate that she even suggested it. I mean, I bet she would never do that with a straight couple" (1.1). While several of The L Word characters could pass as straight in many settings, as Bette's character is shown to be able to, most do not constantly out themselves as Bette does. In addition, to return briefly to the issue raised by the show's race-card approach to racializing Bette, this is yet another moment when Bette repeats the phrase that others "couldn't possibly understand" her experience either of being mixed race or of being a lesbian. Perhaps Bette's scripting reveals that privileged whites cannot understand even when people of color explain ad nauseam. The race-card accusation can also be seen as a privileged white move to counter what feels like an irrefutable claim of exclusive authenticity. The experiences of real mixed-race people trying to communicate their lived realities are always deferred because of the slippage between the representation (with its concomitant accusation of the race card) and the complexities of mixed-racialized experiences.

The issue of outing oneself as opposed to passing—inadvertently or not—is a central idea both inside and outside the text of The L Word. As the rhetorician Charles E. Morris III puts it, "Passing implies peril. . . . It entails a precarious combination of secrecy and disclosure."[57] Indeed, critics and academics have noted the anxiety about the "secrecy and disclosure" in the representation of passing issues on The L Word. The queer studies scholars Susan Wolfe and Lee Ann Roripaugh assert that popular reviews of The L Word "reveal a consistent sense of anxiety about lesbian representation: assimilationist visibility vs. marginalized invisibility, identitarian 'authenticity' vs. Revlon revolution 'passing,' second wave vs. third

wave feminism, lesbianism vs. post-lesbianism, and policing of commodi-
fied mainstream image making vs. the policing of negative stereotypes."[58]
Wolfe and Roripaugh's delineation of multiple modes of passing showcases the anxiety about representation, the "burden of representation"
as Ella Shohat and Robert Stam put it, where minoritized groups feel the
responsibility to highlight their so-called positive aspects simply because
there are so few other images available.[59] But issues of race remain invisible. As in *The L Word*'s struggles to represent Bette's intersectionality, even in Wolfe and Roripaugh's extensive list, racialized identities are
omitted.

Punishing the New Millennium Mulatta

Bette's playing the race card and her other "bad behaviors" do not go without assessment on *The L Word*. Within private, domestic spaces like her
living room and public, work spaces like her boardroom, *The L Word* continually knocks Bette down. For Beals's character, any release into happiness is swiftly followed by a disciplining turn. In a show that revels in
its characters' foibles, the myriad and over-the-top ways it punishes the
haughty and powerful Bette stand out. Bette loses her job mere days before her partner gives birth, she is shunned by all members of her social
circle, and she endures a multimedia installation dedicated to her public
flogging. Even when the show builds her up and grants her some degree of
personal or professional success, it appears to do so just to make her inevitable fall that much more dramatic. At her father's funeral, Bette gets fired
from her job a few days before Tina gives birth to Angelica (2.13). A season later, after she and Tina break up for the second time, Bette looks for
answers in Buddhism and goes on a silent retreat that gives her anguish
instead of peace (3.9). The show positions Bette sympathetically here, but
also hints that she gets what she deserves for her infidelity to Tina and her
snooty, condescending demeanor.

The show's most public punishment of Bette comes from Jodi after
their breakup. At the opening of Jodi's new installation piece, she is introduced by Bette to a crowd of about a hundred people. Bette gushes that
Jodi "redefines the landscape of sculpture." "I am repeatedly in awe of her
fearless choices [and] . . . her audacity, which borders on defiance. . . .
She's made me relive all over again the redemptive power of art." Through
this laudatory introduction Bette asks for forgiveness from Jodi for the
cheating that precipitated their breakup. After granting Bette a vengeful

smile, Jodi introduces her work through her interpreter: "This piece is called *Core* because it's about core values: love, loyalty, honesty, and commitment." At these words Bette blanches as she realized that the words she spoke to Jodi during their breakup, "love, loyalty, honesty, and commitment," will now be used to mock her. As the piece begins, video montages of Bette loop in 360 degrees on floor-to-soaring-ceiling walls. She looks beautiful for a moment, but is quickly fragmented into devolving pieces as the screen splits, multiplies, and crackles. Similarly, the sound is fragmented, looped, and spliced into discordant echoes. With this effect Bette appears to be stuttering "go without me . . . fuck me . . . stop" again and again. The piece resoundingly asserts that Bette is a fragmented liar, someone for whom "love, loyalty, honestly, and commitment" is a mere pretense. Similarly, mixed-race is represented as a fragmented racialized identity that is tricky, treacherous, and never what it really appears to be. Bette is thoroughly humiliated. Her friends and colleagues have seen her flaws magnified and projected literally ten-times larger than life (5.12). Throughout *The L Word* Bette is punished for overstepping her bounds, for using white, male, straight privilege, and for stepping out and not celebrating the golden, white womanhood of Tina. With the representation of the new-millennium-mulatta Bette on *The L Word*, African American mixed-race, balancing between the tragic mulatta and the race-using superwoman, revitalizes the privileges of whiteness.

Reviewing the New Millennium Mulatta

Outside knowledge about Jennifer Beals unquestionably informs the manner in which viewers understand *The L Word* and Bette in particular. While the character Bette is often flogged on *The L Word*, like the fictional new-millennium-mulatta figure, the actress Jennifer Beals is often celebrated in the popular press, even as she is described along historic tropes of the tragic mulatta. Over the course of Beals's career, from her first film role in *Flashdance* to her role on *The L Word*, mixed-racial discourse has significantly evolved. The representational possibility of mixedness in 1985 is not what it becomes in 2005. Certainly the language of "mixed-race" or "multiracial" as it is applied by multiracial activists to collectivities, or as in the case of the census in 2000, national lobbying and interest groups, is an idea that emerged in a large-scale manner in the 1990s. The naming and framing of a multiracial identity emerges from such important multiracial movement texts as Maria Root's anthology *Racially Mixed People in the United States.* And yet, dominant press assessments of Beals, in 1985 or 2005, do not appear to consider collective multiracial identity. Instead they read her by old tropes of mixed-race. This type of treatment from the dominant press reflects, as Catherine Squires notes, "a dominance of white viewpoints in the mainstream news. In the dominant press, the majority of practitioners are white and male; so too are the majority of their sources and contacts, including politicians, civil servants, and businesspeople."[60] Furthermore, Jane Rhodes writes that this positioning, or framing, means that "subjects are placed within a formal frame that focuses attention on selected aspects of visual or verbal texts, or subjects are set up to appear to be something they are not."[61]

Thus, Jennifer Beals's multiracial heritage is cited centrally and consistently in newspaper articles. In the dominant press Beals is represented through the old cliché of multiracial solitude. She is alone in two ways: as an effect of her inherent mulatta tragedy or her utopian, post-racial possibilities. Both tropes are in one of the earliest newspaper articles on Beals, an article that came out after her hit movie *Flashdance*, when she was still an undergraduate student at Yale University. The article begins with a racially coded description of Beals's "flawless tawny skin," then moves into a more explicit narration of the role that race plays in her life: "Beals is the product of a racially mixed marriage. Her father, who owned a small chain of grocery stores and died when she was in the fifth grade, was black. Her mother, who taught public school, is of Irish descent. When she applied to Yale and it asked her to list race, she put down 'other' because 'I didn't consider myself as any category.' . . . Being part of both worlds, however, has given Beals a strong social conscience."[62] She is marked as outside, alone, "other," and tragic with the echoes of her father's death, but she is also racialized as safely multiracial through her relatable, middle-class parents, a businessman and a teacher. She is posited as not using race as a crutch, the critique in anti–affirmative action discourse. With her "social conscience," she is above such ploys, above playing the race card. Additionally, in various popular and scholarly writings on *The L Word*, when Beals and her character Bette are discussed there is never any placing of her within multiracial or black communities. She remains alone in their writings as well. This is a common trope in the representations of mixed-race blackness: a life of isolation.

Newspaper and magazine articles on Beals repeatedly focus on her ostensible feelings of otherness, which are shown to stem from her mixed-race heritage. The leap some journalists take is that Beals can make the race portrait more authentic because she is really mixed-race, and she can make the lesbian portrait more authentic because she experiences alterity. Thus, in an L Word–era article, Beals is quoted as saying, "I completely identify with the state of otherness,"[63] while in another one she remarks that she utters this line "ruefully."[64] Most articles delineate Beals's parents' racial identities and link their racial differences to her otherness. One journalist writes, "The daughter of an African American father and an Irish American mother, Beals grew up in a black neighborhood where her pale skin caused people to wonder what she was doing there."[65]

However, while Beals is presented an outcast because of her mix, she is also represented as reaping the benefits of multiraciality. This amounts to, as one writer asserts, the idea that Beals "treasures her flexibility,"[66] an idea that traps her in a liberal multiculturalist paradigm of color blindness. At least in her press coverage she can be read as both resisting and, to a certain extent, acceding to this. The real-life Beals becomes a good minority in her press coverage, an exceptional multiracial who does not use her race in ways that hurt whites, the apparent victims of the race card.

Despite this framing in the press, in direct quotes Beals seems to read herself against definitions of herself as the other. She is quoted in one article, for example, saying, "I know what it is to be the other. . . . I realize we all feel different. No one ever feels like they are in the center of the circle, because there is no center of the circle."[67] Her comments here are reminiscent of Stuart Hall's commentary that "the representative modern experience" is actually one of being "dispersed and fragmented."[68] In other words, the representative experience today is one of dislocation. Beals is also described as a role model because she is invested in issues of representation. One reporter quotes her explaining, "What's really exciting is that people are vocal about how they want to be represented after they've been invisible for so long."[69] If, as Sika Alaine Dagbovie writes, "the reception of mixed-race celebrities in popular culture reflects a national inclination to define blackness,"[70] Beals's interviews indicate a rescripting of mixed-race blackness to the race card.

Concluding the Bad, New Millennium Mulatta Race Girl

While Stuart Hall points out that minority consumers of media must be wary of celebrating a text just because it is produced by "us,"[71] the critic Sarah Warn writes that audiences should celebrate the victory of visibility that occurs when Bette is portrayed as mixed-race: "Bette's ongoing presence on the series as an openly identified biracial character chips away at America's practice of casting race in black-or-white terms, regardless of whether the topic is ever explicitly addressed again."[72] But Lisa Henderson, following Hall, complicates such notions of positive imagery, writing that for minoritized subjects, "'Positive images' are better understood . . . as . . . a shift from the static logic of 'good' role models (doctors, lawyers, elected officials) to a more dynamic articulation of symbolic value, in which goodness is liberated from conventions of status to become contingent on narrative context and identification and in which the social terms of goodness are themselves open to question."[73]

Bette Porter demonstrates how televisual diversity is managed in sophisticated and power-laden ways in so-called post-identity America, and yet she is unable to function without clear echoes of the tragic mulatta, "the race card," and the superwoman. While Bette might satisfyingly speak back to power structures, she is punished for such speaking out of turn and is put back in her place. Such punishment lays bare the intersecting and conflicting narratives and ideologies surrounding the televisual, twenty-first-century multiracial African American character. Bette's punishment ultimately illustrates that while the new millennium mulatta might exhibit racial flexibility and superwoman strength, as blackness muddles her whiteness, her downfall is inevitable.

Bette's representation on *The L Word* functions as a type of multiculturalism-mitigating tragedy, where race falls in and out of the storyline seemingly at the mixed-race African American character's will. The result is a rolling out of the conservative ideology of the race card and a concomitant dictate of black transcendence for the mixed-race African American subject. The television character's behavior is coded for the new millennium mulatta through traits of oversexed, impulsive, spoiled, and irrational (for the passing, tragic mulatta) and alpha female, unbreakable, and resisting punishment (for the superwoman). These portrayals showcase echoes of the past (tragic mulatta) and future (superwoman) because the intersectionality of a mixed-race African American character cannot be understood in the present. Jennifer Beals's portrayal of Bette Porter on *The L Word* reveals a twenty-first-century post–affirmative action ethos that ultimately dictates multiracial African American subjects to transcend blackness.

CHAPTER TWO

≡

THE SAD RACE GIRL

Passing and the

New Millennium Mulatta

in Danzy Senna's *Caucasia*

I was usually performing . . . and when I heard those inevitable words
. . . nigga, spic, fuckin' darkie — I only looked away into the distance, my
features tensing slightly, sometimes a little laugh escaping. Strange as
it may sound, there was a safety in this pantomime. The less I behaved
like myself, the more I could believe that this was still a game. That
my real self — Birdie Lee — was safely hidden beneath my beige flesh,
and that when the right moment came, I would reveal her, preserved,
frozen solid in the moment in which I had left her.[1]

Danzy Senna's novel *Caucasia* (1998) illustrates another type
of new millennium mulatta: the sad race girl. While black-
white actress Jennifer Beals's portrait of multiracial African
American Bette on *The L Word* can be read as the bad race
girl, whose mixed-race anger erupts all over innocent bystand-
ers, the black-white novelist Senna's portrayal of multiracial
African American protagonist Birdie in *Caucasia* can be read
as the sad, self-hating, perpetually passing race girl, whose
mixed-race gloom tortures her internally. White-skinned
Birdie transgresses assumed and so-called normative cate-

gories of gender, class, and sexuality, as white-skinned Bette does, and ends up punished, also like Bette. But Birdie lacks Bette's defiance, her sense of self, and her superwoman-like strength. Also unlike Bette, Birdie attempts to pass as monolithic, essentialized notions of white and black, and subsequently Birdie must suffer passing's effects. She metaphorically disappears altogether or doubles into a second form. Passing is at the very root of Birdie's pain.

While Senna does not use the terms "multiracial" or "mixed-race," she suggests that a third category might challenge the binary of black and white, which would sometimes create fluidity, and sometimes crisis. Senna presents Birdie's physical body as the vehicle for what Patricia Hill Collins dubs the inclusive "both/and," which Collins characterizes as a core aspect of black feminism, as opposed to an exclusive "either/or," which she characterizes as a core aspect of the hegemonic culture that misunderstands black feminism.[2] Marjorie Garber gives another name to Collins's both/and: "the third." This model provides white-appearing subjects who identify as African American with greater flexibility in moving between many categories, including gender and sexuality, not just race. Garber contends that the third not only "questions binary thinking" but also "introduces crisis."[3] This crisis is a "failure of definitional distinction, a borderline that becomes permeable, that permits border crossing from one (apparently distinct) category to another: black/white, Jew/Christian, noble/bourgeois, master/servant, master/slave."[4] The third is not an embodied identity or a new category; instead it is a "mode of articulation, a way of describing a space of possibility."[5] This "space of possibility" is a "disruptive element that intervenes, not just a category crisis of male and female, but the crisis of category itself."[6] In other words, by showing the interstitial subject's inability to fit into categories 1 or 2, the third illustrates that categories themselves are flawed. Senna weds Garber's notion of a third "crisis of category" with an acknowledgment of the material realities of living in a racialized and gendered body.[7] The third can produce a crisis of passing or the possibility of racial, sexual, and gender fluidity (or both). Senna resolves this question of fluidity, and the concomitant crisis of passing, by having her protagonist unabashedly embrace blackness.

Caucasia tells the story of young Birdie growing up in the 1970s and 1980s. The novel is told from her point of view and is divided into three parts, "Negritude for Beginners," in which Birdie learns how to adopt certain signifiers of blackness in order to be accepted by black friends; "From Caucasia, with Love," in which Birdie reluctantly abandons external signifiers of blackness in order to pass for white; and "Compared to What," in which Birdie leaves behind her staid ideas of blackness and whiteness to explore dual identification as both African American and mixed-race. Birdie's attempts at race passing, which signify insecurity about both her ostensibly inauthentic blackness and her multiraciality, are the cause and effect of her lack of a central sense of self. By having Birdie preserve her black-identifying self "beneath [her] beige flesh," Senna illustrates both the importance of a multiracial African American subject maintaining a "real" blackness even, or especially, in a racist climate, as well as the resilience of African American identity. Thus, even in moments when Birdie must perform as white, she protects and loves her blackness. However, at the same time, the blackness that she hides remains a staid, "frozen solid" image instead of a vibrant, constantly changing racialized identity. Such inauthenticity leads to Birdie's silent participation in anti-black racism. To safely pass as white, she pretends to be amused when those around her spew racist epithets.[8] The barriers between blackness and whiteness are constantly enforced in the novel so that the mixed-race African American subject cannot embody any racialized identity without tragedy befalling her. *Caucasia* illustrates that for the new millennium mulatta like Birdie, race is always a performance structured by pain and sadness.

When *Caucasia* opens, Birdie is a precocious, home-schooled eight-year-old whose world revolves around her sister, Cole, who "looks black." Birdie and Cole are weathering their parents' tumultuous relationship and imminent divorce. Although their immediate family shields them from the racism in Boston, within their household, Birdie's white mother, Sandy, and black father, Deck, wage their own race war. Deck, a Harvard-educated anthropology professor whose specialty is racial issues, expresses his guilt and frustration over marrying Sandy, a blond radical whose blue-blooded Cambridge background embarrasses her. When Deck and Sandy separate, Birdie and Cole's world expands beyond the inner racialized turmoil of their household. They end their homeschooling experiment with their mother, attend public school, and are subsequently exposed to outside racism and sexism. Faced with "the real world," the sisters discover how they are racialized and gendered, just as they figure out how to claim and perform "appropriate" blackness and femininity.

In the second part of the novel, and soon after first facing people beyond their immediate family, the sisters are split apart. The FBI is allegedly hot on Sandy's trail because of her underground revolutionary activities. In order to blend into society, Sandy and Deck decide to each take a daughter who "looks like" them: Black-appearing Cole goes with Deck while white-passing Birdie goes with Sandy. While on the run, Birdie is forced to claim a white identity and live alone with Sandy. Cole disappears from the novel because she lives with Deck. In the third part Birdie finds her father and sister, and the novel abruptly ends before articulating how exactly Birdie will perform a nonessentialized form of blackness or whiteness so that she does not remain trapped as the sad race girl. Traveling from Boston to New Hampshire to the San Francisco Bay Area, Birdie spends the novel manipulating her image of race, femininity, and sexuality, and trying to find her father, sister, and her own true race.

Caucasia takes place during a contentious racialized moment, 1975–1984, and in contentious racialized spaces, Boston and New Hampshire. Boston in the 1970s and 1980s, Senna tells us, is a city "in black and white, yellowing around the edges" (1), a racially segregated and stratified "battleground" (7). Even in homogenously white New Hampshire, where one might assume that the absence of people of color means the absence of race talk, Senna writes, "the white folks needed no prompting" to discuss race, which "came up all the time, like a fixation" (248). Just as geographic locations are explicitly racialized in *Caucasia*, so are all of the characters and the situations in which they find themselves. The racism that Senna illustrates is not politely post-racial, hiding behind coded words and phrases. It is extreme and stark, often in the form of racial epithets and violence. At the same time, the mixed-race African American subject is given no option but to ignore and therefore silently participate in such racism. Politicized modes of blackness are presented as incredibly desirable to Birdie, but just out of her reach. What remains the available and undesirable option is whiteness, which bears down upon Birdie so intensely that it is manifested into a physical place, as the novel's title denotes.

The epigraph illustrates that *Caucasia* is a story that represents far more than a white-appearing mixed-race African American becoming white. *Caucasia* engages in and disrupts the conversations about passing from the vast body of passing novels by referencing and paying homage to fictional passing works such as the novels *Plum Bun* (1900) by Jessie Redmon Fauset, *The Autobiography of an Ex-Colored Man* (1927) by James Weldon

Johnson, and *Invisible Man* (1952) by Ralph Ellison, as well as the two film versions of *Imitation of Life* (1934 and 1959). Following these works, *Caucasia* investigates how whiteness is akin to invisibility while blackness means visibility. However, deviating from these works, Birdie not only tries to pass as white but also as black. In addition, Birdie performs various racialized personae from blackness to in-betweenness to whiteness, various gendered roles from hyperfeminine to androgynous, and various sexual identities from in-control with a girl to pinned down by a boy. Each identification is intertwined with the others; Birdie's race and sexuality are gendered just as her gender is raced and sexualized.

In *Caucasia* race, gender, and sexuality interlace as simultaneous constructions and bodily realities, real in their effects and yet imaginary in their shifting performances. With heterosexual and feminized accoutrements such as boyfriends, makeup, clothes, hairstyles, and jewelry, Birdie's attractive, mixed-race body helps her magically transform into different races; Birdie's adolescence made her "more conscious of [her] body as a toy, and the ways [she] could use it to disappear into the world around [her]" (65). Birdie's racialized performance is entirely contingent upon her performances of gender and sexuality, because acting appropriately femininely facilitates a successful racial pass, and failing to act femininely leaves her race in question. Her intersectionality is one of the many ways in which *Caucasia* deploys black feminist theorizing: Birdie learns how to perform race through gender and sexuality, and vice versa.[9] At the same time, while race, gender, and sexuality are performances, they are not inconsequential ones. Instead, they are painful, difficult forces in the lives of Birdie and her loved ones; they tear families apart and cause emotional and physical violence. Although Birdie appears to wear a racial identity as easily as a costume, she suffers internally for using her gendered identity as a means to facilitate racial change.

Senna's Birdie provides readers with multiple ways to understand passing in a contemporary moment. Birdie's attempts to be recognized as black and perform as white constitute the moments of her passing. In both cases the trauma of the pass causes her to forsake her physical form so much that she must imagine leaving it by doubling or disappearing: she becomes the sad race girl because of passing. Passing and its effects do not present an exceptional multiracial, striving for a raceless subjectivity, or an angry new millennium mulatta, lashing out at all in her path. In *Caucasia*, multiraciality is not the means to becoming a successfully deraced, degendered person of the new millennium. Rather than floating freely above racial categories, she must constantly attempt to pass by performing fluctuating and essentialized ideals of both blackness and whiteness. A liminal, in-between, middle racialized space is not available until the very close of the novel, and then Senna barely articulates how a figure such as Birdie can be both mixed-race and African American, or how she can move away from the monolithic ideals of blackness and whiteness. The doubling and invisibility that Birdie suffers are problems of the new millennium mulatta, and then the solution that Senna offers is to resolve the crisis by stepping back into race. In *Caucasia*, sadness structures the new millennium mulatta's racialized identity.

Passing as Black, Passing as White

The most common form of passing is, of course, the historic passing of Jim Crow–era African Americans from a "black world" to a "white world." Scholars such as Amy Robinson argue that this passing, whether recorded in historic or literary forms, illustrates that race is far from stable and monolithic. If the mixed-race body can move from a "black race" to a "white race," race cannot be a singular reality. Instead, according to Robinson, a racial "politics of substance" moves to a fluid "politics of optics." In other words, the look and the reality of race do not always align.[10] Robinson states that the "most rudimentary lesson of passing [is that] the visible is never easily or simply a guarantor of truth."[11] Similarly, Samira Kawash writes that passing narratives are actually about the inability of either blackness or whiteness to provide a stable, coherent identity.[12] Building on both Robinson and Kawash, we can see that for the white-appearing, mixed-race African American protagonist, "the truth" of race remains in question throughout *Caucasia* because passing is an always present, and always painful, reality. Following the logic of the one-drop rule, despite looking white, Birdie is really black. But Birdie tries to pass not just for white, as in the historical cases, but also for African American. Thus the novel tweaks the idea of passing. The incongruity and poignancy of trying to pass for black complicates both the ideas of passing and the notions of blackness.

The multiracial African American protagonist is not the only character searching for racial authenticity in *Caucasia*: while Birdie's parents do not switch races, they do perform racialized transformations. Whereas Birdie transitions from being black in the first part of the novel to being white in the second part, her mother transforms from overweight, disdained, interracially married Sandy Lee into thin, desirable, white-male-dating Sheila Goldberg. After leaving Boston and her black ex, Sandy undergoes a dramatic physical change, losing seventy pounds and becoming "willowy, fragile, feminine, a shadow of her former self" (145). Sandy claims that she "lost the weight out of grieving for Cole" but Birdie thinks that her weight loss "was more intentional than that, just another piece of her disguise, to go along with the auburn hair and horn-rimmed glasses and the new name" (139). Sandy's weight loss helps proclaim her unspoken break with blackness and alliance to whiteness; here Senna follows the cultural assumption that straight African American men are attracted to larger women.

Senna also describes Birdie's father with careful details about racialized looks: Deck "was not very dark, and his features were not very African — it was only his milk-chocolate skin that gave his race away. His face spoke of something other — his high cheekbones, his large bony nose, his deep-set eyes, and his thin lips against the brown of his skin. . . . His hair wasn't so wooly either[,] . . . black ringlets pleasantly curl[ed] into his scalp" (34). The book posits this "something other" as the reason why Deck tries to prove how authentically black he is, with the added burden of having a daughter who passes for white. Sandy derides Deck's attempts at performing identity politics, hissing to Birdie, "your papa's too busy trying to grow a fucking afro" to take care of his family (77). These details illustrate how many of the novel's characters struggle to find so-called genuine racialized selves; performing authentic race is not solely the purview of the mixed-race African American character.

Nonetheless, Birdie is the only character in the book given the mandate to pass as another race: first as black, and then as white. Throughout the novel, mutable Birdie lacks a center and becomes what she believes people want her to be. Looking at children outside her mother's car window, Birdie wonders "which one of them [she] would become" (37). When, after her parents' divorce, she attends an alternative public school in Boston, the Nkrumah School, she endures initial teasing because of her white appearance. At this Black Power school — named after Kwame Nkrumah, the foremost proponent of pan-Africanism in the twentieth century — she struggles when she is not seen as black, or seen as "one of us." At first she suffers with insomnia brought on by the isolation that stems from her "white looks." Senna writes that Birdie literally tries to consume her white-appearing exterior in order to arrive at the true black interior: Birdie "often found [herself] alone, chewing on [her] hair and nails with an insatiable hunger, as if trying to eat [herself] alive, picking at [her] scabs with a fervor, as if trying to find another body buried inside" (48–49). She so desires to be identified and accepted as black that she cannibalizes herself. Her desire is essentially defensive, as she learns that she will be punished, physically by the bullying children in the school and figuratively by Black Power, if she does not appropriately articulate and perform a monolithic version of blackness. In this moment *Caucasia* articulates Black Power solely through the lens of Birdie's identity crisis, so that it becomes a dehistoricized threat to white-appearing subjects, and nothing more.

Birdie learns how to become black by dressing as her image of a young, African American girl from Roxbury and soon learns "the art of changing at Nkrumah, a skill that would later become second nature" (62). When faced with fitting in with African Americans, essentialized blackness becomes an important performance that both Birdie and her visibly black sister, Cole, enact. With help from Cole, Birdie learns how to become black through employing commercial signifiers, such as Jergens lotion, *Jet* magazine, "Sergio Valente jeans, a pink vest, a jean jacket with sparkles on the collar, . . . spanking-white Nike sneakers," and gold hoop earrings (54). A femininity born through such commercial markers helps this mixed-race African American subject produce the appropriate racialized identity. Birdie's material-accented, racialized femininity also creates straight male desire. At Nkrumah, when the popular boy Ali wanted to "go" with her and she agreed, she joined the Brown Sugars, a clique for girls who have boyfriends: "A new boyfriend had catapulted me into the world of the freshest girls in the school. Now that I had been knighted black by Maria, and pretty by Ali, the rest of the school saw me in a new light." At the same time, Birdie suffers with this new racialized and gendered performance: "[I] never lost the anxiety, a gnawing in my bowels, a fear that at any moment I would be told it was all a big joke" (64). Yet passing as black does not take the same psychic toll on Birdie that passing as white does later in the novel.

Hair, one of the most tangible signs of the lure and danger of identity fluidity, functions as another loaded signifier of black performance and authenticity in *Caucasia*. Just as in the independent film *Mixing Nia*, in *Caucasia* hair signifies (in)authentic and (in)appropriate race and gender.

Birdie's naturally straight hair, signifying whiteness, is neither ambiguous nor mutable. Because the book is set in a time before the mass popularity of hair extensions, the one thing Birdie cannot buy is new hair, and so she wears "a tight braid to mask [her hair's straight] texture."

Birdie, and the novel, largely understands the hair politics of authentic blackness through her other half, her visibly black sister: "When Cole was very little, [our] mother had simply let her run around with what she called a 'dustball' on her head. She had thought the light and curly afro adorable and didn't quite understand the disapproving glances of the black people on the street" (50). Like the stereotype of inept white mothers of mixed-race African American children, Sandy appears neither to understand black hair nor the significance of hair for gendered and racialized identities. Cole is portrayed as the victim of Sandy's ineptitude: along with her ashy legs (Sandy doesn't understand the importance of lotion for brown skin) and "white speech" (Sandy doesn't understand the importance of code switching for brown subjectivity), Cole was teased at Nkrumah for being "Miz Nappy" (53). Even though she looks black, in order for Cole to pass as a "real black girl," she needs to have her hair done in what is read as an appropriately African American manner. When Cole becomes an adolescent she resents her mother for not knowing how to do her hair and sees it as proof that Sandy has no clue how to raise a black daughter.

Birdie watches the racialized power play between Sandy and Cole. Although she is torn between her mother's dismay and her sister's anger, and despite her intense love for her sister, Birdie tells Sandy, "It's okay, Mum. You can do my hair" (52). Over the issue of racialized beauty, Birdie aligns with her white mother. However, in one scene, in her mother's absence, Birdie manipulates her hair in order to become the black girl she always fantasized about being. When spending the night at Maria's, her Cape Verdean best friend from Nkrumah, Birdie is thrilled when Maria cuts, curls, and styles her hair, because she looks like she could pass as black. She thinks, "when I grew up . . . I [would] be just like Maria's mother, who I imagined looked like [African American singer and actress] Marilyn McCoo" (70). The way for Birdie to perform appropriate black beauty is to pass into the body of another woman: Birdie can only become African American if she physically transforms into Cole or Maria's mother. However, in the novel, Birdie's dreams of transforming into a visibly black girl are thwarted by family dynamics that necessitate her passing as white.

The Sad Race Girl

—

Passing as (authentically) black thus remains an ultimately unviable option for the sad race girl, new millennium mulatta Birdie.

Performing as authentically black is the first iteration of passing in *Caucasia* and masquerading as white, the historically expected mode of passing, is the second.[13] To pass as white, Birdie "lets her body speak for her" while she protects her true black identity inside. In the very first lines of the book, Birdie says,

> A long time ago I disappeared. One day I was here, the next I was gone. . . . The next I was a nobody, just a body without a name or history, sitting beside my mother in the front seat of our car, moving forward on the highway, not stopping. (And when I stopped being nobody, I would become white—white as my skin, hair, bones allowed. My body would fill in the blanks, tell me who I should become, and I would let it speak for me.) (1)

Birdie's passing for white seems to work more for the convenience of the plot machinations than for internal realities of the characters. These machinations veer toward the melodramatic as the characters are running for their lives from the FBI after Sandy helps a Weather Underground–type organization hide arms. Sandy tells Birdie that her "straight hair, pale skin, . . . general phenotypic resemblance to the Caucasoid race, would throw [the FBI] off [their] trail . . . [as her] body was the key to [their] going incognito" (109). In this and other ways, Birdie's passing as white does not just affect her, and her parents have strong opinions about it. Despite Birdie's need to pass as white for her safety, in her father's parting words to her he asserts that she does not have to accept her racialization as white. To Deck, passing as white threatens Birdie's core cultural and historic identity. Her mother, however, sees Birdie's passing a bit differently. It means Birdie is using her whiteness as a strategic tool.

Birdie's appearance does the work of passing her even before she has to pass to be safe, and the way outsiders read her race informs how she passes. Indeed, everyone except for her sister has an opinion about Birdie's racialized looks. Birdie's racist white grandmother is thrilled that her granddaughter looks as if she "could be Italian." "Or even French" (107). And her WASP landlords in New Hampshire describe her appreciatively as having "such classic features." "Almost old-fashioned. She looks Italian" (195). On the other hand, before fleeing Boston, Birdie's parents are far from thrilled by how white their one daughter looks. When discussing how Birdie is capable of passing as white, her mother dismissively scoffs that Birdie "looks like a little Sicilian," and her father rants, "no daughter of mine is going to pass" (27). With these comments Birdie is exotically non-Anglo but still safely "white," within contemporary U.S. definitions. As much as her family obsesses over her racialized and gendered appearance, when Birdie leaves the safe haven of her Boston home, passing, or performing authentic race and gender, becomes the focal point in her life. This is indeed the problem that Birdie is faced with as she changes from black Birdie Lee from Boston to Jewish Jesse Goldman from New Hampshire.

Effects of Passing: Disappearing and Doubling

Throughout much of African American history, the idea of passing, or passing as white, accompanied the notion of invisibility: "black" people who passed disappeared from their African American communities. Accordingly, one of the first ways that *Caucasia* interprets passing is through allusions to disappearance and invisibility. A rhetorical device that Senna employs is the metaphor of "Elemeno," Cole and Birdie's secret language named "after [their] favorite letters in the alphabet."[14] Senna describes Elemeno as "a complicated language, impossible for outsiders to pick up—no verb tenses, no pronouns, just words floating outside time and space without owner or direction" (6). This is an insider language for two racial outsiders, and a metaphor for disappearing. Elemeno is not just a language but a group of people:

> The Elemenos . . . could turn not just from black to white, but from brown to yellow to purple to green, and back again. [Cole] said they were a shifting people, constantly changing their form, color, pattern, in a quest for invisibility. According to her, their changing routine was a serious matter—less a game of make believe than a fight for the survival of their species. . . . [T]heir power lay precisely in their ability to disappear into any surrounding. (7)

Foreshadowing Birdie's escape into the "white world," the Elemenos' chameleon-like behavior was a matter of life or death.

Elemeno also functions as a signifier of escape for the two girls. The sisters want to flee their parents' constant bickering. On another level, Elemeno is a symbol for an escape from the racial reality of their lives, and in particular, Birdie's life. She becomes a racial chameleon throughout the novel just like the Elemenos. In the same way that Elemeno makes no sense to outsiders who don't know the grammar rules, race makes no sense to the racial outsider Birdie if she doesn't know the race rules. Birdie figures out a way to circumvent the confusing rules of race: become a chameleon like the Elemenos.[15] At the same time, racial chameleonism, or disappearance, is a performance fraught with tragedy, or as Birdie puts it in a question about the Elemenos to Cole that never gets answered: "What was the point of surviving if you had to disappear?" (8).

The responses of family members to Elemeno shows the different ways that the children's mixed-race signifies to various people in their lives, because in *Caucasia* race is never just "inside," and racialized identity is formulated in relationship to racial ascription. Birdie's father calls their language "a high-speed patois," racializing Elemeno as a black and mixed language by referring to it by the name used for hybrid languages in the Caribbean. To Sandy, trying to figure out this confusing language "was like trying to eavesdrop on someone sleeptalking, when the words are still untranslated from their dream state" (6). Sandy's children's mixed-race is similarly familiar but strange to her: as with Birdie's described Italian looks, their mixed-race bears traces of whiteness but is still beyond her grasp. Their white grandmother thinks that their language is pathological and wants to call in a child psychiatrist to help; Granny also sees any attachment to blackness, particularly by Birdie who can pass as white, as pathological. Hearing that the sisters are attending an Afrocentric school in a black neighborhood, Granny fears for Birdie and screams at Sandy, "It's crazy, child abuse, to send your child into a neighborhood like that. She could be robbed or killed or anything!" (106). In this estimation Granny equates blackness with violence.

Birdie's ability to blend into her surroundings means that she is exposed to inappropriate things. As a young child she wanders around unseen by adults and spies contraband guns at her Aunt Dot's party (15). As a young adolescent in New Hampshire, she is not spotted when she sees her friend Mona's mother having sex with the local bartender in a truck (289). Birdie's passing strips away her innocence about issues like violence or sex. In other words, Senna implicitly argues that mixed-race African American subjects should be wary of assuming that they can shunt aside racialized identities in a quest for invisibility.

The external invisibility of passing fails Birdie at various points, in particular when she is on the road and on the run with her mother. Birdie becomes a race-neutral tomboy on the road in between performing a hyper-feminized black persona in Boston and an equally hyperfeminized white persona in New Hampshire; Senna describes her as invisible or effectively de- or e-raced and de-gendered. In these moments Birdie is "incomplete—a gray blur, a body in motion, forever galloping toward completion—half a girl, half-caste, half-mast, and half-baked, not quite ready for consumption" (137). In a liminal state, Birdie is not a girl but a "body." She is not racialized as a living skin color but is morbidly "gray." In this in-between realm of disappearance, passing means invisibly existing in some unnamed, halfway state.

Again, gender and race performance are linked. When she is on the road and lacks a prescribed racial identity, Birdie also describes herself as androgynous, "a twelve-year-old-girl who might be a boy if it weren't for the scraggly ponytail falling down her back" (180). She imagines one scenario in which her gender is indiscernible and a gas station worker observes that Birdie "might be a guy." In this same fantasy, the worker describes Birdie's mother's van, the very vehicle of their escape, as "sorta gray or black or something" (145).

Without adolescent female peers and the expectation to perform a specific, singular racialized identity, Birdie appears awkward, unfashionable, and androgynous. She has no girlie signifiers such as makeup, feminine clothes, and a trendy hairstyle to do the work of passing her. Senna describes Birdie at age twelve as being embarrassed that she dressed "like a much younger child, in high-water dungarees and a pair of hot-pink Converse sneakers [her] mother had stolen off a rack at Mammoth Mart. . . . [She] appeared wild and ill-fitting, like a girl raised by wolves" (144). Birdie's shoddy appearance implicates her mother since she is, by extension, the wolf. Good mothers are supposed to hand down privileged notions of beauty and help create their daughters' visibility through a cultivated femininity. However, white Sandy must struggle to be an appropriate role model for mixed-race Birdie. In other words, Senna's portrayal of Birdie's invisibility through her racialized or gendered liminality does not just illustrate the mutability of race or gender as identity categories; it also warns of the danger of such mutability, especially for those who occupy an interstitial space.

Passing affects Birdie not just by making her invisible, when she loses herself, but also by making her double, when she gains another self. Senna signifies Birdie's multiplicity through a core device: her main characters' names, which are metaphors for racialization. While Cole's name is a shortened version of the name of the frizzy-haired "octoroon" author Colette,[16] it is also a homonym for "coal," and Cole is Birdie's standard for blackness in the novel. As opposed to Cole's clearly racialized single name, Birdie has three names to which she answers "with a schizophrenic zeal." Senna morbidly describes how Birdie's official name was "Baby Lee[,] . . . like the gravestone of some stillborn child," because her parents could not agree on a name. While her father "wanted to call [her] Patrice, as in Lumumba, the Congolese liberator," her mother "wanted to name [her] Jesse, after her great-grandmother, a white suffragette." Neither racializing force wins, so she becomes Birdie because Cole wanted a parakeet more than a little sister (19). Later in the novel, "Birdie" takes on more symbolic heft as Deck compares, in his words, "mulattoes" such as Birdie and Cole to canaries in a coal mine used "historically [as] . . . the gauge of how poisonous American race relations were" (393). When Birdie and her mother go into hiding, at her mother's suggestion she takes on the moniker Jesse after all, her mother's chosen name for her as a baby, just as she takes on her mother's white race. Birdie suffers from a protracted namelessness because of the way in which her parents render her invisible by refusing to acknowledge her multiple racialized identities.

Doubling is an extreme effect of passing as either black or white, as opposed to living as both black and white. Until she learns the rules of racialization, and how to consume commercial signifiers in order to perform gender and race appropriately, race is elusive to mixed-race Birdie, who desperately longs to be black but looks white. At times *Caucasia* essentializes blackness by having Birdie see it as a completely separate entity from whiteness that can be frozen whole. She survives by treating blackness like her own little secret. Doubling is particularly an effect of passing when Birdie is passing as white. When Birdie has to perform as white, she must abandon her external signifiers of blackness and instead hoard her secret blackness inside. At times this is a dirty little secret that she must hide to protect her mother's freedom; at most other times her secret is a precious sign that she is different from the racist white people who surround her in New Hampshire. The physical manifestation of Birdie's doubling is a box of black family memorabilia, or "Negrobilia," that her father and Cole leave for her: "a black Nativity program from the Nkrumah School, a fisted pick . . . , a black Barbie doll head, an informational tourist pamphlet on Brazil, the silver Egyptian necklace inscribed with hieroglyphics . . . , and a James Brown eight-track cassette with a faded sticker in the corner that said 'Nubian Notion'" (127). Birdie's hidden blackness is like the contents of this box, constructed through popular culture, broken artifacts, and disposable signs and easily hidden away. By doubling into a white person on the outside and preserving a black person on the inside, Birdie becomes a race spy, a racial double agent.

Doubling enables Birdie to become white and also to create another hyperfeminized persona: if she engages in sexualized relationships with straight males, she can become another body who is appropriately white. In New Hampshire, her relationship with Nicholas Marsh, a coveted, privileged white boy, helps her gain access to the clique of popular white girls. Nicholas is a racist, angry boy who confides to Birdie that he lost his virginity to "this fat black chick from Africa or something" in Amsterdam, whom he and his friends "all took turns with" (199–200). Birdie feels uncomfortable hearing Nicholas's racist stories but stays mute. She later gets high with him and laughs uncontrollably when they look at a racist comic book. Soon after the laughter she must double: when he wants to go further sexually than she feels comfortable with, Senna writes, "touching him felt too real, proof that the game had gone too far. It wasn't Birdie, but Jesse, who lay beneath him" (203). When Nicholas asks Birdie to perform oral sex on him, he calls her "Poca," or Pocahontas, his nickname for her, because as he puts it, she turns "all brown in the sun. Like a little Indian" (193). Nicholas marks her as a miscegenating Indian princess, brown and valuable, not an intimidating African prostitute, black and dispensable. Like Birdie, Pocahontas "is positioned between cultures";[17] she bears the same privilege and burden by residing in a similar in-between state and partnering with a white man.

In *Caucasia*, doubling is not only about performing straight white femininity but also about transgressing norms of race, gender, and sexuality. The pain of passing, which registers in the novel through doubling, nevertheless solves the problem of the multiple racialized demands placed upon Birdie. After Birdie first leaves her black self behind in Boston, she doubles, feeling as if she is "watching [herself] from above" and critiquing herself "with the detachment of a stranger." In one of these moments she describes her "faint, dusky mustache that made [her] look dirty in the wrong light" (190). At another moment, talking about herself in the third person, Birdie describes "the dark trace of a mustache over her lip and eyebrows that met faintly in the middle" (180). Her "mustache" is not a neutral signifier of masculinity or androgyny (a form of gender passing). Rather, when true femininity is valued, as it is by outsiders in *Caucasia*, Birdie's mustache signifies as her outright failure at femininity. Indeed, it made her look "dirty," and by extension, "black." Senna's use of the word "dirty" marks Birdie's failure as lurid and wrong, and so a failure of not just race and gender but also of sexuality. Suzanne Bost points out that "the symbolic associations of whiteness with purity and blackness with evil and filth fueled the taboo against interracial associations."[18] When Birdie closes her eyes, eager for a kiss from her white crush Nicholas, he instead licks her cheek. Nicholas then points out her "mustache" and tells her, "I like it. It makes you look dirty, like I could lick you clean" (200). In this moment it is unclear if a white boy wants to rid her of her dirt, or her blackness, or instead wants to consume her. Nicholas's erotic, cleaning gesture demonstrates Birdie's desirability, as transgressive, taboo object, to straight, white masculinity.

Caucasia's Black Transcendent Reception: "Skin Color," Not Race

The burden of representation weighs heavy on the shoulders of authors such as Senna who both create fictional versions of multiracial African Americans and are multiracial and African American. The fictional mixed-race African American character Bette on *The L Word* and the real-life mixed-race African American actress playing her are presented in similar fashions in the popular press, and Senna and Birdie have also been conflated. However, while Birdie is firmly cemented as the sad new millennium mulatta race girl, in reviews of *Caucasia*, Senna is celebrated as the exceptional multiracial. Post-*Caucasia* Senna has written a memoir that pushes back against her scripting as either tragic or exceptional.[19] Interestingly, before her star rose, Senna herself satirized the phenomenon of seeing multiracial people as the bridges to a future racial utopia. In her essay "The Mulatto Millennium," published, like *Caucasia*, in 1998 and cited widely,[20] Senna describes the "mulatto fever" that hit the United States at the end of the twentieth century: "According to the racial zodiac, 2000 is the official Year of the Mulatto. Pure breeds (at least the black ones) are out and hybridity is in. America loves us in all of our half-caste glory. The president announced on Friday that beige is to be the official color of the millennium. Major news magazines announce our arrival as if we were proof of extraterrestrial life. They claim we're going to bring about the end of race as we know it."[21] Senna's essay, which mocks the celebration of "mulattoes" as bringing "an end to race," prophesized much of the critical consensus that would surround mixed-race African Americans in the public sphere from her own novel *Caucasia* to the forty-fourth president of the United States during his 2008 election campaign. Obama and Senna have been heralded by major news outlets as in vogue because they were safe minority voices that could be read as predicting the end of race: they were valuable because they had transcended their blackness.

Despite *Caucasia*'s vehement argument against the impossibility of post-race and against the idea of black transcendence, the majority of Senna's critics, hungry for a race-transcending ideal, celebrate *Caucasia* and Senna herself as emblematic of a post-racial United States.[22] This phenomenon can be at least partially attributed to the desire of what bell hooks calls "eating the other," where "there is pleasure to be found in the acknowledgement and enjoyment of racial difference."[23] At the same time, the urge toward post-raciality is also a power-evasive desire in contemporary multicultural attitudes of white Americans in which they see racial difference as something so tradable that it remains on the level of voluntary hobby. The sociologist Mary Waters calls this attitude one of "optional ethnicity," where "if your understanding of your own [white] ethnicity and its relationship to society and politics is one of individual choice, it becomes harder to understand the need for programs like affirmative action, which recognize the ongoing need for group struggle and group recognition, in order to bring about social change."[24] Following Waters's argument, the implication is that mixed-race African Americans can choose to transcend blackness, because power, history, or structure makes no impact on race.

Popular reviews and academic analyses of *Caucasia* illustrate this desire to transcend blackness. Some reviewers set out to designate *Caucasia* as an emblematically race-transcendent or post-racial text. Some described *Caucasia* as a prophetic tale where paying too much heed to race, or perhaps more specifically, paying too much heed to blackness, ultimately lands one in trouble. Senna was also celebrated in reviews as the perfect facilitator of a post-racial state. Few of *Caucasia*'s laudatory comments completely eschew talk of race and gender, but the novel has also been celebrated as a universal (read: color-blind) success. *Caucasia* won a number of awards where Senna's race and gender were not foregrounded.[25]

Employing no identifying terms of race, one *Newsweek* review says that Senna "tells this coming-of-age tale with impressive beauty and power."[26] Perhaps *Caucasia* is particularly beautiful and powerful because the contentious issues of race can be read as deliberately underplayed; after all, the protagonist passes for white and many whiteness studies scholars have pointed out that white is not coded as a racialized identity.[27] Another reviewer in *The Women's Review of Books* gushes, "With the arrival of Danzy Senna, the fiction-writing talent in the room is put on notice: the standard of achievement has just been ratcheted up a couple of notches." This review goes on to state: "[Senna] approaches [*Caucasia*] with gimlet-eyed scrutiny, be-here-and-now detail, a bemused and hopeful compassion for each person she conjures warts and all, and not an ounce of sentimentality. How can she have developed such chops this early in the game? Read *Caucasia* and marvel."[28] Race and gender are not mentioned here, so one can assume that according to the critic, this book is a success with a universal audience, regardless of race or gender.

Combining the idea of *Caucasia* as a universal human novel with power-evasive notions of multiculturalism, an article in the *New York Times Magazine* acknowledges that while "biracial and bicultural issues are trendy right now," *Caucasia* and other contemporary end-of-the-millennium mixed-race novels are "trying to forge an identity that reconciles the basic human desire to fit in and yet to remain separate, distinct, special."[29] Deployment of the word "trendy" makes multiraciality seem like a passing fad, an ephemeral fashion statement as opposed to a racialized reality. This reviewer's language also echoes "separate but equal." Although race and gender are not named in this *Caucasia* review as the "distinct [and] special elements," these elements are clearly the subtext. As subtext, they remain a hobby or choice, as opposed to ascribed, impactful identity categories.

However, most reviews did talk of race and gender. By and large, *Caucasia* received rave reviews from mainstream journalists who celebrated the novel as a coming-of-age story and a racial saga. Even so, where in *Caucasia* themes of adolescence and racial awareness are inextricably linked, in the reviews the issues remain separate. Some reviews invoke the roles of race and gender in the novel simply to dismiss them. For example, one reviewer from *Booklist* states: "This courageous and necessary tale about the color of skin and the variations of love is full of sorrow, both personal and societal, and much magic and humor."[30] *Caucasia* is "courageous" and "necessary" because it is merely about the color of skin, an individual quality, and not race, a group attribute imbued with issues of power. "Sorrow" can be read as a code word for tragic, or tragic mulatta, but according to the reviewer, Senna moves beyond this racialization into a deracialized realm of "magic and humor." Another review from *Library Journal* maintains, "Senna combines a powerful coming-of-age tale with a young girl's search for identity and family amid a sea of racial stereotypes and cultural ideas of beauty."[31] Here the coming-of-age and racialized identity tale is at odds with issues of beauty and race as opposed to them being imbricated with each other. In other words, while in *Caucasia* performing racialized beauty is precisely how Birdie searches for herself, this reviewer reads Birdie as "searching" for two isolated elements. Prevalent desires to keep race and gender separate are why the critical race theorist Kimberlé Crenshaw argues we need a theory of intersectionality: "When the practices expound identity as 'woman' or 'person of color' as an either/or proposition, they relegate the identity of women of color to a location that resists telling."[32] *Caucasia* illustrates intersectionality while its reviews deny it.

Some reviews celebrated the novel because it seemed to surpass ostensibly typical issues of racial animosity. To these reviewers, *Caucasia* did not showcase the assumed anger of other race books written by "real minorities." In other words, Senna is not just another angry black woman. One particularly post-racial review in *Publisher's Weekly* opens with, "This impressively assured debut avoids the usual extremes in its depiction of racial tension. . . . Senna's observations about the racial divide in America are often fierce but always complex and humane."[33] Indeed, to many critics, Senna's appeal comes through the middle ground that she and her protagonist Birdie are described as inhabiting. *Caucasia* is celebrated as a fine novel precisely because Senna manages to reject the "extreme" racial points of view and keep her "fierce" (or black) aspects in check. For example, the *Library Journal* review says, "Senna's first novel explores life in the middle of America's racial chasm."[34] Implicitly, Senna is the one to fill the gaping racial abyss; if she refuses an essentially deracialized placement, then she is left stranded in the depths of her middle hole. What is implied here is that the appropriate post-racial position for the mixed-race body is the bridge, imagined to magically bring two disparate and often warring groups together. Indeed, a voluminous biography of Barack Obama, the ultimate mixed-race connector, is titled *The Bridge*.[35]

This image of multiracials as model minorities, bridge people, or safe, interstitial interpreters who can help translate between two disparate worlds has been deployed not just by monoracials describing mixed-race people but also by some multiracials themselves. For example, Jill Olumide describes how "some [of her mixed-race interviewees] have occupied the moral high ground and offered skills assessments of themselves as 'bridge builders' or 'peace makers' in situations of prevalent race thinking."[36] The bridge image is a seductive one. Racialized inequality can be ignored in the service of valorizing a multiracial bridge hero whose mere presence is all it takes to hide a gaping racial abyss.

In many of the reviews, Birdie and Senna are often elided. Indeed, part of the way that race and gender are deployed in these reviews is by referencing Senna's own ethnic identity and phenotype as a mixed-race woman who passes for white. Typical of the majority of the reviews, one *Booklist* critic writes, "Like her strong-minded young narrator, Birdie, Senna is the daughter of a black father and a white mother, and the lighter-skinned of two sisters."[37] Another review in *Newsweek* points out, "Senna, herself the more fair-skinned daughter of a biracial couple, knows racial politics first-hand, but she's more interested in their real-life consequences."[38] Both reviews leave Senna's own racial identification unnamed, but identify her parents by racial labels; Senna, labeled by proxy, is not given her own ethnic descriptor. The former review interestingly points out that Birdie longs "for acknowledgement of her mixed blood."[39] And yet, in *Caucasia* Birdie simply has "mixed blood" but truly aches for blackness and sisterhood. By placing Senna into her ficitionalized work, *Caucasia* is purposefully situated amid the slew of mixed-race memoirs rather than in the fiction section. This is a way of compartmentalizing Senna—she can write about certain things like autobiography but not others like fiction. Reading Senna into Birdie is a way of racializing her as a safe, nonminority person of color. Celebrating mixed-race is an important post-racial move, because mixed-race would appear to be divorced from "traditional" (or parent) racial communities, and therefore not demand resources or challenge white privilege.

The *Booklist* review is interesting because of its reliance upon describing the looks of race(s), or, as the reviewer puts it, *Caucasia*'s "visual conundrums." Without specifying precisely how, the critic writes that Birdie "takes after" her white mother's side while her sister Cole, "takes after" her African American father's side.[40] The assumption, of course, is that "takes after" means looks like the same race.[41] However, although Birdie might resemble a general perception of "whiteness" (with dark eyes and hair and "beige" skin she is described as "looking" white, although not the pale, blond whiteness of her mother's family), she does not take after her mother in political or physical ways. Birdie's radical mother hides illegal guns and revolutionaries, and she could be described as a second wave feminist who is deeply committed to her political causes, while Birdie hides her unpopular racialized identities and could be described as a post-feminist who uses her racially malleable looks as a means to fit in. In a similar way, Birdie's sister is portrayed as "looking" black like her father; but as a caring, sensitive girl, she does not necessarily "take after" her aloof intellectual father in any other way. Physically, despite the fact that "people generally didn't comment on their resemblance to each other," Cole and her mother share "high foreheads and deep-set green eyes, . . . [and] small and delicate [hands]" (94). Likewise, Birdie and her father "have the same eyes" (387), and at the end of the novel Deck remarks to Birdie, "You look a little like my mother. . . . Same skinny body, broad shoulders. Same eyes" (395).

Mixed-race itself is often described as a visual phenomenon. It is a mixed look that causes people to do a double take at an unfamiliar mixture of features, skin color, body type, and hair texture. Different racial looks influence someone to question why a father looks so different from his daughter. When Birdie and her visibly black father spend the day together at Boston's botanical gardens, a white couple calls the police to find out what this black man is doing with a little white girl. The police officer harasses and humiliates Deck while Birdie is asked, "Did the man touch you funny?" (61). While a television show, such as *The L Word* or *America's Next Top Model*, or a film, such as *Mixing Nia*, can more obviously highlight or downplay the nuances of a particular racialized phenotype through elements that include casting, lighting, clothing, hair extensions, tanning, and makeup, a novel can negotiate race through careful language. *Caucasia* demonstrates that the visual, especially the visual nature of race, is open to interpretation. The novel maps how entities such as education, accent, makeup, jewelry, geography, profession, and music, map race, and not just phenotypic features, such as skin color, facial features, body type, and hair texture. And in contradiction, the characters' race(s) and gender(s) are not always just costumes but are also essential signifiers of the characters' "true essences." In *Caucasia* the multiple iterations of race, gender, and sexuality occur through visible bodily performances. *Caucasia* reflects the words of Oyeronke Oyewumi: "Sheer physicality . . . seems to attend being in Western culture" where, as a physical, visual marker, "the body is given a logic of its own. It is believed that just by looking at it one can tell a person's beliefs and social position or lack thereof."[42]

These issues surrounding the look of mixed-race blackness surface in the marketing of Senna's photograph along with her novel. In *Mulattas and Mestizas* Suzanne Bost contends that "an important part of the marketing of *Caucasia* is the appearance of the light-skinned Senna, whose photo accompanies some reviews of the best-seller."[43] In the paperback version of *Caucasia*, Senna's photograph is featured on the back cover. Occupying a relatively small space, the black-and-white photo is placed prominently on the upper-left-hand corner, so that before reading any of the excerpted rave reviews by James McBride (the author of *The Color of Water*), *Newsweek*, *New York Times Book Review*, *Glamour*, or USA *Today*, one has to first peruse the photograph. Senna is looking contemplatively toward one side. Her hair appears straight and black while her skin color is some indeterminate shade of off-white. The effect of the black-and-white photo is that one cannot discern gradations of color, or of "race," because Senna's skin and clothes are shades of gray.

Despite many black transcendent assertions from *Caucasia*'s critics, and although *Caucasia* came out in our so-called post–civil rights moment, the novel is quite concerned with the issues of civil rights. A handful of reviewers, the majority of whom identify themselves in their articles as women of color, wrote against *Caucasia* as a post-racial or post-feminist novel. One article identifies that "little is stable or certain in [Birdie's and Cole's] lives" and this is largely, if not exclusively, because of race.[44] The way the sisters manipulate their gendered identities with clothes, makeup, and boys helps to stabilize their identities simply because these accessories help them to fit in. This critic, acknowledging how strongly Birdie is wedded to her invisible blackness, also identifies Birdie as having "a kind of nostalgia for a lost blackness she never really owned."[45] One reviewer remarks, "What Ms. Senna gets so painfully well is how the standard-issue cruelties of adolescence . . . are revitalized when they encounter race."[46] Again, Birdie's coming of age is particularly marked by race and gender, and is not universally applicable to all.[47] Another article also sets itself apart by looking at Birdie's racialized and gendered adolescence: "More than a coming of age story[,] . . . *Caucasia* . . . addresses themes of coming into consciousness within the U.S. ethnoracial landscape." At the same time, while this critic proclaims that "*Caucasia* interrogates, displaces, and transforms the normative meanings of whiteness,"[48] she fails to see how the novel similarly exercises concepts of blackness and mixedness.[49] Because mixedness is such a slippery concept, some of the reviews end up missing the book's argument about the performativity and historicity of race, gender, and sexuality in the new millennium United States entirely.

Alternative Models to Passing

While the problem of mixed-race blackness is solved in the popular press by marking Senna as an exceptional multiracial, Senna does not take that same route in solving Birdie's problems with passing. The in-between causes Birdie plenty of problems, as does passing as both black and white. For example, when Senna describes Birdie as androgynous, she fails to seamlessly pass as white. *Caucasia* is intimately concerned with the trap of binary notions of race, gender, and sexuality, so Senna posits a certain identity fluidity as an alternative, but not a solution. However, at the same time, passing as black or white is so ineffective and torturous that it produces emotional, social, and psychological dissonance. The effects of Birdie's passing, her disappearing and doubling, reveal the pain that passing, and embracing an interstitial state, causes for the sad new millennium mulatta. Birdie's answer, while it is still a conflicted one, lies not in passing, but in loving blackness, and understanding the simultaneity of mixedness and blackness.

Even though Birdie's race transforms but is far from permeable (her race performances are based on staid notions of blackness and whiteness), Senna describes Birdie's sexuality as having greater porousness. From a young age Birdie is attracted to both girls and boys. In one fluid space between Boston and New Hampshire, the Aurora Commune for abused women and their children, Birdie plays "honeymoon" and learns how to kiss with her white female friend. As many of her identity changes happen in her own imagination, Birdie describes how she was in love with a male character in a novel that she wrote (required by Sandy to graduate from her home-school seventh grade), but "also dreamed about his sexy, abused girlfriend." Furthermore, "it wasn't clear to [her] which one [she] was supposed to be identifying with" (172). This fluidity, representing a break from heterosexual norms, is not simply an extension of the historical sexualization of the tragic mulatta.

In an interesting echo, Suzanne Bost has written about a "natural" proclivity of fictional multiracial characters toward gender androgyny and bisexuality. Calling these figures "the transitive bi-," Bost writes, "mixed identities cross conventional definitions of sex, gender, sexuality [and] race."[50] Thus, just as race is a constantly changing construct for Birdie, so are sexuality and gender. Bost asserts that for mixed-race characters, flexibility within and between identity categories is a "resonance produced by the racial contingency of sexual norms: answering simultaneously to more than one set of racial assumptions, as people of mixed race do, leads to answering simultaneously to different definitions of sex and gender."[51] In other words, because the idea of race is multiple, and performative for mixed-race characters, other ostensibly impermeable categories such as gender and sexuality are also multiple.

While Senna posits this sexual fluidity as liberatory for Birdie, such liberation is only viable for a short period of time. Fluctuating definitions of identity can be read as ultimately liberatory because, according to Stuart Hall, the "recognition of difference, of the impossibility of 'identity' in its fully unified meaning, does, of course, transform our sense of what politics is about."[52] This new politics is itself transformative and fluid, where although we are conscious of our own subject positions, we are able to move beyond those positions to work for social change. For *Caucasia*, though, the transformative politics involve embracing blackness, not transcending it.

Some readers might assume that because Birdie "plays the game of race," she easily claims a third, liminal position, treating race as a costume. However, although Birdie switches racial personae with apparent ease, she feels guilt, frustration, and pain for her masquerades: she is tied to her new millennium mulatta sadness. Historically, in the racially bifurcated black-white United States, a third option has largely not been allowed for "mulattoes" and "mulattas."[53] Like Birdie, they are either black by way of the one-drop rule of hypodescent, or they are white by way of passing. Scholars have written of passing as both shameful and an economic necessity. Senna illustrates both of these views in *Caucasia*.[54] The third space that Senna tenuously stakes out for Birdie speaks out against the framing of the new millennium mulatta vis-à-vis the tragic mulatta. Birdie thus pushes back against the Victorian-era mulatta characters that Jennifer Brody examines in *Impossible Purities* (1998).[55] Brody coins the term "mulattaroon" to demonstrate how the mixed-race cultural figure is "an unreal, impossible ideal whose corrupted and corrupting constitution inevitably causes conflicts in narratives that attempt to promote purity."[56]

The conflicted, tragic mulattaroon is not a reflection of reality, but rather a carefully crafted construction who "is perpetually being erased or effaced in an effort to stabilize (reify) the tenuous, permeable boundaries between white and black, high and low, male and female, English and American, pure and impure (or passionate)."[57] Birdie, as a new millennium mulatta, represents a greater reality than Brody's mulattaroon. She is a demographic category to be reckoned with.[58]

Therefore, just as the identities of Birdie, the sad race girl, keep shifting, identity, in the words of Stuart Hall, is a "production" that is perpetually in process.[59] Racialized identities, like gendered ones, are performative. *Caucasia* reflects Hall's sentiment—with more than a little sadness. As a new millennium mulatta text, Danzy Senna's *Caucasia* appears to argue against black transcendence, but the author's mixed-race African American protagonist's slippage into tragedy prevents resistance to the stereotype.

PART II

THE EXCEPTIONAL MULTIRACIAL

CHAPTER THREE

≡

TRANSITIONING TO THE
EXCEPTIONAL MULTIRACIAL

Escaping Tragedy through

Black Transcendence

in *Mixing Nia*

The camera pans across black faces and white faces at a dinner table littered with Chinese food takeout boxes, bottles of half-empty wine, and errant chopsticks. The diners, including an older white man; a younger, curly haired, mixed-race African American woman; and a younger, dreadlocked African American man, look tense. They do not blend into the low-lit, intimate ambiance of what appears to be a candlelit dinner. The woman, Nia, sighs and says, "here we go again,"[1] as the topic of race rears its ugly head. The two men argue passionately while Nia listens passively. The older man, Nia's father, Harvey, a civil rights attorney, expresses optimism about the success of American integration, the gains of the civil rights movement, and the power of "choice." The young man, Nia's boyfriend, Lewis, an African American studies professor, expresses pessimism about the state of contemporary black America and proposes that African Americans were "better off" during segregation.

Nia remains silent. She alternates between glancing uncomfortably at her plate, twirling her wine glass, and gazing off at some unseen point in the middle of the table. She does not engage in eye contact with either her father or her boyfriend but seems hopelessly caught in the middle of the discussion. This scene, located a little more than halfway through Alison Swan's independent film *Mixing Nia* (1998), is one of many that showcase the protagonist Nia's discomfort with the trappings of race. Swan initially portrays Nia as a mixed-up young woman who is caught between a staid notion of authentic blackness, which her boyfriend represents, and a deracialized philosophy of post-race, which her father symbolizes. Like the new-millennium-mulatta protagonists, in the first part of the film Nia is portrayed as a stuck-in-the-middle, mixed-race African American woman, whose racialized identity remains painfully in question. However, unlike the new millennium mulattas, Nia is presented with greater agency, and greater abilities to transcend the problems of racialized identity, or, more specifically, the problems with her blackness. In other words, as the film progresses Nia becomes an exceptional multiracial, who leaves behind the troublesome issue of blackness to achieve true freedom.

The writer, producer, and director Alison Swan's *Mixing Nia* is an end-of-the-twentieth-century film about an identity-crisis-ridden young black and Jewish woman who struggles with how she should mix and perform her racialized identity. Investigating black authenticity and color blindness in what Swan describes as the hybrid "dramedy" genre (drawing from late 1990s television shows like *Ally McBeal*), the film is part satire, part parody, and part melodrama. The hybrid form of the film parallels the content. Nia is played by the multiracial actress Karyn Parsons, who is recognizable to many viewers because of her over-the-top portrayal of the eldest daughter and spoiled young socialite Hilary Banks on the television sitcom *The Fresh Prince of Bel-Air* (1990–96). *Mixing Nia* is a post-collegiate coming-of-age story that takes place over the course of a number of months in New York City in the 1990s.

As the film opens, Nia works as a copy writer in an advertising agency. She is the only person of color in her office, and she quits her job after her conscience prevents her from working on a campaign for Slam Malt Liquor, which is targeted at young black men. Nia proceeds to find herself racially and sexually by changing her hairstyles, writing stories, and dating men. As Nia's racial identities fluctuate, and as the film toys with notions of African American authenticity, external signifiers of Nia's identity also change. Her sexual partners vary from black to white to Latino men. Her hair transforms from straight to curly to braids to slicked back and inconspicuous. Nia's racialized identity play is represented through her imagined book plots. She changes the plot of the novel she is writing from an interracial love story to a Black Panther tale to a modern urban "ghetto" narrative to a Jim Crow South account to a post-racial and post-feminist autobiography. In the final scene, the film embraces post-raciality in lieu of an essentialized black identity. *Mixing Nia* critiques staid, controlling images of blackness. However, instead of positing a true heterogeneity of African American identities in lieu of stereotypes, the film rejects any racialized identity by embracing an empty and impossible ideal of post-raciality, or the view that race no longer matters. In contrast to the embraced blackness in *Caucasia*, blackness in *Mixing Nia* remains something that must be transcended in order for the multiracial African American character to escape the anger and sadness of the new millennium mulatta.

Swan enacts a number of signifiers of black authenticity. Her film, engaging with a mixed-race African American identity crisis, tells us quite a bit about black hybridity in popular culture, which is, in the words of Herman Gray, a "contested terrain" of "competing claims" for blackness.[2] Such claims change with shifting historical moments. *Mixing Nia* was released during a historically critical time in the United States. The popular press was abuzz with the news from the Office of Management and Budget (OMB) that the 2000 U.S. Census would allow for multiply raced people to account for all of their racialized backgrounds; this was institutionalized acknowledgment of mixed-race. The film performs old tropes of mixed-race, which stem from paradigmatic portrayals of mixed-race women in films such as *The Birth of a Nation* (1915) and *Imitation of Life* (1959). However, reflecting its historic moment, the film also dramatizes a new subject position, a movement away from the angry and sad new millennium mulatta and toward the exceptional multiracial of the presidential candidate Barack Obama, who rose to prominence almost a decade after the film's release. *Mixing Nia* comes at a moment of late multiculturalism, where naive but hopeful rainbow politics have been replaced by vehement erasures of affirmative action. This film is an ideal text because it is symptomatic of the exceptional multiracial ethos surrounding mixed-race blackness. Although it was never released theatrically, it did find a niche audience as an independent film on a film festival circuit and cable run. *Mixing Nia*'s importance in the discourse of mixed-race African Americanness is heightened because it is the *sole* late-twentieth-century feature-length film to explore multiracial blackness in the United States, notably, through a female protagonist.[3] Nia's visible racialized and sexualized choices, from hair to men, facilitate her movement from the new millennium mulatta to the exceptional multiracial, which in the film means a state of black transcendence. *Mixing Nia* therefore challenges the most harmful tenets of racial essentialism, but it still produces racialized and gendered stereotypes of blackness and ultimately espouses the reactionary racial discourse of the exceptional multiracial's success because she achieves black transcendence.

The Filmic Past of the Tragic Mulatta

What has been cinematically written on the African American mixed-race woman's body? *The Birth of a Nation* (1915) and *Imitation of Life* (1959) provide landmark portraits of mixed-race African American women in film that produce and reflect mythical images of sex, shame, exceptionalism, poverty, and privilege.[4] In *The Birth of a Nation*, the mulatta rises from U.S. slavery, the product of forced relations between a slave woman and her white master. In *Imitation of Life*, as the unsuccessful passer, the mulatta is poor and cast out from all monoracial communities. In *Mixing Nia*, the multiracial African American figure is imagined as a child of "the movement," who represents civil rights–era optimism bound up in a rainbow-colored package of cultural fusion. In all three films, depicted as sufficiently light and deliciously dark, the multiracial black woman finds her answers in heterosexual coupling. These films demonstrate the important role that the imagined mulatta plays in exercising white fears of black infringement in each time period.

Filmic myths of the tragic mulatta reflect, reproduce, and circulate a specifically mixed-race African American female racialization and sexualization. The tragic-mulatta characters in *Birth of a Nation* and *Imitation of Life*, like many other tragic mulattas on screen, share certain features: they were often played by white women; they were viewed as beautiful and were hypersexualized; they were emotionally unstable, fragile, or hysterical; they were manipulative liars; they were angry at the social structure of which they imagined themselves victims; they attracted black men and white men alike; they were mired in psychological pain and distress; and their struggles often represented the struggles of the entire film, and the struggles of the entire nation. Eva Saks describes how "scientific, legal, and popular mythology deemed this offspring of an interracial union to be

. . . a monster ultimately deviant and inferior. . . . The mulatto monster was . . . the other of the other. . . . [S]he was virtually an *infection*."[5] *Mixing Nia* both deploys and critiques filmic tragic-mulatta characteristics. The film doggedly embraces ambiguity and multiplicity alongside singular, controlling ideas of racialization and sexualization.

There is close continuity in the portrayal of Lydia in *Birth of a Nation* and Sara Jane in *Imitation of Life*. The representations of mixed-race black women in these two highly successful studio melodramas illustrate that despite differing historical contexts, multiracial black women were largely viewed the same way: as a menace to the stability of American racial boundaries. Because they represent threat, both women are portrayed as hypersexual and mentally unstable. Both characters long for whiteness, attained through sexual relations with white men. Both characters are played by women racialized by their studios as white in their press materials, providing the audience with a safe understanding that something truly transgressive is not really occurring, and that the boundaries between white and black are kept intact. The women's passing for white resonates against Birdie's post-*Loving* attempts at passing for black.

Reflecting their historical moments, *The Birth of a Nation* and *Imitation of Life* provide powerful blueprints for future filmic representations of black-white mixed-race women. The singularly over-the-top, aggressively heterosexual manner in which *Mixing Nia* embraces mixed-race sexuality is reperformed — men as sexual partners are essential to Nia's understanding of her racialized selves. In addition, as illegitimate bodies emerging from the extralegal shadows, these mixed-race characters demonstrate a common insecurity or confusion about their identities. The filmmaker Alile Sharon Larkin notes, "seeking her/his identity becomes the primary preoccupation [of the tragic mulatta]."[6] In all three films the tragic mulatta is portrayed in opposition to "pure" white and "pure" black female foils, from Elsie and Mammy in *The Birth of a Nation* to Lora and Annie in *Imitation of Life* to Nia's white best friend, Jen, and black childhood friend Renee in *Mixing Nia*.

However, the portrayals of Lydia and Sara Jane do differ from Nia. Nia understands her race through her sexuality, but it is not her sole defining characteristic. Nia does not explicitly desire white power, as she does not long for whiteness. But she does desire a certain colorless power, and ability to transcend the confusion that comes with acknowledging her blackness. Just as Swan changes Nia's racialized hairstyles and boyfriends, she also changes the sexualized performance of her protagonist from chaste to libidinous to in between these two extremes. Nia is played by an African American actress who is biracial, and whom contemporary audiences could likely identify as such; seeing this light-skinned black woman on the screen as opposed to white women imitating blackness is quite a different experience for the audience, although in *Mixing Nia* Nia does imitate certain so-called authentic forms of blackness.

The genres of the films also differ. Linda Williams notes that the earlier two films are melodramas,[7] while Swan describes *Mixing Nia* as a dramedy, with comedic elements tempering the more dramatic aspects of the film. This change in genre perhaps prevents viewers from labeling Nia as too tragic. Nia, a self-reflexive character, appears to be both tortured by and in on the joke that she inadequately performs assimilationist and authentically black roles. Another interesting difference is the trajectory of parents, all black women and white men, in these three portrayals: while both of Lydia's parents are absent from the screen (but present in our imaginations), Sara Jane's father is never shown (but is referenced), and Nia's mother and father are both featured (but her white father receives more screen time). As time progresses the audience is forced less and less to imagine the border-breaking parents; because they are featured on screen, their act becomes less illicit. They are real characters and not simply figments of an American imagination, making miscegenation less taboo.

The directors and their understanding of the representations of mixed-race women also differ quite drastically. Most strikingly, the auteur of *Mixing Nia*, Alison Swan, is an Afro Bermudian woman and not a white man like *Birth of a Nation*'s filmmaker D. W. Griffith and the second version of *Imitation of Life*'s filmmaker Douglas Sirk. As opposed to Swan, neither Griffith nor Sirk portrayed their mixed-race female character as a lead. Perhaps because of this, where the previous two films were studio blockbusters, *Mixing Nia* was never picked up by a distributor and was instead sold to the more African American–friendly space of television. While Nia, a late-twentieth-century representation of a mixed-race African American woman in film, is certainly, in Sandy Flitterman-Lewis's words, a "simultaneous signifier of racial and sexual difference alike," her "sexual and racial allusions" reconfigure from the tragic mulatta to the exceptional multiracial.[8]

Mixing Nia opens with a scene bathed in serene blue light. Soothing music and the sound of splashing water accompany the incongruous sight of a bulbous white polar bear swimming gracefully through water. After about thirty seconds the camera cuts to a profile shot of a light-brown-skinned girl of about six—her curly hair peeks out of her pigtails as she leans up against the glass of an aquarium's underground viewing area. Enraptured by the sight of the bear, the girl touches the glass and delightedly speaks to herself, although we do not hear what she says. The calm music, blue colors, and happy child tell us that this is a place of safety. There are no adults present, only an innocent little girl, Nia, who is enthralled by the sight of a magical polar bear. In this otherworldly space, questions of race, gender, and sexuality, and the anxiety these identity categories will cause for Nia when she is an adult, are absent. This is the moment that Nia remembers as the day before her parents told her they were getting a divorce. This is her last moment of innocence, of complete safety, and throughout the film Nia seeks to return to the feelings embodied here. Little-girl Nia identifies with a nonhuman, endangered species perform-ing alone in its underwater box for the spectacle, display, and visual con-sumption of an unseen audience. Swan moves from this strange safety into a world marked with utter uncertainty.

Immediately following the aquarium scene are several scenes filmed in Nia's advertising agency. The camera only takes us into the small spaces of a confined hallway, a stuffy office, and a claustrophobic conference room, portraying the agency as a constricting place. Conservatively dressed white men populate the office, with the exception of one white woman, most likely a secretary, who is briefly seen filing in the background. Nia's business clothes, muted in color and loose fitting, and straightened hair, shoulder length and unobtrusive, mark her effort to blend into her white, male, professional workplace (fig. 3). She is a woman trying to pass not directly as white or male, but as another executive, who, in the Ameri-can popular imagination, is coded as white and male. However, as hard as Nia tries to fit in at her white office, her boss and officemates see her as the black spokesperson, evidenced in their desire for her to create racist stereotypes in the advertisements she pitches. Swan self-reflexively locates Nia at an advertising agency where she manipulates images, com-

FIGURE 3 Nia's conservative look in the advertising agency.

merce, and marketing for a living; this presages Nia's own adventures with racialized, gendered, and sexualized identity performances.

When Nia is first assigned to create an advertising campaign for Slam beer, targeted at young, black men, she is excited about the opportunity. However, her excitement wanes when her boss essentializes her as embodying "the" black experience; he tells her that she has the edge in this malt liquor campaign because "the closest Charlie and Nick [her white coworkers] have ever gotten to the black experience is through a sitcom." At this comment her mouth offers up a perfunctory, good-natured smile. Her eyes, however, look away uncomfortably, offering silent resistance at his assumptions of her authentic blackness.[9] Black authenticity, as a form of essentialism, reproduces hegemonic categories. In the words of J. Martin Favor, "rather than undermining blackness or whiteness by calling attention to and complicating the relationships between these categories' constitutive parts, an overly simplistic race consciousness may risk the reification of 'race' and the closing out of possible coalitions across gender, class, geographic, color and other boundaries."[10] There are no coalitions offered up in the film; in the agency Nia is seen as authentic, safe, and just black. Nia, a beautiful, straight-haired, mixed-race African American woman, is the acceptable minority chosen by corporate America to market black working-class masculinity.

Nia is first excited by the professional opportunity to sell beer to an abstracted "them," and she creates a campaign that plays on racist images of black men desirous for basketball and beer. Later she balks at marketing cheap alcohol to "us." Although in the agency Nia never references herself with any racial label, her white coworkers quickly point out that her blackness gets her what they believe to be special favors, such as being chosen to pitch the Slam beer campaign. Nia grimaces when she overhears two of her many white male coworkers bitterly whispering, "The only reason she's getting this is because she's the only black in Creative." Their repetition of "only" underscores Nia's racialization as only black by her coworkers, calling into question her qualifications, and referencing contemporary post-racial complaints of affirmative action as unfair reverse discrimination. Nia acquiesces to her white male officemates at one level by assimilating with her clothing and hairstyle, but her facial expressions demonstrate her resistance.[11]

However, Nia's attempts at assimilation only last so long because *Mixing Nia* ultimately critiques white desires to stereotype blacks. Racked by a guilty conscience fueled by her daydream of a ten-year-old African American boy drinking Slam beer and gleefully stating, "I'm your target audience, ages six to fourteen," Nia abruptly quits her job in the middle of her Slam pitch. As her coworkers reject her, Nia immediately rejects feeling that she has to act "too white" in order to stave off their ascription of her as "too black." As soon as she leaves her office building she allows herself to connect with her blackness and humanity: she gives money to the African American panhandler whom she brushed past and avoided eye contact with in an earlier scene. Thus, the film's very first scenes equate authentic blackness with poverty, and the film fails to question the structural factors linking them, or interrogate what blackness means to professional, middle-class African Americans, such as Nia's own mother, who is a lawyer.

After Nia quits her job, she finds herself lost and in the midst of an identity crisis. The identity crisis Swan creates for Nia calls on old cinematic, literary, and social scientific tropes of mixed-race, which dictated that multiracial people are doomed to insanity because of their unnatural mixture of races. While the filmic tragic-mulatta predecessors Lydia and Sara Jane were driven to the brink of insanity, with an exceptional-multiracial tinge, Nia's multiracial blood leads only to a crisis of identity. In addition, while Sara Jane rejects and abandons blackness, at times Nia embraces it. Thus, Nia's identity crisis cannot be dismissed as simply typical of another twenty-something career woman seeking to find herself. Instead we must recognize the mitigated models of deviance that Swan employs alongside essentialist visions of blackness and color blindness. Unlike past representations of tragic mulattas, this contemporary multiracial protagonist never longs to be white. Instead, she aches for a notion of color blindness; *Mixing Nia* presents no alternatives outside of critiquing authentic blackness and embracing a vision of black transcendence for the exceptional multiracial.

Race Crisis, Part II: Acting Too Black

After leaving the advertising agency, Nia becomes an aspiring novelist. There is no explanation of how she is supporting herself financially, but it is apparent that money is not an issue. Her first idea for a novel, which is an allegory for finding her voice or discovering her racial identity, is an interracial love story based on her now-divorced parents' experiences living in Greenwich Village in the 1960s. Nia finds her way into all-black spaces for the first time in the film: because she is suffering from writer's block, she agrees to accompany her friend Renee, whose constant comments about how to be black position her as the authentic black woman in the film, to an African American writers' workshop. At the workshop Nia listens to a lecture by the professor, Lewis (played by Isaiah Washington), with an enraptured gaze reminiscent of the six-year-old watching the polar bear at the zoo. Nia nods almost imperceptibly when Lewis lambastes "the Man." When she meets him after the lecture she touches her straightened hair self-consciously, instinctively knowing the assimilation it must proclaim.

Immediately after this scene she dons a "natural" hairstyle that is more in line with Lewis's philosophy of authentic blackness. Viewers are led to believe that she is letting out her true, unprocessed self, although the cultural studies scholar Kobena Mercer reminds us that "nobody's hair is ever just natural, but is always shaped and reshaped by social convention and symbolic intervention."[12] Whether a signifier of privilege or of punishment, of sexuality or of repression, African American women's hair is far more than mere adornment. Hair, as a sign of race, has real material consequences and historical effects. Hair stories illustrate, as Deborah

FIGURE 4 Lewis lecturing.

Grayson argues, that "because we live in a culture where visual images affect our relations as human beings, the choices black women make about hairstyle or body appearance often mean the difference between acceptance or rejection by groups and individuals."[13] Similarly, the psychologist Maria Root writes that for mixed-race women, "a particularly difficult issue may have to do with hair, particularly for persons who are of African-American or Asian-American heritage. Hair can determine physical identity by others with a specific ethnic and racial group, and thus becomes a vehicle through which symbolic integration of a multiracial identity occurs."[14] For multiracial African American women, with imagined allegiances to insiders and outsiders, us and them, blacks and whites, hair denotes not just beauty or style, but racial authenticity, politics, and desire. As a malleable and yet clearly racialized mark, multiracial African American women's hair expresses the tangled threads of the personal and the political, the pain and the privilege.

Lewis is a handsome and aggressive man who flirts with Nia in the middle of his lecture, erotically dubbing her "café au lait" (fig. 4). Smart, driven, and arrogant, his many external signifiers, from his dreadlocks to the African masks displayed in his apartment, demonstrate that he is authentically black. Lewis only finds value in books written by black authors and shows contempt for all things white, including Nia's father. Swan depicts Lewis, a caricature of Black Nationalism, as petty, irrational, argumentative, and one dimensional. While he hates whites, he exclusively dates very light-skinned women. In a parodic representation of authentic blackness, he even segregates Nia's books into separate shelves for black and white authors and de-Anglicizes her music collection by ousting her Grateful Dead records. While the film could have entered into a nuanced interrogation of Lewis's own identity crisis, it fails to linger on that angle. During this phase of the film, her Jewish father complains that the couple spends time with her African American mother while he feels left out.

Although none of the other characters question the fact that Nia is black, Lewis asserts that to truly be black, Nia must have certain essentialized interests, behaviors, and alliances, which she understands must accompany a certain hairstyle, romantic partner, and book plot.[15] This is the same philosophy that the advertising agency espoused, where she was given a similar dictate to perform essential blackness. Nia embraces a new authentically black lifestyle solely because she is attracted to Lewis and what he represents. She stops straightening her hair and cultivates its curly texture, and she changes the topic of her novel to the Black Panthers, the emblematic symbol of authentic blackness. While the film desexualizes Nia in her white advertising agency phase, the film hypersexualizes her when she "gets in touch with her blackness." Her clothes become tighter and expose more of her body. Nia and Lewis have sex on their first date; wrapped in his *kente* cloth patterned sheets, she utters phrases that seem to come more from Lewis than from her, telling him that she "thinks [she] might have caught the spirit" and that she was "speaking in tongues" (fig. 5). In this scene the film associates authentic blackness, marked by the libidinous black man Lewis's and the oversexed mulatta Nia's performances, with an uninhibited, aggressive, and excessive sexuality.

Authentic blackness is also marked by Nia's free, curly hair.[16] In her attempt to be authentically black, Nia has three fantasies in the form of imagined book plots, in which she stars as various icons of blackness. The fantasy sequences in which actress Karyn Parsons performs the role of Nia, who in turn performs the fantasy roles, introduce yet another level of performance and highlight the fluidity of race, gender, and sexuality. As hard as Nia tries to play an ostensibly truly black character, she never manages to be Lewis's ideal black subject. Her hair, Swan's signifier of

FIGURE 5 Nia and Lewis wrapped in kente cloth sheets.

Nia's racial alliance, changes in each fantasy to match the appropriate ambiance and demonstrate that switching hairstyles necessarily accompanies switching racial personae. The punch line of all three sequences, played for comic appeal, is that even in her imagination, when she is supposed to be freed of the confines of reality, our mixed-race protagonist can never quite play an authentic black role; in other words, she cannot seamlessly perform a stereotypical, essentialized version of an African American woman. In order to highlight her gender, Swan surrounds Nia with men. The sequences also feature male-propagated physical violence, the metaphoric violence committed to Nia's identities; because of this violence the viewer understands that authentic blackness is unequivocally a wrong choice for Nia. While these fantasy sequences are critiques of racial authenticity politics, ultimately Swan suggests that Nia would just be happier if, as in color blindness, race did not matter in an identity-based way.

Nia's first fantasy occurs immediately after the African American writers' workshop, when the subject of her novel changes from an interracial love story to the Black Panthers. A Jimi Hendrix–esque electric guitar whines as Nia imagines herself as "Roberta," a woman with a huge Afro and all-black attire, whom gun-toting and black-beret-wearing Afri-

FIGURE 6 Nia's Black Panther fantasy.

can American men surround (fig. 6). Swan shoots this scene with very little light, so the audience understands that the characters are doing something dangerous. Conspiring in a dark room, the characters appear to be on a lookout, as one man cautiously peers out the window, rifle in hand. Roberta tries to wear a tough expression, but wilts when called to action with her fellow Panthers; as they run off, cocking their guns, she freezes and looks uncomfortable. Blackness equals male violence that Nia as Roberta resists or cannot participate in. Even in her fantasies she cannot fully realize each persona—she is just playing dress-up with an Afro wig. As fantasy bleeds into Nia's reality, her hair turns curly after this sequence, or as Nia tells Matt, a white friend she later dates, "I'm just letting it go natural, you know, part of the new me." Nia questions herself while wearing her shifting racial personae on her head, struggling futilely to be authentic.

The second fantasy occurs after Nia sees Lewis's friend Loquesha, a crude stereotype of an angry black woman, perform at a poetry slam. Because Nia had been struggling with her story about the Panthers, Lewis suggests that she write something more contemporary. She comes up with a new story idea set in the same ghetto she visited for insight while

FIGURE 7 Nia's ghetto fantasy.

working on the Slam beer commercial. Nia changes the name of her character, who is clearly inspired by Loquesha, from Quesha to Shoquesha to Shoque. Shoque wears cheap-looking synthetic braids, a red knit hat, and gold doorknocker earrings. Rap music plays as this stereotypical black ghetto princess reclaims her power from the street. However, despite Shoque's tough walk up to the black man who "gunned down" her boyfriend, his curses and screams easily scare her away, and she ends up apologizing (fig. 7). The threat of physical violence, coded again as black and male, frightens her off. At a moment of reckoning, Shoque falters just as Roberta did in the previous sequence. After this fantasy, we see Nia, who now has braids in "real life." Swan's transfer of Nia's fantasy hair to her real-life hair demonstrates the tangible effect that fantasy plays in all of the film's diegetic layers.

Nia's third fantasy sequence comes after an argument between her father and Lewis, the scene at the dinner table. Nia envisions herself as an unnamed woman in the Jim Crow South while a banjo twangs away in the background. Wearing two scraggly braids and an old-fashioned, tattered cotton dress, she is comically refused entrance into a whites-only bathroom by dirty, white, overall-clad men who cock their shotguns at her

The Exceptional Multiracial

—

FIGURE 8 Nia's Jim Crow South fantasy.

(fig. 8). Again, she cannot stand up to these violent men in her fantasy, just as she cannot stand up to anyone in her life. While Nia's unkempt pigtails do not make it into her real-life scenes, the audience understands that despite changing her hairstyles, along with other external signifiers, Nia cannot fulfill so-called authentic black roles. In this fantasy sequence, the film most clearly posits the post-racial ideology that Nia cannot truly be black because she has not experienced oppression, or anti-black racism, which is marked as solely existing in the Jim Crow South.

Swan's comedic fantasy sequences indict authentic blackness as a superficial performance. Post-feminism acts in concert with post-race as feminized accoutrements, like Nia's hairstyles, to facilitate her movement through authentic black personae. Nia's inability to adequately perform stereotypes can be read as a form of what Stuart Hall calls "the end of the innocent notion of the essential black subject" in order to move away from the politics of authenticity.[17] In his work, Hall deconstructs mediated monolithic portrayals of black identity and explicates the true diversity of black communities.[18] By contrast, in *Caucasia*, while Danzy Senna does critique black authenticity and gesture toward a fluidity with identity and identification, her critique exhibits a residue of longing for the blackness her protagonist will never fully be able to inhabit; Senna's longing falls back upon Hall's description of the one-dimensional "essential black subject."

Swan seems to question the current avenues available to African Americans to express racial loyalty far more than we saw in *Caucasia*. Unfortunately, in doing so Swan falls short of illuminating true diversity within the category "black." Additionally, although Swan mocks popular imaginings of the essential black subject, she does not allow Nia to verbalize this struggle. Nia remains mired in her confusion, shouting at herself and her characters, "you're supposed to stand up to him, you idiot!" Part of her frustration is that she cannot assert herself in her relationship, and the violent men in these fantasies represent Lewis. Nia's identity crisis is also rationalized as somehow understandably mixed-race: her confusion gets blamed on her multiraciality.

In addition, although Nia fights against narrow understandings of what it means to be a black woman, she does not know how to discover herself outside of men's definitions of her. Swan briefly critiques Nia's post-feminist power, which came from embracing a newfound sexualized identity. Nia's temporary fix of an authentic black identity crumbles as her relationship with Lewis falls apart. Her loss of control over her race, gender, and sexuality is illuminated when she admits, "I feel like I'm getting so caught up in who [Lewis] wants me to be that I'm losing who I am." Ultimately, just as acting what Nia believes is "too white" in the advertising agency is an empty proposition, acting what she soon sees as "too black" cannot last either.

Race Crisis, Part III: Exceptional Multiracial Found

After *Mixing Nia* thoroughly critiques authentic or essentialized blackness, the film proceeds to eliminate any articulation of an African American identity in lieu of a deracialized ideology of black transcendence. Nia sees post-raciality as her answer when she breaks up with Lewis. Frustrated with Lewis's denigration of all things not black or not black enough, and longing to not have to measure up to his barometer of blackness, Nia laments, "Why can't people be people? Like humanity!" In response, Lewis says, "The only thing you know about being black is from a book," suggesting that her mixed-race body will always prevent her from being authentically black.

Immediately after breaking up with Lewis, Nia takes out her braids,

FIGURE 9 Nia smoking Matt's cigar.

shaking her head at the mistakes she just made. She brings the bought hair to a trashcan outside her apartment building, seeming to want the hair, like her relationship with Lewis, as far away as possible. After the breakup, Nia dates her white former coworker Matt, who exoticizes her because of her blackness, and the difference he feels she represents. Nia uses her newfound sexuality, unleashed by a libidinous black man, to turn herself into a sexual subject for a white man — on her date with Matt she even smokes his cigar (fig. 9).

Hair, race, and sexuality come to the forefront when Nia realizes that Matt could never be the man for her. Matt insists that she ride to a party with the top of his convertible down, despite her concerns about her hair. When they arrive at the party, Nia's hair is huge and unruly. Nia is distraught and insists that she looks as if she's "been struck by lightning," while Matt enthuses, "I think it looks really cool" (fig. 10).[19] Matt does not understand the racialized significance of Nia's wild hair, and he thinks her problems are solved when he finds some twine for her to tame it. Matt's suggestion of twine seems more appropriate for an inanimate object than human hair. The problem with Matt is still the problem with black authenticity; instead of Nia not being black enough, as with Lewis, she is only

FIGURE 10 Nia's wild hair.

black with Matt. *Mixing Nia* exposes the collusion of race, hair, men, and heterosexual desire. However, Swan grants Matt the dignity of changing and growing; he quits his job after Nia lambastes him for working with a racist, while Lewis stays the same throughout the film.

Nia looks for answers with yet another man: her new truth comes from Joe (played by Diego Serrano), a Latino musician who embodies some mythical nonblack and nonwhite, post-racial and hybrid, combination. In keeping with post-raciality, Joe's Latinoness is presented as devoid of history—he tells Nia he is adopted, posited as a blank slate akin to color blindness, in order to avoid relating his racialized identity questions to hers. Joe's hybridity bleeds into his career as a classical composer who plays rock music. He also seems to instinctively know Nia. In one scene approximately two-thirds of the way through the film, Nia perches on Joe's couch, falling into the role of patient to Joe's therapist (fig. 11). She confesses, "All I feel is confusion. . . . I've got all this black-white crap to deal with. . . . I don't know a goddamned thing about the black experience and I'm black."[20]

In response, instead of questioning what it really means to be black, Joe proclaims that race is immaterial to her identity crisis, which is signified

FIGURE 11 Nia in therapy with Joe.

through her writer's block. He tells Nia to "go with," which she interprets
as go beyond, her ambiguity and confusion.[21] In other words, acknowledging racial difference means that she can move beyond it to become
the exceptional multiracial. Because no heterogeneous black expression
exists in the film, performing as black *and* multiracial is dismissed as such
a dismal option that Nia's only viable alternative is to abandon blackness,
which Nia does by writing an exceptional multiracial autobiography,
dating a (neither black nor white) Latino man, and tying back her hair in
order to reflect her new nonracialized identity.

After Nia discards both Lewis and Matt, symbolically rejecting black
authenticity in favor of color blindness, it initially appears as though she
is going to define herself outside the confines of a sexual relationship.
However, in the film's final scene when Nia performs a monologue at a
poetry slam, Swan utilizes a shot/reverse shot convention that leads the
audience to believe that Nia is speaking directly to Joe. In this scene Nia
iterates a form of prototherapist Joe's earlier advice: she is ignoring her
mixed-race confusion.[22] Nia confidently types away on her laptop as the
scene changes to a voiceover of her closing monologue. The camera cuts
to a low-lit shot; everything is in darkness except for Nia's exposed skin

FIGURE 12 Nia's final monologue.

on her hands, face, and chest and a few tendrils of curly hair (fig. 12). Her hair seems to have almost disappeared in this final scene: in order to fully embrace post-raciality she must rid herself of racialized signifiers, like her hair. She slowly and confidently performs her piece, refusing to place a racialized label on her newly found self: "Now with my feet planted firmly toward the direction of my chosen fate I see in the faces of passing people my maternal ancestors bound in shackles, standing on the shore, weeping for the freedom they've lost, my paternal ancestors weeping for the freedom they have gained. And as I catch my reflection in the glass of a storefront it is like I'm seeing myself for the first time. And what I see, I like. The End."

Nia's first-person address proclaims that she has solved her racialized identity crisis. She acknowledges the painful history of "shackles" inscribed in her African American heritage just as she recognizes the lucky opportunities of "freedom" marked by her white background. Blackness equates to struggle while whiteness, even the Jewish whiteness of her father's family, equates to opportunity. Nia remains a "reflection" whose "chosen fate" is strikingly without a racial label. In addition to her words, other diegetic elements bespeak Nia's growth beyond the confines of singular racial choice, or any racial choice at all. She speaks from a poetry café where Lewis once taught her how to be "authentically" black. Now, literally spotlit, she steps into the role of teacher and reclaims the space, following a new lesson plan of color blindness. After her reading ends, the camera cuts to a beaming Joe, who is visually conjectured as her new boyfriend. Nia has addressed her words to Joe, whose presence has turned this previously black space into a multicultural space: when she was at the poetry café with Lewis the camera only took in the three African American bodies of light-skinned Nia, dark-skinned Lewis, and the brown-skinned performer Loquesha. With Joe the camera takes in a wider audience peppered with people who appear to be African American, Asian American, Latino, and white.

When Nia visited this café with Lewis, she committed the faux pas of what Lewis suggested was mainstream clapping instead of bohemian snapping at the end of Loquesha's performance. Lewis admonished her, silencing her clapping hands by gathering them into his. In stark contrast, at the end of Nia's monologue Joe begins a loud, slow clap that overtakes the snapping audience, and quickly leads to their clapping. Comparable to the critique of authentic blackness espoused in *Mixing Nia*, Joe's gesture forges a critique of racialized categories of behavior. In Nia's revelatory moment, she speaks to Joe, who is implicitly credited with ending her identity crisis. This scene illustrates the antifeminist slant of postfeminism: Nia is not allowed to act as her own teacher (although her positioning in this scene references her as such). Instead, she mouths Joe's earlier words. Her gendered, sexualized, and racialized identity is defined by her sexual relationships.

The music swells as a mix of conga drums, Native American wind instruments, and the *kora*, a Senegalese gourd instrument, aurally mark the space as transnationally hybrid. But this is mere empty multicultural positioning because they are ahistorically infused into the background. Nia's various identities, particularly her performances of authentic blackness, are personal, not structural, articulations. Seeing African American as a monolithic, essentialized identity causes Nia's identity crisis, manifested in her writer's block. After forging a critique of, as Hall puts it, "the essential black subject," Swan illustrates how the problems of authentic blackness are answered by transcending blackness. Nia's post-feminist performances showcased through her novel plots, hair, and sexual relationships facilitate transitions through her racialized identity changes. Despite launching a critique of monolithic ideals of blackness, *Mixing Nia* proposes black transcendence as the answer instead of black heterogeneity. When mixed-race African American identity remains largely unlinked to structural issues, as in *Mixing Nia*, race, gender, and sexuality can be dismissed as personal and ultimately irrelevant for the exceptional multiracial.

"Who Is the Market for This Film?"

Before writing and directing her own film, Swan worked as the vice president of production for RSO Films, the company that produced such blockbusters as *Evita*, *Grease*, and *Saturday Night Fever*. Swan and her white producing partner, Gabriella Stollenwerck, raised $600,000 by bypassing Hollywood financing and receiving funding from Wall Street.[23] Swan and Stollenwerck "got nonindustry types like Wall Streeters to write checks — big checks."[24] Swan's funders were primarily friends and family who "liked the financial package" that she and Stollenwerck put together; Swan also noted that very few of these people actually read the script and most did not expect to get their money back.[25] Swan said that they targeted "high net worth" individuals with diverse portfolios and an interest in high-risk ventures such as this one. Swan also told me, "I made quite a bit of money working for my father" (she acted as his press secretary after attending film school at NYU). Personal connections afforded Swan a budget for her first film.

Swan's $600,000 budget produced, according to *Essence* columnist Tara Roberts, a "slick piece of moviemaking" with a cast and crew of more than 150 people. As a result, *Mixing Nia* "has sweet touches that many up-and-coming filmmakers can't afford—like using a split screen to indicate that we're inside Nia's head, or shooting in 32 locations around New York City, or having an original music score and a music supervisor."[26] These "sweet touches" would also seem to make the film more appealing to distributors, because it looks like a mainstream Hollywood film. Swan scored talented actors, including Karyn Parsons, famous from *The Fresh Prince of Bel-Air*,[27] and Isaiah Washington, notable at the time for high-caliber independent films.[28] It was not amateur filmmaking elements that prevented *Mixing Nia*'s theatrical distribution.

And yet, Swan failed to hook a distributor for *Mixing Nia* because it was not a film that easily fit a singular marketing niche. She said, "We had a lot of trouble distributing the movie because the executives and the distributors said, 'who is the market for this film?' And . . . I told them that (a), the film is very universal, and (b), that it's not only biracial people, but that black people, white people would relate to it because there is so much of it in our families and in our lives and our friends. And it's just fun, you know what I mean?"[29] In an attempt to secure a theatrical distributor, Swan described her film as a text that encourages a color-blind reading: universalism, where all viewers, regardless of race, relate to and enjoy the film. Swan's reading speaks back to Hollywood's sentiment that films by women of color must be narrowcast into niche films. However, distributors rejected *Mixing Nia* as both too black to feature as a universal independent film and not black enough to feature as a black independent film.

I was able to interview Swan at her home and a restaurant in the Los Angeles area over the course of an afternoon in March 2001.[30] During our time together, Swan asserted to me that much of her experience speaks to the viability of color blindness.[31] Swan is the daughter of the former prime minister of Bermuda; a graduate of an elite boarding school, university, and film school; and the wife of a prominent white film producer, Robert Tietel, whose partner in State Street Pictures, George Tillman, is African American. Thus, Swan explained to me that *Mixing Nia* was "not just a black film." Nia's struggle served as a metaphor for Swan's own transnational discontinuity as she traveled back and forth between schools in the United States and home in Bermuda. Swan explained to me that Nia's mixed-race was a metaphor for her own transnational and class discontinuities, which she felt prevented her from identifying with African Americans:

> And growing up at boarding schools, very white boarding schools, and going to white schools in Bermuda, even though I wasn't biracial, I felt very torn between these different worlds. You know, between the black world and the white world. And I just wanted to like everybody. And I wanted to just be judged as a person and to judge people as people, as naive as that was. And so I really struggled for a while. And so when I thought about doing *Mixing Nia*, it was like, how can I put my struggle to find myself in an American perspective that people can get? Because I can't give them my whole baggage, and my history, because they wouldn't get it. And so I thought, I can make this girl biracial because

people would get that, people would get that she'd be torn, people would get that she'd be sort of struggling to sort of figure out what her place was in the world.[32]

Swan relied upon the stereotypes of the tragic mulatta—that she is torn and caught between two cultures. Interestingly, directly after making this statement, Swan provided a disclaimer: "I didn't want to get into this whole tragic-mulatto stereotype, and I was so petrified of that." Thus, by having Nia triumphant at the end of the film, Swan ostensibly flips the new-millennium-mulatta script on its head and instead produces the exceptional multiracial. Swan's two statements illustrate the dialogic nature of the new millennium mulatta and the exceptional multiracial.

This flip did not, however, resonate with distributors. Swan searched for a distributor for the sole late-twentieth-century film that delved into mixed-race African American identity just as the biggest multiracial battle of the 1990s waged around the country—the creation of a multiracial category on the 2000 U.S. Census. The mid-1990s ignited already existing controversies about claiming and naming a multiracial identity. For example, at this time newspapers largely represented "the" white response from critics such as David Horowitz, who wrote a newspaper article in 1997 about "the controversy over a multiracial category on census forms shows that racial and ethnic advocacy groups aren't worried about fairness as much as they're worried about spoils."[33] By belittling civil rights struggles as petty fights for unjust rewards, Horowitz's larger thesis is that because race, and with it, mixed-race, no longer matters in the color-blind society of the United States, Americans should simply stop discussing this heated issue. Meanwhile, according to many newspapers, "the" black response primarily came from equally vehement critics like the then-NAACP president Kweisi Mfume, who spoke out against mixed-race defection from the "black" category and the subsequent decline of political power for all African Americans. Mfume asked, "Will we be able to identify black votes in terms of fair representation?"[34] The two primary metaphors in the newspapers were those of mixed-race people watering down and defecting from African American culture and political power. This was the political tide as Swan sought a distributor for *Mixing Nia*,[35] making it very unlikely that audiences would view Swan's film with a color-blind eye.

The universal moniker is well known to all filmmakers. Gina Prince-Bythewood (the writer and director of *Love & Basketball* [2000], an intra-racial, black, heterosexual love story with a basketball-playing female protagonist), describes how in selling a film "the word *universal* is very important." In agreement, Kasi Lemmons, the writer and director of the African American Southern gothic film, *Eve's Bayou* (1997), states, "You have to say to them, 'This is a movie for everybody; just like you related to the script, anybody can relate to the movie.'"[36] Prince-Bythewood's and Lemmons's comments suggest that somehow, if pitched appropriately, monoracial black films can be marketed as universal. These directors understand the importance of selling the film as universal. However, unlike *Mixing Nia*, these films comfortably fit under the rubric of unquestionably "African American films."[37]

Swan's personal racialized history plays out against her statement that Hollywood distributors who carry black independent films critiqued *Mixing Nia* as not black enough. One producer told her that he would be interested if she made Nia's white love interest into an African American character. Thus, an authentic black film does not feature interracial relationships, especially when the protagonist processes through her in-authentic, mixed-race identity.[38] In contrast, critiquing *Mixing Nia* as too black, film executives who produce ostensibly universal independent films told Swan that Nia's pairing with two white men would make the film more appealing to Hollywood sensibilities: "One producer called and was interested in the film, but he wanted me to change Isaiah's character [Nia's African American love interest] to a white guy, and I was like, sorry, I don't think so."[39]

Additionally, studio executives told Swan that her film was not marketable as an independent film because it did not fit into a niche marketing scheme (when a film is designated as appropriate to a small, marginalized demographic group).[40] Swan explains, "They like the niche market thing. So [it might have been picked up if it] was purely, if they could say it's an *urban* film."[41] In other words, the film is not black enough because it does not fit the code word for authentically African American. Furthermore, a mixed-race film does not necessarily mean there will be multiracial bodies in the theater. Because of this imagined lack of a niche audience, Swan's deployment of the term "universal" was unsuccessful with distributors. To

Swan, the phrase "the film is very universal" means that her audience is "intelligent, college-educated people from their early twenties on up."[42] In opposition, the distributors' refusal to release the film theatrically demonstrates that a mixed-race protagonist who questions her racial identity and dates interracially is unrelatable to demographic niches.

As a marketing label, Swan's classification of *Mixing Nia* as universal calls on a liberal modern notion that there are certain experiences, values, and narratives that transcend race; in other words, all people can relate to filmic images of dating, love, and sex and can rise above their own racial alliances. But subjects experience even universal events through racialized bodies. With the enlightenment ideal of universalism, one strives for notions of justice, community, and common good, which offer up the possibility of emancipation. Ignored in these democratic notions is the fact that racialized and gendered subjectivity often prevents egalitarianism, precisely because American society is structured around the lines of race and gender. The impact of this structure would make it difficult for a white male, part of the demographic Swan identifies as her target audience, to identify with the black-white woman he sees on the movie screen. In stark opposition, Obama's presidential campaign was able to spin mixed-race blackness, or, more specifically, his mixed-race black maleness, as emblematic of the racial experience of the United States. Maleness works like whiteness in this estimation: men are the default people. Obama can be representative of all America, as a mixed-race African American *man*, in a way that a mixed-race African American *woman* simply cannot be.

Monoracial Marketing Success

Despite the fact that it was never released theatrically, *Mixing Nia* did achieve some success in other arenas. Just as Nia changes her racial identity throughout *Mixing Nia*, various executives and Swan herself changed the film's marketing strategy in order to receive successful financing, film festival play, and video and cable runs. Ironically, despite Swan's statements to the contrary about the text of the film, much of the film's success stems from marketing it as just black, or with African American content that targets a black audience. Subsequently, *Mixing Nia* scored well at film festivals when labeled as a black film, including the Planet Africa Program at the Toronto Film Festival, and the Urbanworld Black College Tour where Swan estimates that approximately twenty thousand people saw

The Exceptional Multiracial

—

Mixing Nia. It won the Magic Johnson Theatres "Best of Festival" award at the Acapulco Black Film Festival. However, paradoxically, Swan was later told by a film distributor, "we couldn't put this movie up at the Magic Johnson theater [located in a working class African American area]," illustrating the differing racial politics of movie theaters and black film festivals.[43] *Mixing Nia* also found an assumed African American audience on cable television. It was first sold to Black Entertainment Television (BET), and then to Home Box Office (HBO), and then to Lifetime Television. Implicitly understanding how *Mixing Nia*'s cable audiences are postulated as black, Swan explains, "the cable companies like HBO and Showtime become so important because they're the only people who are [showing black films]. Because they know that a large segment of their audience is black, they can cater to them." Swan's sentiment is echoed by Herman Gray, who describes how "blacks watch television at rates far higher than the rest of the population,"[44] and Krystal Brent Zook, who identifies that rate as 44 percent.[45]

For its video and DVD distribution, Swan sold *Mixing Nia* to Xenon Entertainment Group,[46] a video distribution company that markets harder-to-find films that attract an African American audience.[47] Xenon's niche marketing technique is evident on the video case for *Mixing Nia*. The front cover features a large picture of light-skinned Nia embracing dark-skinned Lewis. The skyline of New York City is barely visible behind them, and the only colors are their skin and Nia's chocolate-brown sweater. Both actors are smiling, but while Lewis's eyes appear to be watching something off in the distance, Nia's eyes are closed in rapture — she is entirely giving herself to Lewis. The back of the video case features a large picture of tank-top-clad Nia next to text that describes her desire to write "the great African American novel," a label Nia never lends to her book. The Xenon website's summary adds to this idea: "A young biracial executive . . . quits her lucrative job to write the great African American novel. But first she has to learn a little about being black."[48] From the front of the video case it appears that Lewis is the one who teaches Nia how to be black. Also on the back, against a black background, there are three small pictures: a shadowy still of Nia and Matt (her white friend from work then love interest) and then a still of Lewis and one of Nia. Her Latino love interest is absent from this video case. The successful video marketing requires this "just black" facade.[49] And yet, despite the move to market *Mixing Nia* as a black film, Nia's narrative in the film makes the case for the exceptional multiracialism and black transcendence.

The Transition Is Complete

Mixing Nia reflects and creates our contemporary political atmosphere: the United States in the twenty-first century brings daily erasures of race-equalizing measures, such as the continuous and overwhelmingly successful attempts to eradicate affirmative action. Paradoxically, or perhaps appropriately, despite its post-feminist and post-racial leanings, *Mixing Nia*'s message about black transcendence appears through its loaded signifiers of race, gender, and sexuality. In *Mixing Nia*, Swan changes external, yet racialized, signs, such as Nia's hairstyles and sexual relationships, to denote her racial- and sexual-identity transitions, and then her movement beyond racial-identity changes to color blindness. Nia's choice of hairstyles and sexual partners are elaborate cultural performances that facilitate these complicated moves; identity is largely understood as the effect of personal volition and not structural or historical forces. Changing these elements of her identity is a bid to embrace, articulate, and perform her shifting notions of blackness until, at the end of the film, blackness is completely excised: throughout *Mixing Nia*, Nia transforms from failure to success, and from the new millennium mulatta to the exceptional multiracial.

≡

CHAPTER FOUR

RECURSIVE RACIAL TRANSFORMATION

Selling the Exceptional

Multiracial on

America's Next Top Model

The climax of every episode of the popular reality television show and model competition, *America's Next Top Model*, occurs during judging when a panel of former models, photographers, runway coaches, stylists, or assorted fashion industry types tears down and builds up the photographs, outfits, hairstyles, personalities, accents, and bodies of each remaining contestant. The judging period begins with a photograph of Tyra Banks, the center judge, former supermodel, current media mogul, and star of the show, enacting some version of the contestants' challenge of the week. Although Banks's own racial background is not first-generation multiracial (both of her parents are African American), she signifies on the show as mixed-race African American. This signification is not because of her light skin, eyes, and hair color, but instead because of her ability to constantly shift racialized codes, the key attribute of the exceptional multiracial. The exceptional multiracial of *America's Next Top Model*, whether in the guise of Banks or her mini-me contestants, sheds racialized particularity, and often blackness, even more than the exceptional

FIGURE 13 Tyra Banks's doubled races.

multiracial of *Mixing Nia*. This exceptional multiracial is not simply trying on various black personae in order to metaphorically graduate to a post-racial state. Rather, the exceptional multiracial of the *Top Model* variety switches races so that she can recursively transform, in the case of Banks, from ambiguously light brown to unambiguously white or black, and back again to ambiguously of color. However, on *America's Next Top Model*, the exceptional multiracial is produced through the white, black, Latino, Asian American, and multiracial contestants learning how to perform racial transcendence. She does not have to *be* mixed-race, but she must evoke the racially transcendent quality of the exceptional multiracial.

Figure 13 illustrates Banks's visual interpretation of "race switching," the theme of a spring 2005 episode from the fourth season (or "cycle" in the specialized language of the show), and the main subject for this chapter.[1] The contestants in this episode "switched" to another race for their photographs. But in Banks's interpretation of the challenge, she instead splits in two. Rhetorically, the bifurcation of the image denotes its dichotomization; in other words, slicing the picture in two means that the two halves function as stark opposites. On the left side Banks is a blue-eyed, peaches-and-cream-complexioned young white girl with a playfully looped red braid. Her makeup seems to be natural and unobtrusive. On the right side Banks is a brown-skinned black woman with an unruly tangle of auburn hair. Her eye makeup is thick and smoky and her lipstick is copper brown. The looped braid and wide open-eyed gaze racialize whiteness as young, clean, and virginal. Banks transforms into a storybook image of a European mountain girl: Pippi Longstocking or Heidi. Meanwhile, the disheveled hairstyle and smoky, seductive eye makeup in the other half of the photograph racialize blackness as older, dirty, and wild.[2] In this half, Banks looks like a woman after a hard night of partying—this is a morning-after look. Thus, the bifurcated image of white versus black womanhood, which relies here upon racialized and gendered stereotypes, becomes operative because of the assumed racial flexibility of the multiracial African American body.[3]

America's Next Top Model, which first aired on the now-defunct television network UPN on May 20, 2003, begins each season with a multiracial assortment of around fourteen aspiring contestants, "the girls," who are put through a series of thematic challenges in photo shoots.[4] After assessing the pictures from the week along with the racialized, classed, and gendered personae of each contestant, the judges confer, and Banks hands out pictures to the grateful, weekly winners. *America's Next Top Model* is an incredibly popular, pleasurable, and powerful text, particularly among the two demographic groups of eighteen- to thirty-four-year-old women of all racialized identities and African American households.[5] The show bears the distinction of being a crossover hit on the former UPN network, which, around the time of *America's Next Top Model*'s inception, was transitioning from marketing itself as a black network to a post-race, post-feminist, young women's network. Banks leads the judging panel and alternately plays big sister, mother, mentor, object of desire, and perhaps most importantly, transformation disciplinarian to the aspiring models. Following the film scholar Richard Dyer's argument that the ultimate function of stars is to be signs, Banks is the sign of the exceptional multiracial.[6]

Through the course of the show, the judging panel proclaims that the eventual winner is not necessarily the most beautiful or even most photogenic of the contestants, but instead is the one who is able to transform enough to fulfill the image of America's model as a malleable and marketable spokesperson in the mold of Banks. She explains in a voiceover in the race-switching episode that the issue of transformation lies at the very heart of *America's Next Top Model*. "Transformation," the historian Henry Yu points out, is also at the heart of mixing, "a taking of two previously unlike things and making something new out of them."[7] Banks, whose ubiquity qualifies her as a "celebrity-commodity" in the words of Graeme Turner, quickly created an incredibly popular brand. She performs as particularly African American, or desirable to a niche market, and universally post-racial, or accessible to all racialized audiences.[8] Following Banks's celebrity-commodity lead, the show dictates that the winner must be able to transform her own racialized looks and ultimately appear post-racial. On *America's Next Top Model* the exceptional multiracial is presented as the perfect candidate to do just this, in both this race-switching episode and the show generally. This race-switching theme is one of two race-switching episodes thus far on *America's Next Top Model*,[9] and is a practice common enough in popular culture that scholars identify it not only through the historical practices of blackface minstrelsy but also through a variety of terms denoting more contemporary performances (for example, Michael Awkward on "transraciality," Susan Gubar on "racechange," and Cherise Smith on "enacting others").[10]

Television programs, even so-called reality shows like *America's Next Top Model*, construct their narratives though careful editing, staging, scripting, and coaching. Such artifice positions viewers to accept preferred meanings of the text. *America's Next Top Model* imparts the message that race appears not by structure, institution, family, or culture but by essentialized signifiers and performances. On the show, doing race means, essentially, performing racialized stereotypes. With Banks at the helm, *America's Next Top Model* circulates new millennium notions of race, gender, sexuality, (dis)ability, and beauty alongside a variety of older stereotypes, and assesses what it means to attempt to transform beyond staid and singular identity categories. Following the ideology of transformation, race is at once deeply embedded in the racialized codes of *America's Next Top Model* and yet it is still a changeable and exchangeable commodity. Racial tropes are paradoxically constant, integral, and transcendable. *America's Next Top Model* suppresses these apparent contradictions in an effort to produce a commercially viable notion of race transcendence, which means, for the mixed-race African American contestants, transcending blackness and becoming the exceptional multiracial.[11]

Banks's race-switching picture, functioning as the visual summation of the episode, provides a flat and dangerous perspective that is now popular in American culture: because race can be traded and performed, we all must be post-race. Banks's coded mixed-race African American heritage thus becomes emblematic of the exceptional multiracial. The image, which documents Banks's transformation, from multiracial (outside the picture) to white and black (inside the picture) and back to multiracial (outside the picture), illustrates that in order to become real models the contestants must transform (in accordance with corporate sponsorship).[12] The transformation that bolsters the entire series is deeply mired in performances of race, gender, (dis)ability, class, color, and sexuality, and it becomes possible through the purchasing of specific commodities, advertised in the commercials that underwrite the show. In the corporate sphere of commercial television, marketing post-race translates to widening profit margins. In other words, treating race and other identity categories as neutral, tradable entities simply makes smart financial sense in a new century.

Within the logic of the race-trading episode, race is presented as devoid of history, politics, and power. Racial difference is merely a makeup effect. Post-race, exceptional multiracial style is sold as the prescribed version of race for multiracial African Americans in this particularly representative episode. The aspiring models are asked to "switch ethnicities" in a photo shoot for "Got Milk?" The women are told by Mr. Jay, one of their "beauty instructors," that their true "challenge here really is taking on the persona of that other ethnicity while in the photograph and *owning* it." As the play on the term "own" illustrates, the logic of capitalism fortifies the models' racialized and gendered performances: the show's product integration, the placement of a commercial item into the narrative of a media production, demonstrates that not just any products, but those of the show's sponsor, CoverGirl, enable such a post-racial transformation. In addition, to facilitate the racial masquerade and pass more successfully, the aspiring models are posed with children who ostensibly reflect the biology that the models have assumed. Is there any transgressive possibility in the *America's Next Top Model* race switch?[13] The show dramatically demonstrates that race is constructed (the same point *Caucasia* demonstrates with passing). More so than in *Mixing Nia*, *America's Next Top Model* demonstrates that racial performance is playful, fun, and profitable. This episode is emblematic of contemporary American popular culture where race (blackness in particular) becomes the focus of a narrative simply to demonstrate that it no longer holds any importance. Thus, *America's Next Top Model* sells a particular version of multiracial African Americanness as exceptionally multiracial: a malleable, performable, transformable escape from blackness.

Each episode begins with a piece of "Tyra Mail," which alludes to Banks's task of the week for the models. In the race-switching episode, it reads: "You all have assets but you also have flaws. See if you can make up for them." Makeup, which can hide certain "flaws," is the key to this challenge. Following the convention of the show, there is a warm-up challenge before the main photo shoot. Quickly inserted into an establishing shot is a sign for Make Up Conservatory, a sponsor of the episode. The women arrive at a makeup studio, where they meet a balding and bearded sixty-something white male makeup expert named Paul Thompson. In the middle of Thompson's droning lecture on lip liner, the camera cuts to the incredulous faces of the contestants, who are used to receiving their beauty advice primarily from young gay men of color who look, behave, and speak quite differently. Capitalizing on the young women's confusion, Thompson pauses awkwardly while the camera scrolls the models' faces. "Thompson" then dramatically reveals himself to be "Mr. Jay," Jay Manuel, the makeup-wearing model coach who ordinarily leads the aspiring models through their tasks—and is, in fact, a young gay man of color.[14]

To reveal his "true self," Mr. Jay snaps his fingers, saying, "y'all betta work it, girls," echoing the phrase popularized by the African American drag queen RuPaul's song "Supermodel (You Better Work)." Mr. Jay's language and snaps are racialized and sexualized in a manner incongruous with his straight, white drag, so that even before he removes his guise he marks himself as brown and queer.[15] In the next shot the screen splits, and we see the "before," blond-haired, brown-skinned, youthful, and glamorous Jay, and the "after," gray-haired, white-skinned, old, and stiff Paul Thompson. This transformation is about race, sexuality, age, and gender performance, from an exactingly made-up, feminine young man of color to an unkempt, masculine old white man (fig. 14). The pictures flip the usual revelations of makeover shows, with "before" Jay polished and "real" while "after" Jay is schlumpy and "fake." The race and sex play is thus up for grabs. Split screens and split images dominate this episode, and the entire series, showing how categories such as sexuality and race are themselves split performances. *America's Next Top Model* plays with the idea that revealing a singular, true identity is actually an assemblage of constructed and performative signifiers of, among other elements, age, sexual identity, gender, race or ethnicity, class, and (dis)ability. Racially ambiguous

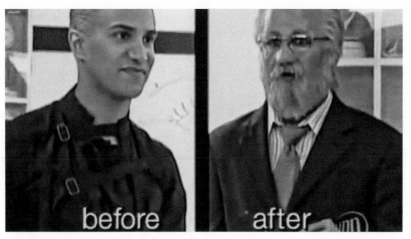

FIGURE 14 "Real" Mr. Jay and "fake" Paul Thompson.

Mr. Jay is set up like Tyra Banks: as an exceptional multiracial via makeup and TV magic.[16]

The drastically shifting cultural landscape of new millennium television gives birth to such postmodern, post-identity play. The content of television has changed dramatically during the past two decades, particularly with the advent of reality television, and the political economy of television has also changed, particularly with regards to the relationship between content and commercials. New millennium technology—from web TV, such as Hulu, to portable TV on iPhones, iPods, and iPads—has allowed viewers to virtually eliminate traditional commercial breaks. Ad agencies argue that the demographic of eight- to twenty-eight-year-old millennials do not consume commercials as older viewers did. The president of Fox, speaking on behalf of television networks, stated in 2006: "We have to be smart and find new ways to monetize the value of our programs."[17] To keep up with the changing marketplace, advertisers have gone beyond the traditional thirty-second commercial spots and embraced the now ubiquitous practice of product placement, the elaborate and ostensibly more subtle or subliminal practice of embedding products directly into storylines, dialogue, and shots. With product placement, merchandise shares screen time with actors. While advertisers term this practice product integration, branded entertainment, or brand casting, media consumer advocates decry it as stealth advertising.[18]

This relatively new practice has become pervasive in television in the twenty-first century. Indeed, Nielsen Media Research reports that from

2003 to 2005, "product placement" spots increased 30 percent, to 108,261 times.[19] One head at a media-buying agency described corporate desire for the "organic integration" of a commercial where the ads complement "the sensibility of a program to broad sensibility. It has more to do with subtext than with seeing a product."[20] Another advertiser stated: "We really look for seamless opportunities."[21] Both statements reveal a desire to create subliminal messages.

Some networks (e.g., the cable channel Showtime) have created corporate positions such as vice president of product integration thus illustrating the mantra from one firm that handles product placement: "The ad has become part of the show."[22] In the fall of 2005, the Writers Guild of America protested the increasing use of stealth advertising both because it limits writers' storylines and because the writers had not received monetary compensation commensurate with the revenues generated from this billion-dollar-a-year business.[23] Even some news programs at local stations participated in stealth advertising by incorporating so-called lifestyle segments with news stories to attempt to sell particular products.[24] Stealth advertising is especially popular in reality television shows like *America's Next Top Model*, where entire episodes can function as extended, involved commercials. In reality television programming, stealth advertising means that producers will go so far as to splice in a voiceover or digitally insert a product into the shot if contestants fail to adequately plug a product at the required moment.

Clearly, advertising underlies all elements of television shows, reality shows included. In Douglas Kellner's words, "commodities, affluence, and conformity . . . constitute the value system of television."[25] Kellner identifies materialism and conformity as twin poles structuring the political economy of television. Materialism and conformity also structure both race and gender roles on *America's Next Top Model*. In this respect post-race and post-feminism function as safe, conformist, and conflict-averse commodities sold to audiences; these two ideologies affirm hegemonic notions of whiteness and femininity, assert that racial and gender discrimination is over, and assuage dominant anxieties and guilt about current privilege and historical inequities. On *America's Next Top Model*, CoverGirl makeup plays an essential role in the "conflict resolution structure," which Kellner says "characterizes both programming and advertising."[26] For example, Mr. Jay will describe a given task of the week not simply as a "makeup challenge" but as a "CoverGirl Great Lash Mascara Challenge." Similarly, racialized difference is reduced to a mere makeup challenge on the show.

Part of this reduction lies in the post-racial and post-feminist ideals of choice that function as fodder for transformation on *America's Next Top Model*. Linked to choice and transformation, surprise is another key element. In *America's Next Top Model* the surprise is racialized, gendered, and sexualized: shifting identity categories amuse and shock. Mr. Jay's surprise transformation serves as a prelude for the "Got Milk?" challenge of the episode. As with so many episodes, this one functions as an elaborate commercial. When the young women are given the "Got Milk?" challenge, Mr. Jay tells them that they have already "learned all about makeup and the power that it has to transform people." After a dramatic pause, Mr. Jay announces, "today you guys are all going to have mustaches." The women explode in a (possibly staged) performance of shock at the thought of enacting this signifier of masculinity, completely at odds with the image of femininity that they must perform on the show. Mr. Jay breaks their apparent shock, clarifying that they will actually wear milk mustaches as part of the "Got Milk?" magazine advertising campaign. The camera then cuts to a shot of the contestants, who are shown rejoicing in relief because the "Got Milk?" campaigns popularly showcase highly sexualized images of female celebrities, such as Tyra Banks, wearing what is supposedly a milk mustache. Mr. Jay presents an additional surprise: the women will be posing with three-year-olds. Their photos thus evoke maternity along with the milk. Makeup, costumes, and children as props will facilitate the women's transformations.

Mr. Jay delivers yet another surprise: the twist in this photo shoot is: "we are actually going to switch your ethnicities." The terminology "switch" immediately evokes binary terms, which in American racial logic means black and white. While the women were shown gasping in shock at the thought of their mustaches, the camera reveals them to be exploding in excitement at this part of the challenge. As a new millennium show, the episode puts a twist on historic notions of blackface minstrelsy by not making all of the white contestants black: simply changing all of the black contestants into white women and vice versa would open the show up for criticism as too transparently racist for network television.[27]

The Big Switch

One of the big moments in the episode occurs when Mr. Jay announces the individual switches. While the switches are described as "ethnic" and not "racial" by Mr. Jay, reflecting the confusion and collusion between race and ethnicity in popular culture, the white women are assigned to be darker "others," the women of color are assigned to be other women of color, and the racially ambiguous and mixed-race women are assigned to be unambiguously black or white. Thus, the opposite race for multiracials is monoraciality. The overall goal is not any particular transformation but the idea of transformation itself. That is, the overall goal is for all women to become exceptional multiracials. They might be either "black" or "white" inside, but by masquerading as another race outside, they get to tap into some fantasy experience of mixed-race.

The six white-appearing contestants are told by Mr. Jay that they will be "East Indian," "African American," "Hawaiian," "Eskimo," "biracial," and "a really dark, tanned, Italian Sicilian woman." The makeup artists and stylists, following the theme handed down by Banks and communicated by Mr. Jay, mark nearly all of the white women as women of color by accessorizing them with dark skin and hair, provided via makeup and wigs. Because the contestants' goal is to successfully pass as their assigned ethnicity, they enthusiastically wear "authentic" clothes, such as a sari on the white woman assigned to be "East Indian" and a fur-lined hat on the white contestant designated as "Eskimo." Most of these costumes are not clearly cemented to a singular time period: they could be referencing contemporary women or those from an unidentified past. Through the logic of the switch, a blond white woman switches to "a really dark, tanned, Italian Sicilian woman." Just as in *Caucasia*, where multiracial Birdie's white family ponders how Italian she looks, this is an anachronistic postulation: the marking of Sicilian as nonwhite ignores the century of racialization in which Italians in the United States have been declared white.[28] Hovering between white and black, Italians stand as a kind of unexceptional multiracial in *America's Next Top Model*. The switch itself proclaims the neutral nature of race (i.e., race transcendence), but to perform the switch the women must employ stereotypical appearances of the "other," which are essentially anachronistic designators of authenticity.

One of the most dramatic switches, which the judges declare to be the most successful one (the contestant wins "best picture" for the week), is white Brittany Brower to African American (figs. 15.1 and 15.2). Brower stands out from the other contestants as the wild one of the group: throughout the season she is portrayed as loud, irreverent, drunk, naked, and generally out of control. Brower's wildness shows that she can logically embody the historical stereotypes of unruly black women.[29] To look "African American," Brower's skin is slathered with light-brown makeup. She wears a late-1960s or 1970s–era large Afro wig. She is dressed in an early-1960s-era ruffled-neckline cocktail dress. Brower is styled as a retro hybrid reminiscent of past moments in fashion, and racial, history, but not of a singular time period. The result is an anachronistic, dehistoricized image that is somehow from the past, but unconnected to a specific, singular time period. While Brower's hairstyle and dress do not match historical moments, they both are from the past, so American blackness remains mired in an imagined "been there, done that" moment. African Americanness is thus posited as irrelevant in the twenty-first century. In a glaring omission, there is no model who is assigned to become a black American woman in 2005.

For this episode, the women are judged not only by how "beautiful" they look in the "Got Milk?" ad but also on how seamlessly they enact the image of the race they are trying to perform. The judges praise pictures in which the women pass for, or really look like, a member of the "race" they are attempting to embody. In the language of Mr. Jay, they must truly "own" the picture (i.e., another race) and its concomitant racial commodification. The panel deems Brower's photograph the most successful. Banks enthusiastically compliments her, switching codes from her previous host mode and saying, "sista, you look like a black girl!" In response, Brower enthuses, "I was feeling it. I loved it." Banks continues, "Brittany this picture reminds me of a picture of me with my mama. It's bringing me back." The screen then splits to reveal a 1970s-era photograph of preschool-age Banks balanced on her mother's hip next to Brower's photograph. Outside of "race," and age, nothing is similar in the pictures. But as black bodies inhabit both photos, Brower's photo is praised as authentic. Post-racial posturing is praised as appropriately real if it, ironically, appears to enact essentialized ideals of race.

While the white women switched to women of color, the two brown-skinned African American models do not transform to their perceived opposite, white, but instead are told they will be featured as Korean (not Korean American) and Native American (with no specific tribal affilia-

FIGURE 15.1 Brittany Brower as white.

FIGURE 15.2 Brower as an African American woman.

tion). Interestingly, while they too will be "switching" ethnicities, they remain racialized as women of color. Unlike Birdie in *Caucasia*, there is no switch to whiteface available for these two women. In the sphere of commercial television, black women becoming white appears so unimaginable, unless it is a broad comedy, that such an inversion is not offered as a possibility. Instead, the models become metaphorical exceptional multiracials by transcending their inside blackness through performances of Koreanness or Native Americanness (figs. 16.1 and 16.2).

In contrast to its praise of Brower, the panel reprimands the brown-skinned African American contestant Tiffany Richardson. The stylists have made up Richardson as Native American, and she signifies as such almost exclusively by her hairstyle: she wears her hair, which was already transformed to long, straight extensions in an earlier makeover episode, in two braids. A black headband, complete with a floral brooch, holds a fluffy black feather in place. When viewing the picture, Banks scolds, "I don't really feel like you're bringing anything from within." Another judge describes her rather demure, floor-length dress, and pose cradling the little boy as evoking an image of a "madam in a brothel." They associate black femininity with excessive sexuality, impeding her ability to successfully pass. Richardson's attempts at racial masquerade are dismissed as inauthentic because of the controlling image the judges read into her body (figs. 17.1 and 17.2). In opposition, Brower more easily becomes black because whiteness is imagined to be a blank slate. Because Richardson falls short of passing appropriately, she fails at her task of becoming Native American. In the words of Philip J. Deloria, she "inauthentically plays Indian."[30] Thus, African American Richardson and white Brower both trade races, but the white contestant is deemed more appropriately post-race, and exceptionally multiracial, both because she passes more effectively and because she performs a stereotypical, time-frozen image.[31]

Exceptional Multiracials and the Switch

While the metaphor of multiraciality looms large throughout the text of *America's Next Top Model*, every season the show also casts multiple mixed-race-identified or racially ambiguous contestants. Because mixed-race is a popular trope on *America's Next Top Model*, in the context of the show it makes sense that Mr. Jay hands out "biracial" as an ethnicity for a white woman to switch into. "Biracial" comes without further racial specification. However, the woman who switches into "biracial" is made up with

FIGURE 16.1 Keenyah Hill as African American.

FIGURE 16.2 Hill as a Korean woman.

FIGURE 17.1 Tiffany Richardson as African American.

FIGURE 17.2 Richardson as a Native American woman.

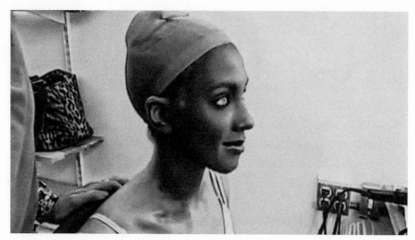

FIGURE 18 Transitioning from "half black" to "a traditional African woman with a head wrap and everything."

brown skin and frizzy, dark hair, so "black and white" is clearly what is intended by this moniker. This woman's look is as anachronistic and incongruous as the contestant masquerading as an African American woman. With her voluminous, unruly tangle of long, puffy hair, she appears to be from the 1960s. But her long gloves, capelette pinned with a butterfly brooch, and demure cocktail dress all appear to be out of the 1950s. Both the "African American" and "biracial" looks borrow elements from the 1950s to 1970s, significant civil rights–era moments, again, marking blackness as safely in the past.[32]

Tellingly, not one of the contestants is switched to a white American. American whiteness is granted reprieve from becoming the stereotypical "other." Instead, two of the three contestants who appear to be ethnically ambiguous or mixed-race are made monoracially "white" or "black." Two are made hyperwhite in their switch: black, Mexican Indian, Irish Naima Mora becomes "an Icelandic Scandinavian" and Latina Lluviana "Lluvy" Gomez becomes "a Swedish milkmaid."[33] The third racially ambiguous woman, Noelle Staggers, is switched from "half black," which the show presents as her own ethnic descriptor, into what Mr. Jay describes as "a traditionally African woman with a head wrap and everything" (fig. 18). The women who are ordinarily racialized outside of the authentic black-white binary are performing and signifying racialized extremes of whiteness and blackness. These women's bodies are forced back into racialized binaries and easy categorization.

The second mixed-race African American contestant, and the season's eventual winner, Naima Mora, becomes "an Icelandic Scandinavian" (figs. 19.1 and 19.2). In a glaring example of how the exceptional multiracial is produced from the mixed-race African American woman, in one part of this episode Mora directly addresses the camera in a convention that reality show viewers would identify as a confessional moment. Following the tradition of the first-person camera address, the audience does not hear the question asked to Mora, who smiles, which appears to be reluctant, and states: "My father is black and Mexican Indian and my mama's black and Irish. To be made up as a white woman is a little mind-blowing. It just goes to show you're ultimately defined by who you are, not by this outside." Mora's answer suggests that she has been prompted to divulge her ethnic background to the camera. She discloses her racialized identity as a product of her parents' black, Mexican Indian, and Irish ethnicities and evaluates her racialized identity as something that does not define her. In Mora's assertion, the word "outside" functions as a stand-in for race. Just as "race" is omitted, the phrase "who you are" signifies a blandly multicultural statement that reflects an ideology of transcending blackness to become the exceptional multiracial.

The television program presents Mora iterating post-racial notions in the exact moment when she is "made up as a white woman": whiteness, as Matthew Frey Jacobson notes, garners its power through its guise as invisible and yet "persistent, naturalized."[34] Mora's reluctantly spoken claims of being passed the "outside" look of race play against her visual presentation of performing the "outside" look of whiteness. In other words, transcending her blackness really means being read as white. In this moment *America's Next Top Model* translates the exceptional-multiracial notion of being simply "who you are" into whiteness, or at least passing as white. In order to pass, Mora can be read as maintaining a secret black inside, much like Birdie in *Caucasia*. To put a finer point on it, Mora's words echo capitalist rhetoric of individualism and choice, which goes hand in hand with the ideology of black transcendence. This ideology works to present race, and, here, African Americanness, as a lifestyle choice and to reconstitute the centrality of whiteness.

But whiteness is not the end of Mora's story: the exceptional multiracial enjoys recursive motion from blackness to whiteness to in-betweenness and back again. To further illustrate such endless motion, Mora fails to identify herself by race (i.e., she does not say "I am black, Mexican Indian,

FIGURE 19.1 Naima Mora as "black-white-Mexican-Indian."

FIGURE 19.2 Mora as a white woman.

Irish") but instead depicts herself by proxy, describing her parents' racial or ethnic backgrounds ("my father is black and Mexican Indian and my mama's black and Irish"). This is the type of shorthand phrase an apparently racially ambiguous person might have to produce multiple times on a daily basis. One reading of her most-likely edited statement is that racialized descriptors are important for her parents but are not necessary for her own self-identity. A generational argument comes into play here: race is named for her parents because it is germane for them and, accordingly, for their generation. As her parents are both multiracially black, she is multigenerationally multiracial. But, as the clip is edited, Mora presents herself as beyond such categories. Her refusal to only name her racialized identity by proxy produces an exceptional-multiracial moment.

Similarly, another racially ambiguous contestant, Lluvy Gomez, a twenty-one-year-old from California whose features are regularly described as "unusual" by the judges, states in a voiceover, "I was born in Mexico." Gomez calls herself neither Latina, Chicana, Mexican, Mexican American, nor a woman of color — perhaps because she does not identify as such or thinks the audience will not understand or believe in such terminology, or perhaps because her self-racializing moment is simply edited out. The show presents Gomez as making her own post-racial move because she fails to identify herself with any American racial nomenclature. In contrast, none of the monoracial or nonambiguous appearing contestants is shown commenting on camera about her ethnicity. Race is only presented as an issue for the mixed-race and racially ambiguous contestants. Furthermore, race is decontextualized, dehistoricized, and depoliticized enough to trade, and yet it is important enough that "coming out" as a clear racialized identity and performing visual signifiers of racialized stereotypes are necessary to understand the multiracial subjects. The off-camera, edited-out "what are you?" question marks the importance of the legibility of race: its invisibility and visibility dictate the relative values accrued in the marketplace.

Myriad texts on mixed-race have addressed the problems and politics of the "what are you?" question since the inception of the multiracial movement in the early 1990s.[35] For the inquirer, the answer to this question sates curiosity, places people into appropriate racial groups, and disciplines for nonnormative, multiracial features. The manner in which the three ethnically ambiguous contestants, who all have quite different racial looks, answer the "what are you?" question is particularly telling. All three contestants leave parts unnamed. Staggers, who probably passes for white in many situations with her long, wavy light-brown hair, pale skin and blue eyes, describes herself as "half black." The other half, her whiteness, remains unnamed because, one assumes, it is self-evident. Interestingly, the white woman who is made up as "biracial" with brown skin and a dark, frizzy wig has a phenotype quite different from Staggers. The white contestant masquerading as "biracial" becomes the chosen signifier for a "biracial" African American woman, and she is marked as more authentically biracial than Staggers. Despite the episode's premise, race cannot be dismissed as inconsequential, because the show relies on authentic signifiers, which are truly racialized stereotypes, in order for the racial masquerade to work.

On *America's Next Top Model* race is real in that it is something that is visually and sometimes orally signified, and it comes with specific commodities, for example, so-called racially appropriate hair, nails, and makeup. However, race is also constructed so that such significations can be switched through performance and commodities. Perhaps it is easier to assert that somehow race does not matter instead of understanding the complexity of race, gender, and power. Furthermore, just like *America's Next Top Model*'s race-switching storyline, our postmodern world produces and reflects cultural representations of race and gender as optional and exchangeable, or in other words, post-identity categories. Postmodernism, says Glenn Gordan and Chris Wheedon, "celebrates plurality, heterogeneity, difference. And . . . the seduced consumer . . . can shop for difference."[36] *America's Next Top Model* produces race and the exceptional multiracial through masquerade in the spirit of free play rather than the material stakes of history, economics, and politics.

Children and Ownership Help Switch Race

Racial masquerade is further complicated by the inclusion of children. The contestants are posed with three-year-old children on their hips. The advertisement is for milk. The addition of the children transforms the models from "just" women to mothers, signifiers of real women who, the dairy industry advertisements illustrate, have the maternal mandate to purchase cow's milk. Each contestant becomes productive object and mother. They are mothers hawking milk; the clear association is mothers' milk. Unlike the mothers, the children do not wear visible makeup, wigs, or costumes, which would help to identify them as a particular national, racial, or ethnic group member or with a particular time period. Instead the children are swathed in fabric, giving them a children-of-the-world feel that proclaims them to be somehow detached from any clear markers of either singular nationality or singular race. They are the new post-race generation. As Georgia Aiello and Crispin Thurlow argue in their analysis of European cities' promotional materials, "children are . . . cross-culturally available icons with the added connotative meaning potential of innocence and, in turn, 'naturalness' and 'tradition.'"[37]

Because the three-year-olds are meant to be racial signifiers for the models, they are simultaneously marked as racialized subjects and as race-less children of the world (figs. 20.1, 20.2, and 20.3). They function as a reflection of the race that the models are striving to embody. Thus, the children help facilitate the racial masquerade or help the models pass. For example, mixed-race African American Mora and Latina Gomez, masquerading as Scandinavian and Swedish, are posed with a blond white girl. The ordinarily brown-skinned African American model who is impersonating a Korean woman is posed with an Asian American boy and the mixed-race African American woman dressed as African is posed with a dark-skinned African American boy.

The transformable and profitable sign of the exceptional multiracial also appears with the child models. The ostensible openness of mixed-race "looks" dictates that the multiracial-appearing children are used to signify a number of different races. For example, a light-brown-skinned boy who appears to be of partial African descent, poses with "African American," "biracial," "Native American," and "East Indian" mothers, and a multiracial-looking girl who seems as though she has some Asian heritage poses with "Sicilian" and "Hawaiian" mothers. The ambiguous-looking children are thus used as racial chameleons while the Asian, white, and black monoracial-appearing children only pose alongside the mother with whom they could be easily racialized. The two racially ambiguous children are posed with more models and hence are more marketable — they are simply in more shots than the monoracial-appearing child models. Their ambiguity bolsters their commodity status. Even though they do not match the phenotypes of the models or the ethnicities the models are trying to embody, they have a valuable racial proximity: they are simply close enough, which in itself is a racially transcendent posture. Since the

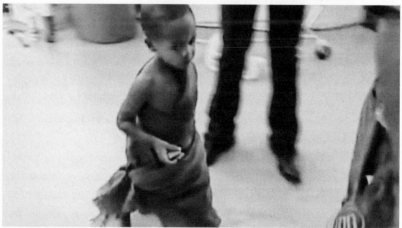
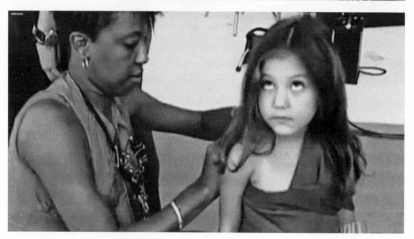

FIGURES 20.1, 20.2, 20.3 Children of the world.

children who can be featured in more shots are more valuable to the advertiser, an ambiguous, mixed-race phenotype is particularly useful in the space of producing race, maternity, and commerce.

But while the episode reflects and produces post-racial ideologies, it also reflects and produces post-feminism. The deployment of children as props in this episode accompanies what media studies scholars critiquing post-feminism have noted as the rising popularity of maternity in popular culture. The feminist notion of choice is key to what Susan Douglas and Meredith Michaels term "the new momism," a post-feminist ideal that "both draws from and repudiates feminism." In the new momism, "the only truly enlightened choice to make as a woman, the one that proves, first, that you are a 'real' woman, and second, that you are a decent, worthy one, is to become a 'mom' and to bring to child rearing a combination of self-lessness and professionalism."[38] Motherhood has enjoyed a recent surge of interest with the rise of infotainment's obsession with celebrity pregnancies and children. Pregnancy and childhood are ripe consumer markets, so profitable that large portions of parenting magazines are devoted to celebrating and rating commercial items, another form of stealth advertising.[39] The maternal aspect of the challenge demonstrates that women are naturally feminine, and naturally maternal. Tellingly, even though she is performing a version of the contestants' challenge, a child is missing from Banks's picture. Neither side of Banks's face is coded as "maternal." If Banks's picture is the visual summation of the contestants' challenge, the true point of the episode is that of racial, and not maternal, transformation.

Banks, as the role model of the show, demonstrates that real success occurs through an important quality of the exceptional multiracial: being able to simultaneously and playfully market oneself as both racially "everything" and authentically black and white. While Banks's own complexion is invisible in her iteration of the task of the week, the audience knows it intimately and understands that it facilitates her transformations. This is especially clear as the camera cuts from Banks's picture to Banks sitting at a raised judging panel. As a woman of color negotiating multiple marketplaces, Banks constantly code switches from a race-neutral CoverGirl to a racially marked African American woman; as an exceptional multiracial, she signifies various races recursively, and not just through the one-way "black to nothing" racialization of Mixing Nia. Mixed-race African American identity, particularly when imagined through the moldable form of the supermodel Banks or the aspiring models, becomes a convenient tool to be wielded by multiracial black women to transcend blackness.

Echoes of a Racist Past or Transgressive Future?

After fully considering this episode of *America's Next Top Model*, the question still remains: is the performance an echo of a racist past or a sign of a transgressive racialized future? The performance of, and ideology behind, race switching is not a new phenomenon in the United States. New-millennium post-race, an attempt to put aside racialization that ironically ends up (re)producing racialized stereotypes, links to nineteenth-century blackface minstrelsy, an attempt to self-consciously execute racialization that not so ironically ends up performing and producing stereotypes. Eric Lott illustrated that performances of blackface minstrelsy changed in appearance, tone, and tenor depending on the needs of various white populations. For example, Lott argues that during the first half of the nineteenth century, "blacking up" functioned as a freeing mechanism for white bohemians who longed "to inherit the cool, virility, humility, abandon, or *gaité de couer* that were the prime components of white ideologies of black manhood."[40] In other words, masquerading as black via makeup, clothing, and other racialized elements of performance enabled whites to explore not only race but also other liberating ways of envisioning oneself.

Blackface minstrelsy paves the way for the type of twenty-first-century post-race produced on *America's Next Top Model*. Like nineteenth-century blackface minstrelsy, twenty-first-century race switching is about far more than the nebulous notion of becoming another race. Following the language of Lott, contemporary racialized masquerade frees television audiences of all racialized identities to envision a highly gendered moment of race transcendence that appears to be completely divorced from the real-life effects of structural racism, institutionalized poverty, and bodily markers. Post-race is ultimately a bourgeois fantasy of choice. Such liberation from the "constraints," not of whiteness but of blackness, occurs in performances of racial masquerade in the late twentieth century and early twenty-first.

Indeed, the racial masquerade that was once historicized in the shady past of blackface minstrelsy has become trendy in popular culture during the past twenty years, the same period that includes discussions of multiculturalism, the disbanding of affirmative action, and the rise of mixed-race subjectivity. Take, for instance, the film *Soul Man* (1986), in which the white actor C. Thomas Howell plays a white high school student who masquerades as African American in order to get a scholarship to Harvard; the film *The Associate* (1996) in which Whoopi Goldberg switches from middle-aged black woman to old white man in order to achieve corporate success; and *Black. White.* (2006), the F/X reality show in which two families switch races in order to perform a "social experiment" orchestrated by the coproducer (and rapper) Ice Cube.[41] Most of these performances employ stereotypical, comedic, and fantastical elements; all are highly gendered, and all are focused along the black-white binary. Along with the race switch comes a switch in gendered performance, often a post-feminist one, and a lesson where the text exposes race and racism as still operative. In contrast, *America's Next Top Model* offers no lesson in this racial-masquerade episode, not even even a clunky, heavy-handed one.

A second, more common form of racial masquerade in popular culture occurs when the masqueraders eschew over-the-top signifiers (e.g., pancake makeup, wigs, and other instruments of passing) in lieu of adopting other signifiers of blackness. Contemporary minstrel performances are often coded, and they are not often as explicit or easy to spot as historic blackface minstrelsy. For example, Daphne Brooks analyzes the white British soul singer Amy Winehouse's unacknowledged mimicry of the sonic quality of African American female soul singers as a type of Lottian "theft." In her music, "black women are everywhere and nowhere."[42] There is no lesson in this race switching, unlike in the over-the-top performances in the previous examples.

In thinking through the question of the regressive and transgressive nature of racial masquerade, Cherise Smith notes the roles of passing and minstrelsy and also of cross-dressing and drag. Designating all four modes as "identity masquerades," Smith writes, "cross-dressing and drag, like passing and minstrelsy, are undergirded by two principles: first, both gender and sexual identity are composed of polar opposites (male/female and heterosexual/homosexual), and second, each category is intractable, impermeable, and inflexible."[43] The identity masqueraders Smith investigates do not "agonize over their boundary crossings," but instead "delight in the disjuncture between their own and their assumed identities because the performance enables, from a sensuous viewpoint, the embodiment of new identities—a practice that is exciting and invigorating."[44]

Smith smartly points out that while such performances might be liberating on a personal, individual level, such liberation does not translate to larger community or communal liberation.

To sum up, while Eric Lott identifies earlier modes of blackface minstrelsy as regressive, Daphne Brooks says that more-contemporary performances erase black women, and Cherise Smith lays out how other more-current performances ignore community processes. But, can *America's Next Top Model* be celebrated as a progressive version of post-race akin to Stuart Hall's notions of racialized identity fluidity? Hall describes identities as neither "armor-plated against other identities" nor "tied to fixed, permanent, unalterable oppositions."[45] In other words, identities are neither dualistic nor antagonistic. Hall also says that one way to transgress staid race definitions is to create "new ethnicities" through "splitting . . . the notion of ethnicity between, on the one hand, the dominant notion which connects it to nation and 'race' and, on the other hand . . . ethnicity of the margins, of the periphery."[46] New ethnicity, both denationalized and deracialized, is a progressive way for racialized subjects to transcend ethnic tensions and work for social change. *America's Next Top Model's* post-race focus seems to fit Hall's ideals.

However, Hall does not convey the sense that all categories are open to and exchangeable by all people, which is how *America's Next Top Model* views race. Hall instead argues that race is not a free space: it is bound up with unequal social relations. Or, as Hall might assert, history shapes ethnicity. He describes social actors reconstructing notions of ethnicity not in a random or volitional manner, but in a manner that takes into account "the place of history, language, and culture in the construction of subjectivity and identity, as well as the fact that all discourse is placed, positioned, situated, and all knowledge is contextual."[47] While *America's Next Top Model* illustrates the constructed nature of race, it fails to illustrate the material effects of race. What contemporary race-switch texts such as *America's Next Top Model* value is a transcendable blackness for mixed-race African American subjects (as on *America's Next Top Model*), or a transferable blackness for whites (as in Brooks's argument regarding Amy Winehouse). Thus, even though enacting racial masquerade in the twenty-first century might appear to be pushing the boundaries of racialization and power, it actually helps reify the conservative tinge of post-raciality. Because racial masquerade means racial conflict is over, such performances remain a "stick your head in the sand" approach to issues of racism in the twenty-first century.

Despite Tyra Banks and her team's persistent attempts to demonstrate that it is a post-racial text where race can be easily switched without ramification, *America's Next Top Model* is not post-racial at all. Instead, Banks's picture reveals what the communication scholars Lisa Flores and Dreama Moon identify as "the racial paradox": "the tensions between exposing the social construction of race while living in a world in which race is as real as our physically different bodies."[48] However, this episode of *America's Next Top Model* supports only one-half of the racial paradox: that race is constructed, fluid, and malleable. The episode fails to illuminate the second half of the paradox, that race has been performed for hundreds of years for the purposes of economic advancement and social division and that it is a reality inscribed in cultural practices and socioeconomic forces. Women of color scholars have long illustrated that the racial paradox is a highly gendered and sexualized notion, as racialized identity and performance is inextricably intertwined with gender and sexual identity. In other words, racialized transformations occur through performances of gender and sexuality. As the critical race scholar Kimberlé Crenshaw suggests, intersectional identity categories always operate concurrently, even if they appear to be experienced separately in any given televised, edited moment.[49]

Sell It, Work It, Own It: Concluding the Exceptional Multiracial

The question about the regressive or transgressive nature of race switching in popular culture is answered most completely by the issue of advertising. The practices and even the language of capitalism are central to playing post-race in *America's Next Top Model*. Mr. Jay coaches the women that to produce a successful picture, "the challenge here really is taking on the persona of that other ethnicity . . . and owning it." "Own" has multiple connotations in this context. On the one hand, ownership comes about through the consumption of specific commodities, in this case, a particular brand of makeup. In cultural representations, messages of ownership come about through, in the words of Georgia Aiello and Crispin Thurlow, "symbolic economies" where "the exchange of capital hinges on the promotion of ideals, images and lifestyles."[50] Thus, happiness is produced through the consumption of CoverGirl makeup, which, as I earlier stated, helps resolve any conflicts in the texts. On *America's Next Top Model*, because the contestants enact another race through symbolic ownership, their performances hinge upon victory in the marketplace. On the other hand, the exceptional multiracial Mr. Jay is employing specific fashion jargon and a phrase racialized and sexualized as black and gay, where "own" is akin to "work" in RuPaul's "Supermodel" song. This is an identity-laden moment that is quite in opposition to the tenets of post-identity: a gay man of color is iterating a catchphrase popularized by another gay man of color.

Nevertheless, because *America's Next Top Model*'s race-switching storyline demonstrates a post-race performance, CoverGirl makeup is the facilitator of such a transition. Of course, despite heavy-handed stealth advertising, it is clear that pancake stage makeup and not everyday CoverGirl makeup is truly necessary for the type of race switch the women perform in their challenge. This inconsistency is simply ignored for the purpose of selling the product. Indeed, the explicit goal of *America's Next Top Model* is owning the lifestyle of a supermodel. All of the women on *America's Next Top Model* are told to draw upon whatever resources they have in order to win. These resources include race enhancing and race changing. Purchasing power makes identity categories (e.g., race and gender) seem to be transitory, inconsequential features in the realm of television, where makeup, clothing, and rented children can turn one into another racialized body.

On *America's Next Top Model*, Tyra Banks prizes beauty when it is shown to easily cross racial and ethnic boundaries and follow her lead, for mixed-race African American subjects, to transcend blackness. The contestants are disciplined to see race as an effect of makeup, wigs, lighting, costumes, props, and acting. In other words, race is divorced from history or the processes of racialization and is instead a very literal performance. Implicit in the racialized performance is a gendered one where motherhood becomes a particularly valid sign that facilitates a smooth transition between races. Elements that help create the racialized and gendered performances, like makeup, can accentuate, enhance, showcase, or diminish beauty attributes or flaws. In *America's Next Top Model* race becomes simply another facet of beauty or a beauty trait that is ultimately malleable, and ultimately a matter of lifestyle choice. While all of the models become metaphorical exceptional multiracials, the mixed-race women are the most easily shapeable. For example, Mora states that her ethnic background is "black," "Mexican

Indian," and "Irish," but she can be "made up" to be a white woman. In other words, her minority status can be exchanged for whiteness. Even though this change might seem mind-blowing at first, the episode shows Mora assuring us that physical racialized identity is actually superficial and, ultimately, irrelevant.

In many ways *America's Next Top Model* is a "minority" show. This marketable series features an African American female supermodel, a team of beauty experts who are primarily gay men of color, and aspiring models with a variety of ethnic backgrounds. Banks herself has frequently remarked that the show aims to make a space for women of color in modeling.[51] Banks also comments regularly about her appearance on virtually every big magazine cover in the world and yet also laments discrimination in the fashion world. In other words, racial stratification in the world of modeling plays against a philosophy based on personal responsibility, transformation, and success. Banks illustrates both to women of color and to white women that they must learn how to transform or transgress "the outside" looks of race in their quest to win. Banks's racial identity is fluid, transitory, and incredibly marketable. For Banks, race functions as a counterpoint to the race-switching challenge's anachronistic notion of blackness that remains in a lost, possibly civil rights, possibly Black Power, era, when racial lines were more clear and, it appears the show argues, blackness could more easily be performed separately from whiteness.

As a result, this racial-masquerade episode tries to showcase the particularly new millennium American ideal of transgressing race. This episode explicitly engages with race only to dismiss racialized identity as unimportant, or as Mora says, "it just goes to show you're ultimately defined by who you are, not by this outside." *America's Next Top Model* serves an ideology of sloughing off race and blackness at will, and without concern for the structural, institutional, or historical nature of racism. These types of performances are far more than unfixable, floating signifiers — they are markers of the anti–affirmative action United States today.[52] *America's Next Top Model* demonstrates that performances of post-race are always reliant on racialized and gendered stereotypes and the logic of capitalism (e.g., CoverGirl makeup and the dairy industry). All of the women slip on racial and maternal "costumes." The show illustrates the seductive power of choosing post-race in the United States in the twenty-first century but fails to illuminate its problematic nature. Furthermore, mixed-race blackness provides the perfect vehicle with which to engage race switching.

America's Next Top Model fails to illustrate the complex notion that race is constructed but has material consequences, and instead it promotes the corporate, mass-marketing ideal that the United States is now post-race, and race can be bought and sold just like makeup. The show's metanarrative fails to note the contradiction between identity's essentialist versus social-constructionist nature and denies the complex American reality: we are living in a moment characterized by a theoretical and personal crisis of identity where people of all racialized identities struggle about what is really real about race.

In an advertisement for CoverGirl foundation, Mora is positioned to sell her multiracial African American heritage along with the makeup. The advertisement, which was one of her prizes for winning the season, presents a series of literal and metaphorical splits of the picture, the makeup, and, metaphorically, the model. Mora's beauty shot with its straight-ahead gaze, open smile, and accessible, slightly rounded shoulders composes the left side of the ad while the makeup's beauty shot remains on the right side: the makeup and Mora are paralleled through this placement. Mora, who in this episode reveals her mixed-race African Americanness, is metaphorically split into the brown and white components of the makeup bottle. The makeup and Mora herself are mixed, accessible, and marketable to all: the perfect exceptional multiracial spokesmodel transcends her blackness in this winning picture. Ultimately, while *America's Next Top Model* appears to value race transcendence, and black transcendence for the multiracial African American subject, it remains an untenable fantasy because of the show's reliance upon essentialized ideas of race.

≝

RACIST JOKES AND THE
EXCEPTIONAL MULTIRACIAL, OR
WHY TRANSCENDING BLACKNESS
IS A TERRIBLE PROPOSITION

A year and a half after Barack Obama was elected as the first mixed-race African American president, my family moved to a new, close-knit community in the most diverse, and most liberal, part of Seattle. Obama bumper stickers decorated the cars that lined our street of white, Somali, Eritrean, African American, and Southeast Asian homeowners and renters. We were immediately welcomed not only with smiles and waves but also with genuine inquiries as to how we were and who we were. The neighborhood children knocked on our door offering sidewalk chalk to share while grownup neighbors offered to lend parking passes. Quickly, through these markedly kind interactions, we became a part of the neighborhood. As part of our welcome, one family invited us over for a salmon barbecue with two other families. Our collective toddler-to-early-elementary-school-age children, four white, two African American, and two multiracial and African American, gleefully ran through our neighbors' house and backyard in an endless circuit.

As I relaxed into this seemingly perfect multicultural oasis, I leaned over to get to know one of the other mothers. I had recently met her au pair, who was from Switzerland, and as I had never before chatted with someone up close about live-in childcare, I inquired about how she went about hiring her nanny. With a wry smile on her face, this white woman told me, "Well, we chose by country. We thought about a Latin American au pair. She would love your children but never get them anywhere on time." At this remark I glanced aside to see if my partner had heard this conversation, but I was all alone. Her comments didn't end there: "Then we thought about hiring someone from Asia. But you wouldn't want them driving your car. So we settled on Switzerland. When we visited Switzerland we loved how clean it was and how the trains were always on time. It felt like we belonged there." She paused, chuckled, and continued, "Like Swiss chocolate, our nanny is sweet. And like a Swiss army knife, she's always prepared for any situation." I was shocked by what I heard, but I said nothing. We had just moved to this neighborhood, and I didn't want to disrupt the evening for everyone else. Somehow accusations of racism tend to do that.

Although I tried to keep a smile on my face, the rest of the evening was ruined for me. Questions swarmed through my mind: Why had my neighbor chosen to freely recount such vile stereotypes? Why had she chosen me as her confidante? Later that evening, as I processed that conversation with my partner, I came up with a possible answer for the first question. In the politically liberal but not historically racially diverse Pacific Northwest, race talk is generally silenced. However, some white liberals who choose to live in diverse neighborhoods do not participate in color blindness but instead feel themselves entitled to the prize of racist talk for their lifestyle choice. And my hypothesis for the second question was how I believe the neighbor read my family's race(s). She told *that* story to *me* because of how she did *not* read my family: not Latino, not Asian American, and not monoracially African American, but also not white. She could not have shared such a story with a Latino or Asian American family, because her racism would have seemed out of bounds. She would not have shared this story with another white family because she is not an old-school racist: she did not intend to bond with another white person about "those people." I also don't think she would have shared with a monoracial African American family who would most likely register to her as more "racially touchy" than we. Instead, she assumed that she could make such jokes because she read my family as middle class, mixed-race, and African American, and, as such, post-racial. She assumed that we were members of the exceptional multiracial tribe, who were so above racial sensitivities that we could recognize her as just joking, and laugh at her racism.

This incident is one of scores of similar ones in the post–Barack Obama United States, where white liberal racist interactions with so-called exceptional multiracials make white liberal racism permissible. Images of the exceptional multiracial are far more prevalent today to stoke American understandings of mixed-race blackness than images of the new millennium mulatta. Furthermore, in this case I believe that this neighbor came to the exceptional multiracial read of my family because of representations. Prior to telling her joke, that neighbor had not yet asked about our racial or ethnic backgrounds, our careers, our children's schools, our educations, or our politics. And yet, something worked as a green light to allow her to make racist jokes. I think that something was the representational ubiquity of the exceptional multiracial. Only with a greater, more nuanced representational world reflecting the true diversity of mixed-race African Americans will the sign of mixed-race blackness not usher in the response of post-racial racism.

More than at any other historical moment, with the election of President Obama, popular culture portrays mixed-race black subjectivity as representative of the American experience. At the same time, multiracial African American subjectivity remains historically bound and linked to the controlling images of the mulatto, the in-between, white-desiring, black-loathing, self-loathing, mixed-race body. The representational landscape of mixed-race African Americanness is conflicted, with both problems and possibilities inscribed in its very definition. As *Transcending Blackness* illustrates, throughout U.S. history, mixed-race African Americans have been placed, and sometimes place themselves, on a trajectory from tragedy (a lack of stability, morality, respectability, and black and white community inclusion) to ostensible privilege (an excess of sexuality, light-skinned advantage, and straight white male desire). At heart is an issue of white power: whiteness enables the success of mulatto bodies, mitigating blackness and rendering it accessible, while blackness taints the white, creating a fearful, monstrous being. In the new millennium United States the multiracial population has exploded, and so has, perhaps more importantly, the *idea* of an ever-growing mixed-race populace.

Multiracial is a viable identity category in the twenty-first century because of the inversion of civil rights–era radical politics into safe so-called multicultural ideals of the 1980s and 1990s and post-racial ones of the new millennium. How will these changes affect representations? How can we already see the exceptional multiracial and the new millennium mulatta faring in the new millennium? Are there any glimmers of richer experience here?

Obama and the Trajectory of the Exceptional Multiracial

Even before Obama was declared president-elect in 2008, pundits in virtually all major news outlets and all major political persuasions gleefully announced that Obama's success was proof that barriers of race no longer existed in the twenty-first-century United States. The election of black-white Barack Hussein Obama as the nation's forty-fourth president was almost immediately heralded as the end stage of racial progress in the United States, which means, in the words of Clarence Lusane, that many people believe "race [is] over as a determinant variable in the lives of Black Americans and, presumably, other racial and ethnic minorities."[1] Obama outran his blackness, and his mixedness functioned as the muscles powering his victory. During the campaign season, Obama linked his accessibility and success to his multiraciality, which he coded as post-racial proof of the American Dream. In a country where anti-black racism dictates differential rates of poverty, education, incarceration, and representation, issues that the majority of the American public does not want to associate with the highest executive officer, the ideology of mixed-race exceptionalism provides a distance from and metaphorical transcendence of controlling images of blackness. Mixed-race functioned as a smokescreen for Obama's racialized difference, blackness, and foreignness. What the historic election of Obama shows is not that race and race politics are dead, but rather that multiraciality, and in particular mixed-race African Americanness, resonates with the nonblack American population. Mixed-race is a marker of "us" more than perhaps any other time in U.S. history. While Obama-love proved to be short-lived (soon after his inauguration in 2009 he was dogged by a variety of racialized attacks, such as the constant requests for him to produce his long-form birth certificate), this moment of national post-racial euphoria is an important one to examine.

Obama's presentation of his gendered identity was also key to his electoral success in 2008: yes, he is male, but his performance of his "masculinities," in the words of R. W. Connell and Jackson Katz, a post-feminist brand of nontraditional, nonessentialized maleness, helped mark his gendered progress and distance from the other presidential candidates, including the traditional feminist Democratic contender Hillary Clinton, and the traditional masculine Republican contender John McCain.[2] Obama's performance of his masculinity can also be understood in relation to his partner Michelle's performances of post-feminism; Michelle Obama is presented in the media as a well-educated, professional woman who has *chosen* to be a family caregiver and not a career woman, a "mom in chief," and not an explicitly political part of her husband's administration. Michelle Obama's presentation of her gendered self helps recenter her husband in a traditional, patriarchal role just as he becomes "a new black man," a phrase Mark Anthony Neal coined "to reinforce the idea that myriad identities exist in the same black male bodies."[3] Obama's controlled masculinity has additionally served to distance him from stereotypes of threatening black masculinity. Obama embodies a metrosexuality illustrated in the press by his careful grooming habits, Spartan diet, and cool, unflappable demeanor.[4]

In the popular press, Obama's metrosexual masculinity and multiraciality, which deviate from hegemonic U.S. notions of masculinity and race, have not been read as deviant but rather as valuable and accessible. The first person of color to ever be elected president of the United States is a Kenyan Kansan American man, and his hypervisible mixed-race heritage dictated his mediated perception as a figure who is able to transcend the perceived burden of his blackness. Part of the idea of his specialness comes not from his being alone but from him being representative, or, in his words from his election night victory speech, from his supporters who are "young and old, rich and poor, Democrat and Republican, black, white, Latino, Asian, Native American, gay, straight, disabled and not disabled."[5] Obama's success was about the triumph of mixed-race in America, and his ascendance to the presidency was about the representational paradox of multiracial blackness: mixed-race African American subjects are racially flexible but really black and really black but racially flexible. For the general (white) population, such a paradox had great resonance.

As I have illustrated throughout *Transcending Blackness*, the mythical figure of the tragic mulatta is largely gendered as female, hypersexualized, and hyperfeminized. Unlike Barack Obama, the new millennium tragic mulatta is represented as desperately wanting to, but being patently unable to, transcend "the burden" of her race and gender. Obama, in stark contrast, is king of the exceptional multiracials; he is proof positive that mixed-race can indeed lead to successful race transcendence. His ascendance to the presidency of the United States has provided popular culture with a new model of how mixed-race blackness is read and represented in the United States in the twenty-first century. No longer is the multiracial black body predominantly recognizable through the figure of the new millennium mulatta, whose multiracial heritage portends confusion, strife, and ultimate failure. With Obama, mixed-race is presented through the figure of the exceptional multiracial, a newer model of a post-racial and post-feminist figure after the civil rights era who is unencumbered by race, racism, or traditional masculinity.

Obama is not just represented through the exceptional multiracial, however. He is also figured, in the film scholar Donald Bogel's typology, as a violent, threatening black male brute.[6] While Obama is represented as a post-racial, post-feminist subject, or a race-transcending "new man," he is also understood through old-school, racist tropes of threatening, violent, unintelligent black masculinity. This representational paradox illustrates that the twenty-first-century ideologies of post-race and post-feminism, particularly as they apply to multiracial African American subjects, are reliant upon their dichotomized opposite: racist, hypermasculine images. In other words, because stereotypes are formed through dichotomies, the post-racial is always reliant upon the racial, which often defaults, in the case of Obama's representations, to the racist.

But How Does Obama Racialize Himself?

How does Obama construe his own mixed-race status? The first of his two memoirs, *Dreams from My Father: A Story of Race and Inheritance* (1995) is a fascinating text because of the seeming transparency that comes in this first autobiography. Self-reflexive, precandidate Obama appears to simply be thinking about his own racialized identity and not how to produce "candidate Obama" or "President Obama." Obama does not describe himself in terms such as "color-blind," "post-racial," "racially flexible," or even, for the most part, "African American," "black," or "multiracial."[7] He favors specificity and describes himself as "the son of a black man from Kenya and a white woman from Kansas."[8] In this self-racialization by parental proxy, Obama provides a way to give the facts of his ethnicity and let people come to their own conclusion about what "side" he ultimately chooses.[9] Obama does, however, connect his own mixed-race to utopian futures (both explicitly and implicitly). For the most part Obama does not link himself to larger groups of mixed-race people.

In *Dreams from My Father*, which Obama wrote before he knew that he was to be a presidential candidate, and perhaps even before he knew that he had presidential aspirations. Obama considers his race, class, and gender so transparently. His self-reflexive, engaged, material analysis of race and gender speak back to the press's controlling image of him as black male thug or post-racial messiah. Obama writes,

> When people who don't know me well, black or white, discover my background (and it is usually a discovery, for I ceased to advertise my mother's race at the age of twelve or thirteen, when I began to suspect that by doing so I was ingratiating myself to whites), I see the split-second adjustments they have to make, the searching of my eyes for some telltale sign. They no longer know who I am. Privately, they guess at my troubled heart, I suppose — the mixed blood, the divided soul, the ghostly image of the tragic mulatto trapped between two worlds. And if I were to explain that no, the tragedy is not mine, or at least not mine alone, it is yours, sons and daughters of Plymouth Rock and Ellis Island, it is yours, children of Africa, it is the tragedy of both my wife's six-year-old cousin and his white first grade classmates, so that you need not guess at what troubles me, it's on the nightly news for all to see, and that if we could acknowledge at least that much then the tragic cycle begins to break down.[10]

Obama asserts that we, as Americans, cannot just continue to transplant racialized tragedy onto the body of the African American multiracial — so that the mulatto or mulatta becomes a scapegoat for the seeping race wounds in this country evidenced by the history, and indeed the present, of racialized violence in the United States. He clearly understands the stereotype of the tragic mulatto and does not try to simply toss off the controlling image by offering its opposite: the exceptional multiracial. Rather, he looks at the social aspects of racial identity. So much of what is written about mixed-race is about the individual. The individual is pathological; the individual is exceptional, even messianic as is the case with some mediated representations of Obama during the election campaign. Instead Obama describes the banal, ordinary nature of his mixed-race and the commonalities between multiracial and other racialized experiences, and other experiences with difference writ large (and sometimes these differences are not immediately apparent or might appear invisible — sexuality, disability, and so on). This is one of the many places where Obama rejects stereotypical, controlling, tragic images of mixed-race blackness and re-defines tragedy as the disaster of racialized violence and racialized repre-sentations in the United States. Thus, instead of focusing on mixed-race tragedy as it is historically understood, he writes that if one is to engage with metaphors of racialized misfortune or disaster, we should look at everyone, of all races, in the United States. This strategy of focusing the assumed-to-be-always-inward gaze outward is identified by Robert Terrill when he writes about "A More Perfect Union." Terrill notes that in this speech, Obama "shifts the burden of double consciousness from himself to his audience."[11] This also appears to be what he does in *Dreams from My Father*.

In another part of *Dreams from My Father* where he recalls his college years, Obama launches a critique of mixed-race African Americans' at-tempts to transcend their blackness by identifying as mixed-race instead of black.[12] He presents no third option here, no possibility of identifying as black *and* mixed-race. Interestingly, in *Transcending Blackness*, "third" is what the multiracial position is, not the multiracial-black position. Obama is speaking with considerable passion and anger about those of us who claim multiraciality above other racialized identities. He makes us think about the power of choosing racialized identities and racialized labels. *Dreams from My Father* is a book in which the mixed-race African American author clearly, unequivocally, and fully embraces his blackness. Obama's interpellation as black is not simply a matter of his ascription. It is not a matter of him wanting to enact a "black cool." Instead, his identifi-cation as black reveals a complicated process of racialization—he is black because he is read as black, yes, but also because he chooses blackness. Obama's embrace of blackness resonates against the anti-black landscape of mixed-race African American representations, as evident in the repre-sentations of the new millennium mulatta and the exceptional multiracial in this book. I know far more people like Obama: multiracial folks who identify as black. Although often they identify as black and multiracial, but importantly, because this is often left out of representational understand-ings of African American mixed-race, as black.

In the realm of popular representation, on the one end we have the new-millennium-mulatta character who is ruined because of the stain of her blackness, or the exceptional multiracial, race-transcending char-acter who only gains success because of his or her metaphoric leaping over and beyond blackness. Obama's memoir is neither of these. His embracing of his blackness, which Birdie's father wishes for her in *Caucasia*, means that there are moments that arise where he is fairly militant in his dismissal of mixed-race African Americans who do not identify fully with their blackness. He cuts through the codes of assimilationist multiracialism and calls out the anti-black racism undergirding some celebrations of mixed-race. What ends up resounding most is his unabashed love of blackness.

Obama's racialized identity as unapologetically African American in *Dreams from My Father* can be read against his later statements on the campaign trail. While he does not exactly apologize for being African American, he does signify his mixed-race in a post-racial manner. He, in other words, enacts an exceptional multiracial guise in order to activate the codes of black transcendence. Obama's own campaign was successful at arguing that his presidency would suture the four-hundred-year-old gaping racialized hole in the United States. However, political scientists have illustrated that Obama's electoral success was not proof of an electoral version of post-racial utopia (because not that many whites swung Obama's way) but of all groups of people of color uniting to support Obama.[13]

Mariah Carey and the Trajectory of the New Millennium Mulatta

While mixed-race African American male icons, in particular Tiger Woods (pre–marital infidelity scandal) and Barack Obama, have been fully embraced, mixed-race African American female icons have been derided.[14] The way in which their mixed-race has been pathologized directly contrasts with the manner in which Obama's mixed-race is celebrated for its perceived accessibility to whites, and the way it translates to his logic, fairness, and ability to speak to all people. The pop diva and self-appointed multiracial spokesperson Mariah Carey is in many ways Obama's polar opposite. Carey has been represented in the press as a tragic figure whose multiraciality is both cause for and effect of her erratic behavior, heartbreaking family background, and excessive sexuality. Because of her frequent public references to her mixed-race and her multiracial fans' celebration of her as a mixed-race role model, Carey symbolizes mulattaness, with all its historical baggage in the contemporary public imagination.

On the December 27, 1999, episode of *The Oprah Winfrey Show*, "Mariah Carey Talks to Biracial Teens," Carey's new-millennium-mulatta performance was on dramatic display.[15] Despite the fact that the title of the episode uses the term "biracial" without further descriptor, the audience was primarily composed of mixed black-white girls and young women, implicitly racializing biraciality as black and white. The participants were largely emotional and highly excitable; the camera showed them screaming in exhilaration and crying in distress throughout the episode. Repeated throughout the show were images of crying girls (and crying Carey) bemoaning their perceived exclusion from both *the* black and *the* white communities. One eight-year-old read a poem called "Invisible," articulating her feelings of racial banishment to indefinite exclusion. Throughout the program Winfrey kept insisting that these "pretty girls" were actually "special" and "the future." The show ended with a performance of "Mariah's Theme" from her album *Rainbow*; Carey stated that the song was inspired by her "pain and torment of growing up biracial."

Carey and the audience members performed a gendered and racialized dichotomy of mixed-race African American tragedy and privilege. The two interpretations of mixed-race identity, the tragic experience expressed by Carey and many of the young women on the show accompanied by Winfrey's view that they were a "pretty" and "future" people, articulates a new millennium (and antebellum) racialization of mixed-race African Americans. Because a mixed-race black racialized identity was represented as inherently tragic on this episode, and because blackness and not whiteness has been historically linked to pathology, the performances of Carey and the young women illustrated the necessity to transcend blackness.

"Mulatta" is a loaded signifier that conjures up controlling images that are historic, racialized, gendered, and sexualized. Initially produced by the history of U.S. chattel slavery with white male masters and black female slaves, the image of a mixed-race African American body has been primarily gendered as female. Furthermore, as mixing occurs through the bodies of women, images of mixed-race are hypersexualized, although not necessarily hyperheterosexualized. The mulatta has been imagined in both fiction and nonfiction as innately tragic: for much of U.S. history, the mixed-race African American female body, as a tragic mulatta, has been imagined to be a lascivious, troubled, privileged, unstable, and beautiful creature.

With a hyperfocus on sexual desirability comes an emphasis on sexual partnership and reproduction. In *Transcending Blackness* the portrayal of each character's identity as a mixed-race African American is wrapped up in whom she picks as a mate: the protagonists perform various characterizations of race through their partner choices. Related to partner choice, reproduction is the means by which a mixed-race person can establish her or his racial position. Reproductive capability has also historically played a part in white men's possession of black women's bodies. Furthermore, reproduction is a fundamental site for the social stigmatization of interracial relationships. *Transcending Blackness* explores what possibilities are both opened and closed when the racialized and gendered sign of the new millennium mulatta appears.

The images of Carey on *Oprah* are dramatically different from images of Obama. Even the negative images of Obama are not those of the new millennium mulatto: that image is not his signifier. Because of his superstar status, his male gender, and his 2008 election campaign's successful (if temporary) "use" of his mixed-race instead of its rule over him, images of Obama diverge from all of the other new-millennium-mulatta and exceptional-multiracial representations I examine. Even when blatant racism, such as in the form of attacks by "the birthers," a group of right-wing activists obsessed with disproving Obama's U.S. citizenship, is thrown in Obama's direction, he does not appear to flinch. He is gifted with racism Teflon. Obama's perceived superhero quality is linked to the representation of his mixed-race. Throughout U.S. popular culture, Obama, the paradigmatic multiracial African American subject, is represented as a flexible racialized body, a floating signifier, or an empty vessel who can conveniently be filled with any desired racialized image from hyperraced or starkly racist (calling up controlling images of black masculinity) to de-raced or e-raced (evoking stereotypes of race transcendence, mixed-race, and post-race).

Transcending Blackness demonstrates that attempting some precision with new terminology, particularly newly racialized terminology, is always challenging. The terms I am particularly concerned with in this book can be thought of as close siblings to each other, "color blindness" and "post-race," and their gendered counterpart, "post-feminism." These first two terms, in addition to others, such as "post–civil rights," "post-Soul," "nontraditional," "post-black," "hybrid African American," and "racially flexible," have been applied to Obama and mixed-race African American figures like him to mark basic newness and distance from black Americanness.

"Color blindness," a term that means being unable to see differences in color, which functions as proxy for race, has civil rights–era roots and is frequently cited with regards to Dr. King's dream. And since the campaigns for Prop. 209 in California (1996) and its clones all over the country, including in Washington in the form of I-200 (1998), "color blindness" has been perverted into a slogan for neoconservative anti–affirmative action activists. Sylvia Chong writes that "under . . . 'color-blind' logic, racial consciousness is itself a form of discrimination," and "clinging to one's racial identity is, at best, an outmoded primordial attachment, and, at worst, a voluntary surrender of freedom. This compulsion towards race-lessness reproduces the valorization of whiteness, reifying one particular racial identity into a template for universalism."[16]

As I have illustrated, "post-race" is a term used to denote two times: after the importance or significance of race, and after the existence of racism. These two notions are often conflated so that race, racism, and questions of power are ignored. "Post-race" is used to show that race does not matter and is not a part of any equation of life chances and voters' choices. "Post-race" denotes a genealogy of racial progress.[17] While post-race is an ideology that the media applied to Obama's voters and his voters' approach to him, it is also something his campaign applied to Obama, billing him at times as the so-called post-racial candidate. Although Obama is presented as having a racialized background, because he is always described as black in the same breath as he is described as post-racial, when Obama is coded as post-racial it is as though he *chooses* not to make such a big deal about race, and *chooses* not to make such a big deal about black American issues. Being painted as post-racial means that he is a new model minority, one who embraces traditional ideas of self-help, such as Booker T. Washington's notion of pulling oneself up by his bootstraps, and does not seek out state help, through, for example, policies addressing structural inequality (e.g., affirmative action).

In the new millennium United States, from the "diversity" trumpeted in former President George W. Bush's cabinet, where the mere presence of people of color and women were meant to evidence the end of racism and sexism, to the "fair hiring practices" of the NFL, where the mere interviewing, but not necessarily hiring, of black coaches is meant to eradicate accusations of discrimination, to the election of our first mixed-race African American president, barriers erected by race and gender are now assumed by many to be a thing of the past. What accompanies empty diversity celebrations in popular culture is the idea that for the sake of progress the United States must move beyond racialized and gendered identities to utopian states of post-race, or a time after racialized difference and discrimination, and post-feminism, a moment after gender discrimination. Perhaps nowhere is the phenomenon of post-race and post-feminism more clear than in popular representations of multiracial African Americans, who in their imagined hybridity symbolize the hope that this millennium will not be encumbered by uncomfortable demands for equity and justice. Since mixed-race African Americans were created by merging the two racialized poles of black America and white America, to many, their bodies portend racialized unity.

However, as shown by the persistence of racialized differential outcomes, post-race remains a fantasy propagated by neoconservatives and neoliberals, both of whom wish that race (or people of color) would simply go away. To take one of a plethora of possible examples, in secondary schools, "25% of all African American students, nationally, were suspended at least once over a four-year period" and "more than 30% of sophomores who drop out have been suspended and . . . high school dropouts are more likely to be incarcerated."[18] In addition to racialized discrepancies continuing in, for example, healthcare and housing, they flourish in popular culture.

We live in a paradoxical moment of color-blind ideology and racialized reality. The belief that the United States is beyond issues of race and therefore needs to protect whites from "discriminatory" measures such as affirmative action has infected the nation like a plague. An article in *The Chronicle of Higher Education* from 2004 reported that on the heels of the Supreme Court rulings in 2003 on the University of Michigan (*Gratz v. Bollinger* regarding undergraduate education and *Grutter v. Bollinger* regarding the law school), where "diversity" was prized as a "value" for admissions, paradoxically, programs aimed at leveling the playing field for students of color have been attacked.[19] For example, Yale University's undergraduate dean invited white students to historically minority orientations programs, arguing that the rulings made it "harder to justify programs that separate communities." Yale and about one hundred other colleges acquiesced to "reverse discrimination" claims and demands for white inclusion to minority-focused programming. Two neoconservative advocacy groups, stealthily named The Center for Equal Opportunity and the American Civil Rights Institute, advocated on behalf of the ostensibly dispossessed white students.[20]

When they did so, students of color, including multiracial African American students, lost valuable ground. At Boalt Hall, the law school of the University of California, Berkeley, in 1997, the year after Proposition 209 outlawed race-based measures such as affirmative action, only one African American enrolled, no Native Americans enrolled, and the numbers of Latinos and Asian Americans went down; meanwhile, the number of white law students at Boalt increased 38 percent, from 173 to 239.[21] In spite of this proof that eliminating affirmative action also eliminates fair chances for students of color, ideologues such as the University of California regent and author of Proposition 209 Ward Connerly and frequent online commentator for the American Civil Rights Institute, argue for post-race. Connerly, who himself identifies as multigenerationally multiracial, uses the existence of interracial unions and mixed-race bodies as the evidence that race no longer matters.

Because racial disparities persist, post-race discourse creates a cognitive dissonance for children and others. The child psychologist Allison Briscoe-Smith writes: "We all do notice difference. When we abstain from discussing race with our kids, we may confuse them and implicitly send the message that it is bad or wrong to talk about racial differences."[22] Post-race also erases the mixed-race of those from multiracial backgrounds. Mixing races makes them disappear. Being multiracial, or perhaps more specifically, not being "all black," means that such subjects are not threatening in the same way.

Ending with the Hybrid

Transcending Blackness uncovers the sometimes caustic ideologies of black transcendence during 1998 to 2008, when popular cultural representations of mixed-race African Americans occurred frequently. The ideologies present in such representations, post-race, an imagined time after racialized inequality and race itself, and post-feminism, a fantasized moment after gender discrimination, ignore the reality that race and gender still order life chances and choices in the new millennium United States. I contend that many representations of black-white mixed-race, which largely come transfixed to images of mixed-race African Americans in the guise of the new millennium mulatta and the exceptional multiracial, communicate that racism and sexism are antiquated notions in our new millennium. The representations I examined reveal how the contemporary performance and refutation of the new millennium mulatta and exceptional multiracial myths function alongside denigrations of blackness.

On many levels all the texts were extraordinarily similar. Young, attractive, middle-class, mixed-race African American women star in the novel, television shows, and the film. In varying ways, all of the protagonists search for their place, which almost exclusively circles around hunting for the "appropriate" iterations of their race, gender, and sexuality; they attempt to arrive there through the vehicles of post-race and post-feminism. However, the texts and the actual articulations of race, gender, and sexuality are incredibly different. In *Mixing Nia* and *America's Next Top Model*, blackness is something that can and should be transcended, and racialized and gendered performances help in that process. In *The L Word* and *Caucasia*, race and gender are disturbing forces that torture the protagonists while post-race and post-feminism remain unachievable states.

What might a positive, useful, accurate representation of mixed-race people look like? Counter to what many might assume to be the "natural hybridity" inherent in multiraciality within the landscape of mixed-race African American popular culture, the notion of a bridging, third space, or an interstitial constellation of identities, is almost entirely absent. There is no third possibility. Performing hybrid blackness is not an option for multiracial black characters in contemporary representations. Instead, even when blackness is not pathologized in the text, but more explicitly loved, hybridity is presented as unattainable, and perhaps undesirable. Blackness is shown as the entity that one must rise above in order to reach a more enlightened, better-adjusted, future moment of desirable racelessness. Hegemonic representations fail to provide the counternarratives that the performance studies scholar Daphne Brooks identifies as boundary-pushing "afro-alienation acts" that "call attention to the hegemony of identity categories."[23] However, despite the prevalence of multiracial African American images of black transcendence, in my experience, defiance, resistance, and, yes, hybridity more accurately characterize how most in-between individuals live their lives. The incredibly pervasive representations in *Transcending Blackness* belie the true complexity of race, African Americans, and mixedness. Such essentializing denigrates blackness, delimits mixedness, and ignores hybridity.[24]

So what exactly are the messy parameters of hybridity, the reasons behind the lack of acknowledgment of hybridity as the state to which all Americans belong? Homi Bhabha describes conflict as being at the root of hybridity, which is "produced through the strategy of disavowal" as a "process of splitting."[25] Bhabha defines hybridity as a disturbing, threatening force to power that deforms and displaces traditional notions of forces such as discrimination and domination. Subsequently, the hybrid "is the articulation of the ambivalent space."[26] However, despite its interstitial placement, hybridity is "not a third term that resolves the tension between two cultures."[27] It is instead a "peculiar 'replication' [that] terrorizes authority with the *ruse* of recognition, its mimicry, its mockery."[28] The inscription of anti-black images is a reaction to this terror.

Mixture is not a panacea for racial problems; rather, representations of mixture provide us with a lens into existing racial tensions. The anthropologist Renato Rosaldo explains how hybridity creates "tensions verging on contradictions."[29] These tensions are never "resolved" because "hybridity can imply a space betwixt and between two zones of purity."[30] And Tavia Nyong'o writes: "Hybridity has been repeatedly enlisted in envisioning utopian and dystopian scenarios. This persistent projection of hybridity into a temporal and spatial elsewhere is itself a mechanism for resisting an awareness of the actual and ongoing mongrel past, a history which is neither a moral scandal nor a transcendental panacea, but an uneasy terrain of ordinary and difficult antagonism and conviviality."[31] Furthermore, Jared Sexton points out, "drawing attention to the permeability of racial borders or rendering visible the embodiment of 'racial liminality' does not necessarily render racial categories suspect."[32]

The possibility of moving beyond the "look" of race, for coalition building and perhaps even envisioning racialization in a completely new light, remains an empowering if somewhat elusive possibility. Some mixed-race organizations, such as the MAVIN Foundation, and groups of scholars, such as those producing work in the burgeoning field of critical mixed-race studies, are creating these coalitions and possibilities by, for example, reaching out toward politically progressive people who are mixed-race, transracially adopted, or who identify as allies of underrepresented people.[33] Critical mixed-race studies is an interdisciplinary subfield that reads mixed-race specificity through larger issues of racialization, gender, sexuality, and class.[34] These critical mixed-race studies texts consider power and history in their analyses of multiraciality, eschewing binaries between bad and good, and noting that, as Kimberly Maclain DaCosta writes, multiraciality has "always been linked to the broader system of racial domination that demarcates white from black . . . and the fates of those of African descent (whether one is putatively 'mixed' or not) have always been linked."[35] This type of beyond-ascription political work portends opportunities for future work in mixed-race studies and activism.

Conclusion

—

In a political climate where one is called "racist" for talking about "race," and "sexist" for talking about gender, we have to keep our analytical skills nimble to stay on top of quick shifts in new millennium racism and sexism. Moving beyond the binaries continues to be a challenge in the representations and politicizations of multiracial blackness in the new millennium United States. Thus, as Stuart Hall aptly asserts, "the future belongs to the impure,"[36] so we must refuse to let our multiracial bodies be used against all of our communities.

PREFACE: FROM BIRACIAL TO MULTIRACIAL

This preface is an extended version of the keynote address I gave at the Multiracial Heritage Week at Brown University in 2009. Five years earlier, as a graduate student finishing up my dissertation, I had also given the keynote, a speech where I flexed my almost-Ph.D. muscles. My talk in 2004 was purely academic, as I "impartially" thought through what it meant to assert a multiracial identity in the shadow of the 2000 U.S. Census, particularly with regards to the contentious history of naming and claiming mixed-race. But for the fifteenth anniversary of Multiracial Heritage Week I felt comfortable, even compelled, to reveal my own multiracial journey. This was no small feat for me. Although I had not let the dismissal of scholarship on mixed-race as "sellout work" (by some academics from my own graduate field of ethnic studies, or the accusation of it as "me-study" by anti–ethnic studies, anti–feminist studies, and anti–critical studies scholars) scare me away from writing about the topic, I had only wanted to engage in the scholarly and political, and not the personal and emotional, implications of my work. As I prepared for my talk in 2009, with four years as an assistant professor under my belt, I realized that my previous refusal to talk personally was not just a desire not to be self-indulgent, as I had told myself previously. Rather, my silence operated as a way to extricate myself from the identity-politics fire that surrounds work on mixed-race, just like work on other so-called inauthentic racialized, gendered, sexualized, or classed experiences. In this personal and emotional opening prologue to my scholarly, political book on mixed-race, I revisit those ideas. This preface is inspired by the works of Mark Anthony Neal, especially *New Black Man*. Neal's work gave me permission to take the voice I do here (Mark Anthony Neal, *New Black Man*).

1. Hall, "Minimal Selves," 116.
2. I am grateful to Mike Hurt, one of the founders of BOMBS and my peer mentor, for keeping these documents for all of these years and sharing them with me.
3. Spickard, "Obama Nation?"
4. Sachi is now a professional documentarian working for the *Los Angeles Times*. She continues to make pieces about multiraciality, among many other topics.
5. Maria Root, "Bill of Rights for People of Mixed Heritage," 1993–1994, http://www .drmariaroot.com/doc/BillOfRights.pdf (accessed December 10, 2008).
6. Hall, "Cultural Identity and Diaspora."

7. See Williams, *Mark One or More*, 12.

8. Ibid.

INTRODUCTION: READING MIXED-RACE REPRESENTATIONS

1. S. Brown, "Negro Character as Seen by White Authors," 280.

2. A number of authors are beginning to write about the metaphor of race transcendence (although I have yet to see "black" combined with "transcend"). See, for example, V. Smith, "From 'Race' to Race Transcendence"; Mirza, "Transcendence over Diversity"; Post, "Cultural Inversion and the One-Drop Rule."

3. V. Smith, *Not Just Race, Not Just Gender*, 38.

4. Hall, "The Work of Representation," 15.

5. Hall, "What Is This 'Black' in Black Popular Culture?," 474.

6. Hammonds, "New Technologies of Race," 108.

7. Hall, "The Work of Representation," 1.

8. Omi and Winant, *Racial Formation in the United States*, 68.

9. Through culture the hybrid nature of identity, described by James Clifford, is "mixed, relational, and inventive" (Clifford, *The Predicament of Culture*, 10). In addition, through examining a wide variety of nontraditional "hidden histories of resistance," Robin Kelley gets us "to pay attention to cultural hybridity" (Kelley, *Race Rebels*, 15 and 13). Tricia Rose writes about the syncretic nature of hip-hop culture "as an experimental and collective space where contemporary issues and ancestral forces are worked through simultaneously" (Rose, *Black Noise*, 59).

10. Almaguer, *Racial Fault Lines*, 3.

11. My "new millennium mulatta" is a play off of Danzy Senna's brilliant phrase (Senna, "The Mulatto Millennium," 12).

12. Kawai builds off the work of Homi Bhabha and Stuart Hall here. Kawai, "Stereotyping Asian Americans," 118.

13. Crenshaw, "Mapping the Margins."

14. Beech, "Eurasian Invasion."

15. See Nagle, *American Indian Ethnic Renewal*. This idea becomes important when considering another set of statistics: this millennium is marked by more interracially married African Americans in the United States than ever before: 9 percent of black men and 4 percent of black women. This number is low when compared to the intermarriage rates of all other groups of color, but relatively high when compared to the 3 to 4 percent interracial marriage rate for both sexes of "non-Hispanic whites." To put this another way, from the 2000 U.S. Census numbers, 96.5 percent of all white Americans are married to other white Americans (U.S. Bureau of the Census, "Hispanic Race and Origin of Coupled Households," Census 2000, http://www.census.gov/population/www/cen2000/briefs/phc-t19/index.html). Another study from 2003 shows that the number of interracial marriages of all groups is even higher than the census data, with whites intermarrying at a rate of 5.8 percent, African Americans at 10.2 percent, Asian Americans at 27.2 percent, Latinos at 28.4 percent (Bean and Stevens, "Interracial Marriage by Racial Group and Race of Partner"; also cited in DaCosta, *Making Multiracials*, 9).

16. DaCosta, *Making Multiracials*, 4; and Ibrahim, "Toward Black and Multiracial 'Kinship' after 1997," 23.

17. One additional note on years: I use the phrase "new millennium" throughout the book, even though I start my study in 1998. Representations of multiracial African Americans in the late 1990s name "new millennium" phenomena even before the advent of the new millennium.

18. I use the phrase "anti-black racism" as opposed to "racism" or "prejudice" not just to signal discriminatory feelings of whites toward people of color, but to also signify the institutional, structural, and cultural forces that foment the inequality of people of African descent in our society.

19. Susan Saulny, "Black? White? Asian?"

20. See Berlin, *Slaves without Masters*; and Blassingame, *Black New Orleans*.

21. See Streeter, "The Hazards of Visibility"; and Foreman, "Who's Your Mama?" Foreman notes, "the term [mulatta] seems to be enjoying a vernacular and critical currency that, I fear, both expresses a current racial anxiety and reproduces the politics of exceptionalism. Today, people ask their peers and professors, clients and customers, 'are you a mulatto?' with little sense of meaning or manners, while publishers clamor for novels, autobiographies, and anthologies about living on the color line" (531).

22. Alex Leo and Nico Pitney, "Wanda Sykes Kills at House Correspondents' Dinner (Video)," *Huffington Post*, May 5, 2009, http://www.huffingtonpost.com/2009/05/09/wanda-sykes-video-of-whit_n_201280.html (see minute 1:40 to 2:15). Sykes also performed a closely related version of this joke in her comedy show "I'ma Be Me," which aired October 10, 2009, on HBO.

23. Parker, Sawyer, Towler, "A Black Man in the White House?, 193–217. See also Kinder and Dale-Riddle, *The End of Race*; and Tesler and Sears, *Obama's Race*.

24. Tesler and Sears, *Obama's Race*, 4.

25. Wyatt, "Wanda Sykes Has a Show (or So They Tell Her)," C1.

26. *Will and Grace*, "Back Up, Dancer," episode no. 142, first broadcast September 26, 2004, by NBC, directed by James Burrows and written by David Kohan, Max Mutchnick, Tracy Poust, and Jon Kinnally; *Scrubs*, "My Common Enemy," episode no. 75, first broadcast October 19, 2004, by NBC, directed by Joanna Kerns and written by Bill Lawrence and Bill Callahan. I have been surprised that the term is also used as a so-called neutral descriptor, since its history makes it verboten for me to use neutrally. I have very rarely heard it used by multiracial African Americans in a reclaiming manner; when used, as by Sykes, it has an ironic or comedic tinge. However, I have come across a surprising number of non-mixed-race African Americans who use "mulatto" as a race label, from undergraduate students and senior citizen learners to the Asian American novelist Don Lee's casual reference to his black-white female character in *Country of Origin* (2004) as "a mulatto."

27. And yet, "hapa" is not totally noncontentious. See Kauanui, *Hawaiian Blood*; and Nishime, "Guilty Pleasures."

28. Parker and Song, *Rethinking Mixed Race*.

29. Omi and Winant, *Racial Formation in the United States*.

30. Bobo, *Black Women as Cultural Readers*, 35.

31. Hodes, *White Women, Black Men*.

32. Frankenberg, *White Women, Race Matters*, 71–74. For more detailed information on antimiscegenation laws, see Rachel F. Moran's *Interracial Intimacy*.

33. Gossett, *Race*, 30–31.

34. Genovese, *Roll, Jordan, Roll*, 461.

35. Winters, "More Desultory and Unconnected Than Any Other," 469.

36. Frankenberg, *White Women, Race Matters*, 73.

37. Collins, *Black Feminist Thought*, 50–51.

38. White, *Aren't I a Woman?*, 29.

39. Genovese, *Roll, Jordan, Roll*, 416.

40. Ibid., 430.

41. E. White, *Dark Continent of Our Bodies*, 33.

42. Davis, *Who Is Black?*, 37.

43. Additionally, the history of mixed-race people in slavery has been described as an attempted dissociation with blackness and association with whiteness. While historians such as Joel Williamson and John Mencke argue that there was a separate mulatto class during slavery, Genovese asserts that "mulattoes did not constitute a separate caste in the Old South except among the well-to-do free Negroes of a few cities. Blacks and mulattoes worked side by side in the plantation Big House and in the fields. Those mulattoes who received special treatment usually were kin to their white folks, and the special treatment was not always favorable" (Genovese, *Roll, Jordan, Roll*, 429). Nevertheless, as Genovese illustrates in his discussion of "fancy girls," distinctions between gradations of mixed-race blacks were also articulated on the auction block. At the same time, it was also sometimes financially beneficial to ignore the issue of mixture. Writing about early descriptions of "mulattos as black," Winthrop Jordan asserts that "by classifying the mulatto as a Negro [a slave auctioneer] was in effect denying that intermixture had occurred at all" (W. Jordan, *White over Black*, 178). For more on this topic, see Williamson, *New People*; and Mencke, *Mulattoes and Race Mixture*. There has also been debate among scholars of African American history as to whether mixed-race African Americans were part of a two-prong black-white system (where their allegiances solely lay with the black community), or a three-prong "mulatto elite" system like that of the Caribbean.

44. This myth works itself out in the legal arena of *State v. Scott* (1869) where the mixed-race person is described as "sickly and effeminate," "inferior in physical development and strength," and finally, "productive of evil, and evil only, without any corresponding good" (Saks, "Representing Miscegenation Law").

45. Gossett, *Race*, 49, 61.

46. Mencke, *Mulattoes and Race Mixture*, 9.

47. Ibid., 39.

48. In an interesting comparison, showing that interracial sex was a scapegoat issue in anti-immigration and antimiscegenation laws, Tomás Almaguer notes that Anglo justification for anti-Chinese immigration was the lascivious nature of the Chinese, or that "like Chinese women, Chinese men also were perceived as a threat

to the moral well-being of the white population, and most especially to white women" (Almaguer, *Racial Fault Lines*, 160). The looming menace of race mixing and mixed-race bodies sparked white fear, halted Chinese immigration, and prevented Chinese competition with white workers; in essence, images of mixed-race helped consolidate white privilege. Examining anti-immigration laws alongside anti-miscegenation laws, it becomes clear that the U.S. government desired Chinese bodies solely for labor, and then hoped they would disappear. Fear of miscegenation and multiracial bodies provided a rationale for racist legislation. In American history, for people of color and interracial families, the ostensibly private space of the family has been torn violently open to make their intimacies public. It is interesting to note that white hysteria focused much more intensely around Asian immigration and race mixing and not nearly as much around actual mixed-race Asian and white children. I am hard pressed to even find names for such children at that time as "hapa" is a Hawaiian import and "Eurasian" comes from U.S. military intervention in Asian countries. In contrast, much of the focus of white hysteria about black and white intermixture was indeed about the formation of mixed-race bodies. There have been very precise terms documenting mixed-race black and white children from "mulatto" to "quadroon," "octoroon," and so on.

49. Quoted in White, *Dark Continent of Our Bodies: Black Feminism and the Politics of Respectability*, 33.

50. Mencke, *Mulattoes and Race Mixture*, 77.

51. Davis, *Who Is Black?: One Nation's Definition*, 29.

52. Moran, *Interracial Intimacy*, 54.

53. Indeed, through some estimations, even greater white fear comes from invisible infiltration from "black" bodies as, for example, St. Clair Drake and Horace Cayton thoroughly documented Great Depression–era white fear in Chicago of "black" people "passing" as "white" (Drake and Cayton, *Black Metropolis*, 159–73).

54. Grossman, "A Chance to Make Good," 361.

55. Moran, Interracial Intimacy, 54.

56. Engaging the science of his time, in *The Health and Physique of the Negro American* (1906) Du Bois argues, "All the great peoples of the world are the result of a mixture of races" (37). See also Squires, *African Americans and the Media*.

57. Du Bois, *The Health and Physique of the Negro American*, 16.

58. Bost, *Mulattas and Mestizas*, 68. In addition, while an undergraduate at Stanford University, Danzy Senna wrote her honors thesis "Hiding in the Light: Representations of 'Passing' in African-American Fiction, 1890 to 1930" (Arias, "An Interview with Danzy Senna").

59. Locke, "American Literary Tradition and the Negro," 271.

60. Grossman, "A Chance to Make Good," 357.

61. In "The Reaction of the Negro to the Motion Picture *Birth of a Nation*," Thomas R. Cripps describes Thomas Dixon as "a sometimes preacher, a professional Southerner, and a fretful Negrophobe" (111) who loved to launch diatribes against the dangers of miscegenation.

62. Gish, "The Making of *The Birth of a Nation*," 44.

63. While Brody explains how the United Kingdom and its citizens were never "pure," but rather a compilation of various peoples and cultures, performances of hybridity help construct its very opposite state, a mythical purity. In other words, performances of hybridity somehow make the English "purely" white (Brody, *Impossible Purities*).

64. Bernardi, *The Birth of Whiteness*, 20.

65. Mencke, *Mulattoes and Race Mixture*, 122.

66. Ibid., 125.

67. Reuter, *The Mulatto in the United States*, 88.

68. Using history and sociology and drawing heavily upon census data, Reuter articulates a pseudo-scientific "narrative of tragedy": "[mulattoes] envy the white, aspire to equality with them, and are embittered when the realization of such ambition is denied them. They are a dissatisfied and an unhappy group" (Reuter, *The Mulatto in the United States*, 88).

69. This includes the "Eurasians/Anglo-Indians of India," the "Cape Coloured of South Africa," the "Coloured Peoples of Jamaica," the "Indo-Europeans of Java," the "Part Hawaiians," and the "Metis of Brazil."

70. Stonequist, *The Marginal Man*, 145–55.

71. Some contemporary texts also combine staid, early-twentieth-century notions of marginality with contemporary ideas of multiracial "specialness." For example, in *From Black to Biracial* (1998), the sociologist Kathleen Korgen argues that mixed-race people must make a lateral move from one singular identity to the next, choosing, in her view, one essentially defined ethnicity, "biracial," over another, "black," to aid in the problem that "biracial persons lack a sense of belonging." Korgen also propagates "positive" stereotypes as she describes a multiracial African American "gift of objectivity" and "cosmopolitan" worldview. Korgen illustrates the persistence of Reuter's and Stonequist's ideas in our age of late multiculturalism, where identities are not historically situated but imagined to be tried on and off like outfits. Korgen, *From Black to Biracial*, 76–77.

72. In "'What's the Matter with Sarah Jane?,'" Marina Heung states that this film was "one of Universal's highest grossing films in history" (303). Mulvey and Halliday, *Douglas Sirk*, 109.

73. Berlant, "National Brands/National Body," 197.

74. Ibid.

75. Butler, "Lana's 'Imitation,'" 15.

76. Williams, *Playing the Race Card*, 181.

77. Stern, "*Imitation of Life*," 284.

78. Drake and Cayton, *Black Metropolis*, 173.

79. See Saks, "Representing Miscegenation Law"; and Pascoe, "Race, Gender, and the Privileges of Property."

80. Harris, "Whiteness as Property," 279; Lipsitz, *The Possessive Investment in Whiteness*.

81. See Moran, *Interracial Intimacy*; and Kennedy, *Interracial Intimacies*.

82. Moran, *Interracial Intimacy*, 6–7, 12–13.

83. P. Gabrielle Foreman notes that a number of critics have observed similar phe-

nomena "that the white skin of some slaves acted as a visibly clear symbol of the wrongs of slavery argument" ("Who's Your Mama?," 522).

84. Talty, *Mulatto America at the Crossroads of Black and White Culture*, 3–6.

85. Ibid., 6.

86. Bullock, "The Mulatto in American Fiction."

87. Zanger, "The 'Tragic Octoroon' in Pre-Civil War Fiction."

88. In addition, just like the tragic mulatta, the tragic octoroon plays political purposes: this character "flattered the Northern audience in its sense of self-righteousness, confirming its belief in the moral inferiority of the South" (ibid., 287).

89. Cooper, "The Negro as Presented in American Literature," 150.

90. Hall, "New Ethnicities," 166.

91. Tucker, "Loving Day Recalls a Time When the Union of a Man and a Woman Was Banned."

92. Mixed-race, however, was not the focus of attention in the United States during the years of the civil rights movement, which, in Manning Marable's phrase, was the "Second Reconstruction," the time period from 1945 to 1976 when there were "a series of massive confrontations concerning the status of the African-American and other national minorities . . . in the nation's economic, social and political institutions" (Marable, *Race, Reform, and Rebellion*, 3–4).

93. Squires, *Dispatches from the Color Line*, 29, 53.

94. What mixed-race also owes to civil rights is a type of mythology of race and racial equality. Nikhil Pal Singh describes how, in the creation of the mythology of the civil rights era, Dr. Martin Luther King Jr. has become a particularly central figure. King "has come to stand for the idea of an America in which racial equality has already been achieved" (Singh, *Black Is a Country*, 5). Singh argues that King has been successfully appropriated as "a figure affirming the accomplishments of color-blind nationalism" (17). The myth of civil rights in the United States has been recast as a utopian meritocracy where racial injustice was quickly put to an end in the civil rights movement. This is what Singh calls "reshaping the boundaries of nation," which "has also involved rearticulations of race" (21). In the post–civil rights era, the reshaping of racialization by the United States has come about through neoconservative celebrations of mixed-race.

95. Williamson, *New People*, 195.

96. Omi, "Racialization in the Post–Civil Rights Era," 179.

97. Brunsma, *Mixed Messages*, 2–3 (emphasis in the original). Along with Root's first anthology, I would include Paul Spickard's *Mixed Blood*, Maria Root's *The Multiracial Experience*, Lise Funderburg's *Black, White, Other*, and Naomi Zack's *American Mixed Race*.

98. The multiracial movement denies the existence of racialization in its myopic desire to create a reified multiracial category. Instead of embracing liminality, syncretism, and hybridity, the Multiracial Movement seizes hold of its new "racial" category, denying the reality of multiple allegiances and seemingly contradictory identifications. In "A Critique of 'Our Constitution Is Color-Blind,'" the legal scholar Neil Gotanda argues that "racial categories themselves, with their meta-

phorical themes of white racial purity and nonwhite contamination, have differ-ent meanings for blacks [or all people of color] and whites" (267–68). Thus, the Multiracial Movement's desiring "multiracial" as yet another category links to the same history that reifies white power and sees race as a distinct, biological reality. In addition, Gotanda states that not grounding decisions about racial categoriza-tion in the history of U.S. racism "supports racial subordination . . . by treating racial categories as if they were stable and immutable" (259). Multiracial activ-ists' desire for the "multiracial" category demonstrates how they see a "solution" to the "problem" of mixed-race as inclusion into the political marketplace. They thus seek to mimic the hegemonic structures of monoraciality and cannot think outside the monoracial box.

99. Somerville, *Queering the Color Line,* 167.

100. K. Williams, *Mark One or More.*

101. Ibid.

102. The Campaign for Color Blind America Legal Defense and Educational Founda-tion's website was www.equalrights.com; there they described themselves as a "not-for-profit organization designed to challenge race-based public policies and educate the public about the injustices of racial preferences." The American Civil Rights Coalition's website is http://www.acrc1.org/index.htm; there, above a big picture of Ward Connerly deep in work, the organization states that it "works with grassroots supporters and leaders on the local, state and federal level to end racial and gender preferences and classifications."

103. Critiquing this phenomenon in the anthology *Mapping Multiculturalism,* the con-tributors struggle with the multiple meanings of "multiculturalism," including its conservative incarnations as an ideology that "renewed demands for assimilation in disguise," "avoided race . . . and left the impression that any discussion of cul-tural diversity would render racism insignificant," and "often played into the view that became backlash orthodoxy" (Gordon and Newfield, "Introduction," 1, 3, 4).

104. Bonilla-Silva, *Racism without Racists,* 2.

105. Squires, *Dispatches from the Color Line,* 2.

106. In addition to white authors such as Hollinger and George Will, men of color such as Ward Connerly, Dinesh D'Souza, and Richard Rodriguez also articulate a post-ethnic point of view. These neoconservative men of color use themselves as "authentic" role models who can testify to the existence of color blindness. See Dinesh D'Souza's *The End of Racism;* Richard Rodriguez's *Brown, Days of Obliga-tion,* and *Hunger of Memory;* and George Will's syndicated newspaper column.

107. Squires, *Dispatches from the Color Line,* 2.

108. For some neoconservatives, a desire for the erasure of the color line, or the blur-ring of racial distinctions, results in an imagined color-blind state of post-ethnicity as described by the historian David Hollinger in *Postethnic America.* Proponents of a post-ethnic ideology, who can be both conservatives and liberals, state that twenty-first-century America no longer needs to hold on to issues of race since racism no longer plays a substantial role in "our" lives. Post-race also signifies post–civil rights, or that the goals of the civil rights movement have been fully met; post-race functions as an antidote to race-based programs such as affirma-

tive action. Failing to acknowledge the existence of continually racially stratified inequalities, Hollinger writes, "a post-ethnic perspective seeks to test more systematically the limits of the epistemic 'we' and to stretch its circle as widely as the capacities of nature and its knowers will allow" (111). While utopian sounding in premise, the application of "voluntary identity," to use a Hollinger phrase, is far from racial utopia producing (129). While a post-ethnic America strikes many as nearly utopian in the abstract, the reality is that merely removing "the ethnoracial component in identity," perhaps an impossible notion in itself, fails to eliminate racism on either a personal or structural level in the racially hierarchized United States and perhaps even stokes institutional racism.

109. Frankenberg, *White Women, Race Matters*, 14, 143.

110. Lévi-Strauss, *Introduction to Marcel Mauss*, 63–64; and *Race: The Floating Signifier*, produced and directed by Sut Jhally (Northhampton, MA: Media Education Foundation, 1996), videocassette, 62 minutes.

111. However, as the communication scholars Kent Ono and Derek Buescher illustrate in their discussion of how Disney's Pocahontas functions as a cipher, the cipher figure is not merely "an empty shell of meaning prior to being imported into mainstream U.S. commodity culture" (Ono and Buescher, "Deciphering Pocahontas," 25).

112. Elsewhere I have noted: "A wide array of scholars have interrogated post-race using a variety of related terms, including 'colorblindness,' used by legal scholars such as Lani Guinier and Gerald Torres (2002), 'colorblind racism,' utilized by sociologist Eduardo Bonilla-Silva (2003), 'colormute,' coined by anthropologist Mica Pollock (2005), 'racial apathy,' deployed by sociologists Tyrone Forman and Amanda Lewis (2006), and 'post–civil rights,' applied by journalists, critics, and academics alike. One of the more strident embraces of post-race comes from Paul Gilroy (2000), who challenges the 'crisis of raciology,' claiming that holding onto 'race thinking,' even, or perhaps especially, by anti-racist activists and critical race scholars, fosters 'specious ontologies' and 'lazy essentialisms' (Gilroy 53). These are terms chosen by authors to denote or critique some moment after the importance of race. I favor the term 'post-race' because it highlights the continued centrality of race in this ideology where race is ostensibly immaterial. I contend that in its very denial of the uses of race, post-raciality remains embroiled in precisely what it claims not to be. In other words, 'post-race is an ideology that cannot escape racialization, complete with controlling images or racialized stereotypes" (R. Joseph, "Tyra Banks Is Fat," 239–40).

113. Elsewhere I have noted: "Media studies scholars from Angela McRobbie (2004, 2008) to Sarah Banet-Weiser (1999, 2007), Susan Douglas and Meredith Michaels (2004), Charlotte Brunsdon (2005), and Yvonne Tasker and Diane Negra (2007) are producing critiques of post-feminism, which is also popularly known as girlpower feminism and anti-feminism. While scholarship critiquing post-feminism often makes the effort to mention race, noting, for example, that post-feminist scholarship largely focuses on white women—there has been less attention paid to women of color and fewer sustained critiques of post-race and post-feminism in tandem. . . . While I am focusing here on the parallels between the two ide-

ologies of post-feminism and post-race, I want to be clear that there are also a number of differences between these two post-ideologies. One of the biggest differences is that similarities abound between the power-evasive ideas of post-race and post-feminism, not post-race and post-gender, or a Butlerian-inspired effort to deconstruct gender roles, behaviors, performances, and ideals (Butler, 1990, 1993)" (R. Joseph, "Tyra Banks Is Fat, 240). (See McRobbie, "Postfeminism and Popular Culture," and *The Uses of Cultural Studies*; Banet-Weiser, *The Most Beautiful Girl in the World*, and *Kids Rule!*; Douglas and Michaels, *The Mommy Myth*; Brunsdon, "Feminism, Postfeminism, Martha, Martha, and Nigella"; Negra and Tasker, *Interrogating Postfeminism.*)

114. Koshy, "Race in the Future Perfect Tense."
115. Waters, *Ethnic Options*, 147.
116. Balibar, "Is There a 'Neo-Racism?,'" 21, 17.
117. Douglas, "Manufacturing Postfeminism."
118. See Camille Paglia's *Sexual Personae*; Katie Roiphe's *The Morning After*; and Naomi Wolf's *Fire with Fire* and *Promiscuities*.
119. Wolf, *Fire with Fire*, xvii.
120. Douglas, "Manufacturing Postfeminism."
121. Bellafante, "Feminism," 54, 55.
122. I have heard this phrase in numerous popular and academic settings, including Root, "The Biracial Baby Boom."
123. With the new way of counting multiply raced individuals, the 2000 U.S. Census revealed that nationwide 2.4 percent of the population identify with two or more races (U.S. Bureau of the Census, "Profile of General Demographic Characteristics: 2000, Geographic Area: United States," Census 2000, http://censtats.census .gov/data/US/01000.pdf). These numbers were higher on the West Coast, totaling 4.7 percent in California; in addition, in 2000, 17 percent of births in California were to interracial couples (U.S. Bureau of the Census. "Profile of General Demographic Characteristics: 2000, Geographic Area: California," Census 2000, http://censtats.census.gov/data/CA/04006.pdf). Almost seven million Americans self-identified with multiple groups, thus earning the label of "mixed-race." To put this number in perspective, while the births of multiracial babies in the United States increased 260 percent since the 1970s, the births of monoracial babies have increased 15 percent (Wardel, "Helping Multiracial and Multiethnic Children Escape No Man's Land").
124. Morning, "Multiracial Classification on the United States Census."
125. Du Bois, *The Souls of Black Folk*, 359.
126. Perlmann and Waters, *The New Race Question*, 16–17.
127. See Glazer, "Reflections on Race, Hispanicity, and Ancestry in the U.S. Census."
128. Kimberly Williams, "Boxed In: The United States Multiracial Movement," job talk, University of California, San Diego, January 14, 2000.
129. Brody, *Impossible Purities*.
130. National Urban League, "African Americans' Status Is 73% of Whites Says New 'State of Black America' 2004 Report," March 24, 2004.

131. Ellis, "The New Black Aesthetic," 234. Similarly, Asian Americans' interstitial racialization has long been noted by scholars such as Frank Wu and Yen Le Espiritu.

132. These include the CBS sitcom *The Jeffersons*, where Belinda Tolbert played Jenny-Willis Jefferson (in sixty-eight episodes from 1975 to 1985); the NBC *Cosby Show* spinoff, *A Different World*, in which Cree Summers played Freddie Brooks (in eighty-seven episodes from 1988 to 1993; the show aired from 1987 to 1993); the WB and then CW networks' *Girlfriends*, which featured the supporting actress Persia White as Lynn Searcy from 2000 to 2007; and the Showtime drama *Queer as Folk* in which Makyla Smith played Daphne Chanders (in thirty-three episodes, which aired from 2000 to 2005). In the realm of historical miniseries, the CBS miniseries *Queen* starred Halle Berry (1993), and the Showtime miniseries *Feast of All Saints* (2001) featured a host of multiracial characters, including Nicole Lynn as Marie Ste. Marie, Jennifer Beals as Dolly Rose, Rachel Luttrell as Lissette, and Jasmine Guy as Juliete Mercer. Characters explicitly written as mixed-race African American men are harder to spot in television. They include Giancarlo Esposito in the NBC drama *Homicide: Life on the Street* as Mike Giardello (in twenty-two episodes from 1998–1999; the show aired from 1993 to 1999) and Ernest Waddell in the CW teen drama *One Tree Hill* as Derek Sommers (in four episodes in 2006; the show first aired in 2003 and is still running).

133. Casey et al., *Television Studies*, vii.

134. Miller, *Cultural Citizenship*, 12. Television studies is a methodologically diverse field that, Horace Newcomb notes, draws upon American "literary studies that redirected critical analysis toward the study of popular entertainment forms." Such critical analysis includes the Birmingham School, the Frankfurt School, film studies, and feminist criticism (Newcomb, "Television and the Present Climate of Criticism," 2). The groundbreaking work in black television studies of scholars such as Herman Gray, Krystal Brent Zook, Robin Means-Coleman, and Beretta Smith-Shomade brings to the fore the manner in which public symbolism functions with regard to African American bodies on television.

135. Robinson, "It Takes One to Know One," 719.

136. duCille, *The Coupling Convention*, 7–8.

137. Hall, "Minimal Selves," 114.

138. Hall, "Subjects in History," 292.

139. In "Mixed-Race Women," Maria Root describes this phenomenon as mixed-race women having "flexible looks" (163).

CHAPTER 1: TELEVISING THE BAD RACE GIRL

1. Odenwald, "Girls on Film"; J. Thomas, "Women's Work."

2. Dunn, *"Baad Bitches" and Sassy Supermamas*; See the entries on the Internet Movie Database website (www.imdb.com) for Jennifer Beals and Pam Grier.

3. See the entries on the Internet Movie Database website (www.imdb.com) for *The Bride*, *Vampire's Kiss*, *Troubled Waters*, *The Book of Eli*, *Devil in a Blue Dress*, *A House Divided*, and *Feast of All Saints*.

4. Kort, "Power Lesbian."

5. Stills in this chapter are screenshots from Netflix's steaming episodes of *The L Word*. I will cite episodes with season first, episode second.

6. Crenshaw, *Critical Race Theory*, 357.

7. Wallace, *Black Macho and the Myth of Superwoman*, 107.

8. V. Smith, "Introduction," 39–40.

9. I'm using the term *polysemy* the way my colleague, the rhetorician Leah Ceccerelli, does to mean "a bounded multiplicity, a circumscribed opening of the text in which we acknowledge diverse but finite meanings" (Ceccerelli, "Polysemy," 398).

10. Edwards, "Powell's 'River of Blood' Legacy."

11. F. Brown, "Nixon's 'Southern Strategy' and Forces against Brown"; Carter, "The Southern Strategy."

12. "Interracial Sex Becomes Weapon in Senate Race," ABC *News Online*, October 26, 2006, http://abclocal.go.com/kabc/story?section=news/national_world&id=469 9279.

13. Neubeck and Cazenave, *Welfare Racism*, v.

14. Dei, Karumanchery, and Karumanchery-Luik, *Playing the Race Card*, xi.

15. Ceccerelli, "Polysemy," 399.

16. Ford, *The Race Card*, 7, 8.

17. Williams, *Playing the Race Card*, 4.

18. Hall, "The Whites of Their Eyes," 91.

19. See, for example, Wald, *Crossing the Line*, 13.

20. Lipsitz, *The Possessive Investment in Whiteness*.

21. Mukherjee, *The Racial Order of Things*, 232.

22. C. Harris, "Whiteness as Property."

23. Collier and Horowitz, *The Race Card*, viii–ix.

24. See Alexander, *The New Jim Crow*.

25. Gross, "The Ethics of Misrepresentation," 194.

26. Erndst, "'The L Word' Here Is Limelight."

27. Muñoz, "Queer Minstrels for the Straight Eye," 102.

28. F. Moore, "Jennifer Beals Returns for a New Season of 'The L Word.'"

29. Brooks, *Bodies in Dissent*, 137.

30. McCabe and Akass, "Prologue."

31. Warn, "Radical Acts," 189–90.

32. Warn, "Introduction," 7.

33. See Omi and Winant, *Racial Formation in the United States*.

34. Salamon, "Big House on the Plantation Has a Family Secret."

35. Sedgwick, "Foreword: The Letter L," xxiii.

36. This is according to biographical information listed about Jennifer Beals, Leisha Hailey, Laurel Holloman, Mia Kirshner, Katherine Moennig, and Pam Grier on the Internet Movie Database website (www.imdb.com).

37. Beirne, "Fashioning *The L Word*," 17.

38. The fan website was www.tibette.com, and the Myspace page is www.myspace .com/tibettesoulmates. On August 5, 2008, there were forty such montages and video clips posted on YouTube. See http://www.youtube.com/results?orig_

query=tibette&search_query=tibette+512&orig_query_src=4. Thank you to Wadiya Udell for directing me to celebrations of Bette and Tina online.

39. Bette's constant cursing is significant; linguists note that expletives are often used to construct a stereotypically masculine persona, or to garner masculine power (see De Klerk, "Expletives"; and Kiesling, "From the 'Margins' to the 'Mainstream'").

40. From the position of dominant culture, Bette and Jodi are two triply minoritized women (as mixed-race, female, and homosexual, and deaf, female, and homosexual, respectively). Even though Jodi is white, her disability marks her as different and not an ideal like the desired, golden object of Bette's perpetual affection, Tina. Jodi is shown as having to traverse far more challenges than Bette. In addition, Jodi is far more defiant a character. Bette, an arts administrator, is part of the power structure and Jodi, an artist, refuses to be. Where Bette challenges authority in order to maintain her own position of power or even garner more power, Jodi flouts it in order to remain an outsider. In the social and legal landscape in which The L Word is operating, racialized minoritization is contested. Throughout the Bette and Jodi storyline, Tina is shown to be the answer for Bette.

41. Squires, "Black Is a Country," 82.

42. Bonilla-Silva, Racism without Racists, 71.

43. However, the show does not allow Tina to bond about her racism with other white women. Upon seeing Marcus, the white female receptionist at the sperm bank remarks to Tina, "that's a pretty serious decision to make." When Tina vehemently agrees with her, thinking that the woman meant having a baby with a black man, the joke is on Tina. The receptionist continues, "really big men like that tend to make really big babies."

44. The tension between Bette and Tina continues throughout the episode until Bette's African American half-sister, Kit (Pam Grier), provides the voice of wisdom. First she prods Bette to acknowledge her passing privilege and seeing that that goes nowhere, insisting that Bette needs to reframe the issue around love, which, in Kit's words, is "the one thing that cuts across all our realities. . . . The bridge between all our differences. And you have so much love in your life. Why you trying to tear down that bridge? Why?" Kit's comments are echoed in the opening music for that episode with the repeating line "I've got so much more, so much love, so much more left to give" from Marianne Faithfull's "Pleasure Song." The link to the opening song helps illustrate that giving love must be part of the "real lesson" of the episode. Race is dismissed as a nonissue.

45. While Bette's character, as one of the leads, functions as far more than metaphor in the show, Angelica is indeed a metaphor. This is a popular role for "mulattas" in popular representation. In fact, in Karen Voss's reading of Jennifer Beals in the film noir Devil in a Blue Dress (1995), Voss argues that Beals's mixed-race character "Daphne's biracial status and the viability of her relationship with a powerful white politician symbolize the possibility of integration of African American and white L.A." (Voss, "Replacing L.A.," 173).

46. A similar plotline is explored in the sitcom Modern Family in 2011, when two white gay male dads are convinced that their adopted Vietnamese daughter is a shoo-in

for a tony preschool, until they see an interracial lesbian couple, one of whom is wheelchair equipped, enter into the preschool's waiting room.

47. Chaplin, "Rounding Up the L Girls."

48. Erndst, "'The L Word' Here Is Limelight."

49. Nyong'o, "Queer TV."

50. Foreman, "Who's Your Mama?," 508.

51. This is not to say that many viewers of the show read through the omission of the scripts to see Bette's mixed-race blackness.

52. E. Johnson, *Appropriating Blackness*, 8.

53. V. Smith, *Not Just Race, Not Just Gender*, xv.

54. Robinson, "It Takes One to Know One."

55. Springer, "Divas, Evil Black Bitches, and Bitter Black Women," 268.

56. Ibid.

57. Morris, "Pink Herring and the Fourth Persona," 240–41.

58. Wolfe and Roripaugh, "The (In)Visible Lesbian," 45.

59. Shohat and Stam, *Multiculturalism, Postcoloniality, and Transnational Media*.

60. Squires, *Dispatches from the Color Line*, 5.

61. Rhodes, *Framing the Black Panthers*, 5–6.

62. Janusonis, "A Life without FLASH: Unpretentious Beals Is Just a Yalie."

63. Goodale, "'House Divided' Breaks Down Realities of Race," 20.

64. Peck, "Daughter of Master and Slave."

65. Vaucher, "Showtime's 'House' of a Different Color."

66. Marcus, "A Role She Can Relate To," 3.

67. Vaucher, "Showtime's 'House' of a Different Color," 4.

68. Hall, "Minimal Selves," 114.

69. Sternbergh, "Back in a Flash," 63–64.

70. Dagbovie, "Star-Light, Star-Bright, Star Damn Near White," 218.

71. Hall, "Cultural Identity and Cinematic Representation," 68.

72. Warn, "Radical Acts," 196.

73. Henderson, "Simple Pleasures," 41.

CHAPTER 2: THE SAD RACE GIRL

1. Senna, *Caucasia*, 233.

2. Collins, "Learning from the Outsider Within," S20.

3. Garber, *Vested Interests*, 11.

4. Ibid., 16.

5. Ibid., 11.

6. Ibid., 17.

7. Other authors, such as Yen Le Espiritu, have discussed how Asian Americans, as a non-black and non-white racialized group, fall into a "third" position. Espiritu writes, "Societies tend to organize themselves around sets of mutually exclusive binaries. . . . In the United States, this binary construction of difference—of privileging and empowering the first term and reducing and disempowering the second—structures and maintains race, gender, and class privilege and power" (Espiritu, *Asian American Women and Men*, 108). Espiritu writes that we engage in

"another kind of dualism" when we "treat race, gender, and class as mutually exclusive categories" (108). Instead we need an intersectional type of position. Espiritu argues that "as multiply disadvantaged people, Asians in the United States complicate either/or definitions and categories and carve out for themselves a 'third space' as 'neither/nor' and as 'both/and'"—both like black and like white, as well as like neither. Her primary argument is: "Asian Americans, as racialized 'others' who occupy a 'third' position, both disrupt and conform to the hegemonic dualisms of race, gender, and class" (109).

8. I question terminology such as "passing" and "looks black" to highlight the fact that race is a social construction and just as one cannot really pass for another race, looking like a certain race is also suspect because that presupposes that there are authentic racialized looks. At the same time, I do use racialized labels to acknowledge the reality of racialization.

9. See V. Smith, *Not Just Race, Not Just Gender.*

10. Robinson, "It Takes One to Know One," 715.

11. Ibid., 719.

12. Kawash, "The Autobiography of an Ex-Colored Man," 63.

13. See, for example, Cheryl Harris's discussion of her grandmother passing in "Whiteness as Property."

14. Ibid., 6.

15. In addition to Elemeno, another metaphor for Birdie's race is the van that she and her mother use when they flee to Caucasia about a third of the way through the book. Senna writes, "Our rule all along had been to switch vehicles every six months, but we'd been driving this one for close to two years. It was a paint-stripped van with a cracked and drafty floor and a vague smell of turpentine wafting up from the corners. It once had been yellow. I could tell because some of the paint was left on the interior, a nice buttery chrome yellow. Now it was no color at all; the color of something stripped clean for the sake of starting over" (142–43). Birdie's identity faces a similar transformation when confronted with race and gender. Just as Birdie and Sandy switched vehicles so that they would not get caught, Birdie switched racialized and gendered personas to stay safe. The persona that she had inhabited while they were on the road was explicitly white, Jewish, and tomboyish, but really "no color [or gender] at all" because she didn't confront peers attempting to racialize or gender her.

16. See Thurman, *Secrets of the Flesh.*

17. Bost, *Mulattas and Mestizas.* Stephen Talty also notes: "Blacks and whites mixed their blood from the mid-1600s onward, but amalgamation became official American policy only when it involved Native Americans. Pocahontas, who saved the Plymouth colony and married the Englishman John Smith, became the model. When she abandoned her culture and embraced English values, her blood became the ingredient that enriched the nation's stock. In the 1880s, there was a full-fledged Pocahontas craze: warships and villages were named after her; manufacturers of cigars, perfumes, and flour slapped her name on their products, perhaps the ultimate American compliment" (Talty, *Mulatto America at the Crossroads of Black and White Culture,* 53).

18. Bost, *Mulattas and Mestizas*, 36.

19. See Senna, *Where Did You Sleep Last Night?*

20. See, for example, Harris and Sim, "Who Is Multiracial?"; Mahtani, "What's in a Name?"

21. Senna, "The Mulatto Millennium," 12–13.

22. For example, combining the idea of *Caucasia* as a universal human novel with power-evasive notions of multiculturalism, another article in the *New York Times Magazine* acknowledges that while "biracial and bicultural issues are trendy right now," *Caucasia* and other contemporary end-of-the-millennium mixed-race novels are "trying to forge an identity that reconciles the basic human desire to fit in and yet to remain separate, distinct, special." Deployment of the word "trendy" makes multiraciality seem like a passing fad, an ephemeral fashion statement as opposed to a racialized reality (Cardwell, "Culture Zone," 20).

23. hooks, *Black Looks*, 21.

24. Waters, "Optional Ethnicity," 453.

25. This includes the 1998 Book of the Month Club Stephen Crane Award for First Fiction and an Alex Award from the American Library Association for one of the top-ten adult books for teenagers. *Caucasia* was also a finalist for the International IMPAC Dublin Literary Award. It was one of *Glamour* magazine's three Best Novels of the Year by a New Writer, one of *School Library Journal*'s 23 Best Adult Books for the Young Adult, and one of the *Los Angeles Times*'s Best Books of 1998 (as reported on a web page of Riverhead Books, Senna's publisher, http://www.idiotsguides.com/static/packages/us/about/adult/riverhead.htm [accessed January 23, 2004]).

26. This review is also quoted at length on the back cover of the 1998 printing of the novel. On the front cover, one part of the article is quoted prominently: "impressive beauty and power." Shapiro, "*Caucasia*," 71.

27. See, for example, Toni Morrison's *Playing in the Dark*, David Roediger's *The Wages of Whiteness*, Richard Dyer's *White*, Ruth Frankenberg's *White Women, Race Matters*, and Mary Waters's *Ethnic Options*.

28. Richardson, "*Caucasia*," 24.

29. Cardwell, "Culture Zone," 20.

30. Seaman, "*Caucasia*," 985.

31. Ellen Flexman, "*Caucasia*," *Library Journal*, January 1998, 145.

32. Crenshaw, "Mapping the Margins," 1242.

33. "*Caucasia*," *Publisher's Weekly*, December 8, 1997, 54.

34. Flexman, "*Caucasia*," 145.

35. See Remnick, *The Bridge*.

36. Olumide, *Raiding the Gene Pool*, 9.

37. Seaman, "*Caucasia*," 985.

38. Shapiro, "*Caucasia*," 71.

39. Seaman, "*Caucasia*," 985.

40. Ibid.

41. Another review states, "In the black power school, [Birdie] looks different but feels at home. In the white school, she looks the same but feels alien" (Heyman,

"Novel of the Week," 55). This is, at best, a simplification of Birdie's school experiences. At worst, it essentializes blackness.

42. Oyewumi, *The Invention of Women*, 1–2.

43. Bost, *Mulattas and Mestizas*, 188. See also Boudreau, "Letting the Body Speak." Boudreau begins her article with a quote from Senna: "What's become clear to me through my racial trials and tribulations is that at some point you do make a choice, not between white and black but between silence and speech. Do you let your body talk for you or do you speak for yourself?" (Senna quoted in Postel, "Invisible Sister," the article, however, is no longer available online).

44. Interestingly, Senna has been embraced and labeled as a black female writer in another way: her work has been anthologized in collections of African American writing. "The Body of Luce Rivera," a chapter from *Caucasia*, appears in *Shaking the Tree*, edited by Meri Nana-Ama Danquah. *Gumbo: An Anthology of African American Writing* features Senna's quintessential tragic-mulatta short story, "Are You Experienced?" This is the decidedly disastrous tale of Josephine, a beautiful young woman in 1969 who is "a Negro by race, but pale as butter, with straight black hair that fell to her waist" (Senna, "Are You Experienced?," 517). Jo is abused by her mixed-race husband, and she finds temporary solace one weekend in the bed of the tragic multiracial musician Jimi Hendrix, who ends up fathering her second child. Jo's "good looks" give her access to and prevent her from certain things, and ultimately get her into trouble. Senna is well aware of the huge body of tragic-mulatta and -mulatto literature, and she performs homages to certain works in *Caucasia*.

45. Richardson, "Caucasia," 24.

46. Jefferson, "Seeing Race as a Costume That Everyone Wears."

47. Jefferson's review goes on to say: "Mulattoes aren't only a gauge of race relations, they are a gauge of the cultural complexities you choose — or choose not — to live with. You don't have to have parents of contrasting races to be a cultural mulatto. You have to stand apart from your heritage, study the forces (natural and unnatural) that made it, and then choose to become part of whatever else stirs and compels you, however foreign or distant" (ibid., E2).

48. Arias, "An Interview with Danzy Senna," 447.

49. *Black Issue Book Review* quotes Senna: "Since I was a little girl, I've always identified myself as black. . . . It was a choice for me, since the outside world did not see me as such. My choice didn't come out of a belief in the 'one-drop rule.' . . . Rather, it came out of my understanding — and my parent's [sic] understanding — that racial identity is a matter of consciousness, not skin color. I learned early on that race was a social construction, and so my racial identity was as much based on experience, history, and consciousness as it was based on physical traits" (Bowman, "Black Like Who?," 24).

50. Bost, *Mulattas and Mestizas*, 133. The psychologists Jewelle Taylor Gibbs and Alice M. Hines also problematically and interestingly note, "Choice of sexual partners and patterns of dating and/or sexual activity can also be problematic and complicated for biracial teens. . . . [P]atterns of dating and sexual activity are sometimes expressed as an 'all or none' situation, with some biracial teens be-

coming sexually promiscuous and others becoming celibate to avoid the risks of intimate relationships" ("Negotiating Ethnic Identity," 232).

51. Bost, *Mulattas and Mestizas*, 145.

52. Hall, "Minimal Selves," 117.

53. However, there have been times when, for example, "mulatto" was a category on the census. In addition, in other nations, particularly in Latin America and the Caribbean, "mulatto" has been a frequently used term and category.

54. See Berzon, *Neither White nor Black*; Spillers, "Mama's Baby, Papa's Maybe"; Berlant, "National Brands/National Bodies" and "The Queen of America Goes to Washington City"; and Robinson, "It Takes One to Know One."

55. There are many examples of literary discussions of the representation of tragic mulattoes and mulattas in novels, including Judith Berzon's *Neither White nor Black*, Barbara Christian's *Black Women Novelists*, Hazel Carby's *Reconstructing Womanhood*, and Werner Sollers's *Neither Black nor White yet Both*.

56. Brody, *Impossible Purities*, 16.

57. Ibid., 18.

58. In addition, a mythical white father often causes there to be a "specter of incest" surrounding the mulattaroon, proving that her skin is always stained with "wrong" sex (ibid., 25). In a related vein, the legal scholar Eva Saks describes the association of miscegenation and incest when state criminal codes list miscegenation next to incest as "crimes of blood" (Saks, "Representing Miscegenation Law," 53).

59. Hall, "Cultural Identity and Cinematic Representation," 210.

CHAPTER 3: THE EXCEPTIONAL MULTIRACIAL

1. All of the quotes in this chapter come from my personal transcription of the film.

2. Gray, *Cultural Moves*, 13, 19.

3. Nevertheless, two films do recall Swan's *Mixing Nia*. One is a French film, Mathieu Kassovitz's *Café Au Lait* (1993), where a young biracial woman carries on relationships with an African and a Jew. The second is Spike Lee's first feature film, *She's Gotta Have It* (1986), where the African American protagonist Nola has sexual relationships with three black men. Incidentally, in an interview on March 2, 2001, Swan told me that *She's Gotta Have It* convinced her that she should go into film. I am grateful to Jane Rhodes and Zeinabu Davis for facilitating my interview with Swan. Our March 2, 2001, interview took place in Swan's house, car, and a Greek restaurant in the Los Angeles area. As the anthropologist Charles Briggs writes in *Learning How to Ask*, interviews are a "communicative event" (2). Thus, I would never assert that I discerned any impartial truth from my interview with Alison Swan. I realize that her responses to me were filtered through the fact that she saw me as a mixed-race woman, a feminist, a graduate student, and the first "academic" to write on her work.

4. Although I am focusing on just three films, the tragic mulatta has been featured in a wide array of American films, including *The Debt* (1912), *Hallelujah* (1929), *Pinky* (1949), *Lost Boundaries* (1949), *Showboat* (1951), *Carmen Jones* (1954), *Sparkle* (1976), *Angelheart* (1987), and *Glitter* (2001). See Bogel, *Toms, Coons, Mulattoes, Mammies, and Bucks*; and Cripps, *Making Movies Black*.

5. Eva Saks, "Representing Miscegenation Law," 63 (emphasis added).

6. Larkin, "Black Women Film-Makers Defining Ourselves," 160.

7. See Williams, *Playing the Race Card*.

8. Flitterman-Lewis, "Imitation(s) of Life," 326.

9. In *Authentic Blackness*, the literary scholar J. Martin Favor investigates essentialized African American ideals that are deployed, in the examples he uses, by African Americans instead of whites. Favor asserts that when used by a minoritized group, authenticity politics exist "to create unity in the face of an 'other'" (Favor, *Authentic Blackness*, 7).

10. Ibid., 30.

11. For more on African Americans and assumptions on authenticity in advertising see Chambers, *Madison Avenue and the Color Line*.

12. Mercer, "Black Hair/Style Politics," 105.

13. Grayson, "Is It Fake?," 13.

14. Root, "Mixed-Race Woman," 163.

15. Lewis clearly flirts with ideas of both black nationalism and Afrocentrism. However, in *Mixing Nia*, black nationalism is understood quite differently than Stokeley Carmichael and Charles Hamilton explain it in their classic text *Black Power: The Politics of Liberation in America* (1967). Carmichael and Hamilton assert that "black people in the United States must raise hard questions, question which challenge the very nature of the society itself: its long-standing values, beliefs and institutions" (34). Lewis's philosophy seems to lack questioning at all; he postures as the essential black subject and derides all things white. In addition, in *The Afrocentric Idea*, the prominent Afrocentric scholar Molefi Asante defines Afrocentricity as "placing African ideals at the center of any analysis that involves African culture and behavior" (6). Lewis again fails to engage in anything but the displaying of African iconography in his apartment.

16. Here Swan calls upon the stereotype of a black woman, especially a light-skinned or mixed-race one, as a jezebel, described by the historian Deborah Gray White as "a person governed almost entirely by her libido." White explains how the jezebel was a well-known stereotype particularly before the U.S. Civil War. White writes, "In every way Jezebel was the counterimage of the mid-nineteenth-century ideal of the Victorian lady. She did not lead men and children to God; piety was foreign to her. She saw no advantage in prudery, indeed domesticity paled in importance before matters of the flesh" (*Aren't I a Woman?*, 28–29).

17. Hall, "New Ethnicities," 165–66. Hall also describes how this initially resulted from his family's struggle to acknowledge their lower-middle-class status; he was later aided by his own diasporic existence. Hall states, "I was aware of the fact that identity is an invention from the very beginning, long before I understood any of this theoretically." Connecting identity questions to history and politics, Hall depicts racialized identity's inherent instability in his demonstration that Jamaicans of African descent "learned" they were black during the black Caribbean cultural nationalism of the 1970s (Hall, "Minimal Selves," 115). Nia similarly "learns" black authenticity when she dates Lewis, posited as an expert on blackness because he is a professor of African American studies.

18. Hall, "Signification, Representation, Ideology," 101.

19. In the short story "Drinking Coffee Elsewhere," ZZ Packer describes how white Heidi admires her black friend Dina's hair. Heidi comments, "You should wear it out more often." Dina responds, "White people always say that about black people's hair. The worse it looks, the more they say they like it" (Packer, *Drinking Coffee Elsewhere*, 124).

20. In various literatures, mixed-race people often note that they question what it's like to really be their group of color. For example, Beverly Yuen Thompson starts an article with an anecdote by a mixed-race Asian woman: "I had been wondering about taking part in a student theatre project about being Asian American, and I said to Tommy, 'The thing is, I don't feel as though I've really lived the . . . Asian American experience.' (Whatever I thought that was.) Tommy kind of looked at me. And he said, 'But Claire, *you are* Asian American. So whatever experience you have lived, *that is* the Asian American experience.'" Nia could be seen as producing a similar sentiment as this woman, but she has no Tommy in this film to validate her mixed-race experience as inclusive of being African American ("Fence Sitters, Switch Hitters, and Bi-Bi Girls," 171 [emphasis in the original]).

21. It is interesting to note that even though he is Latino (and played by the Ecuadorian soap opera star Diego Serrano), Joe has an Anglo name and is quite light skinned.

22. After the scene where Nia rejects Matt and Lewis, she dramatically runs home in the rain to find that Joe has left town and sublet his apartment without telling her. He has nevertheless left a present for her: a kora, the Senegalese, "slightly Celtic sounding" instrument that she identified as representing her voice. His note states, "Nia, I hope you find your voice, love, Joe."

23. Greg Merritt writes that other first independent films from the 1990s have significantly lower budgets. For example, Robert Rodriguez made *El Mariachi* (1993) for a mere $7,000, while Whit Stillman made *Metropolitan* (1990) for $200,000 (Merritt, *Celluloid Mavericks*, 374). Most first independent films fall somewhere in between these two sums with, for example, Hal Hartley's *The Unbelievable Truth* (1990) was $75,000 (ibid., 361), Matty Rich's *Straight Out of Brooklyn* (1991) was $90,000 (ibid., 366), and Nick Gomez's *Laws of Gravity* (1992) was $38,000 (ibid., 368). These filmmakers also took different financing routes: for example, young filmmakers, such as Matty Rich and Kevin Smith, are famous for taking out thousands of dollars on their credit cards to finance their films. Although Merritt does provide some information on the budgets of filmmakers of color, he provides no budgets for African American women independent filmmakers (ibid., 369).

24. Roberts, "Independents' Day," 105.

25. Follow-up phone interview with Swan, April 26, 2001.

26. Roberts, "Independents' Day," 105.

27. Perhaps the fact that the film would star Karyn Parsons was also a reason that distributors eschewed the film. Parsons is best known for her television role as the privileged Hilary Banks in the long running sitcom *The Fresh Prince of Bel-Air*. Hilary, the oldest Banks child, was depicted as a shallow, arrogant young woman with a desire for nothing but shopping and celebrities. Intertextuality, sometimes

seen as a draw because audiences are attracted to their favorite performers in different media, possibly worked against Parsons here; the studio executives could not imagine her in any role other than Hilary. Parsons's career shows this typecasting: she has tried to break into films, but outside of her starring role in *Mixing Nia*, she has only been chosen to play stock one-dimensional characters in such comedic films as *Class Act* (1992), *Major Payne* (1995), *Gulliver's Travels* (1996), and *The Ladies' Man* (2000) (according to biographical information for Karyn Parsons on the Internet Movie Database, www.imdb.com).

28. Isaiah Washington's filmography demonstrates a number of savvy choices. He has picked clever independent films, often with racial themes, with some decent mainstream films as well: *Alma's Rainbow* (1994), *Clockers* (1995), *Girl 6* (1996), *Mr. and Mrs. Loving* (1996), *Get on the Bus* (1996), *love jones* (1997), *Mixing Nia* (1998), *Bulworth* (1998), *True Crime* (1999), *Dancing in September* (2000), *Romeo Must Die* (2000), *Texas Funeral* (2000), *Exit Wounds* (2001), *Ghost Ship* (2002), *Welcome to Collinwood* (2002) (according to biographical information for Isaiah Washington on the Internet Movie Database, www.imdb.com).

29. Interview with Swan, March 2, 2001.

30. Ibid.

31. As we turn from the film itself to the reception of the film, I wish that I could draw upon reviews in order to assess if Swan was read through her fictional character (as in my discussions of Jennifer Beals's and Senna's [and *Caucasia's*] reception). However, because *Mixing Nia* was unable to secure a theatrical distributor, the film did not hold the attention of the popular press. My interview with Swan does, nevertheless, fill in some necessary extra-diegetic information.

32. Interview with Swan, March 2, 2001 (emphasis added).

33. Horowitz, "American Apartheid."

34. Kweisi Mfume, NAACP weekly radio address, January 6, 1997, www.multracial .com. See also, for example, C. Thomas, "America Doesn't Need Racial Labels"; Morse, "Kiss Me — I'm White"; Todd Nelson, "A Question of Identity," March 30, 2001, www.pioneerplanet.com; and Schmitt, "Multiracial Identification Might Affect Programs."

35. Swan never explicitly mentioned politics or the census during our interview.

36. In an *LA Weekly* cover story, four African American female directors discuss their work and the role of race and racism in erecting bulwarks against their films (Hardy, "I, Too, Sing Hollywood") (emphasis in the original) found at http://www .laweekly.com/2000–10–26/news/i-too-sing-hollywood/ (accessed April 10, 2012).

37. Ed Guerrero points out in *Framing Blackness*: "If the situation for black male independent filmmakers has proven difficult, then it has been almost impossible for black women. Compared to black men there are few black women filmmakers and, in most cases, they must negotiate the 'triple oppression' of their work predicated on independent vision, race, and gender" (174). Because of this "triple oppression," Swan has chosen to try for, in white Hollywood's eyes, unquestionably universal projects: those that feature white actors. At the time of our interview, Swan was in the process of commissioning a film that she imagined as a love triangle starring Matt Damon, Gwyneth Paltrow, and Ben Affleck. Swan told one

interviewer that while she would like "to synthesize independent vision with Hollywood film-making," she is not "opposed to doing pure entertainment" (Barclay, "Festival's a Reel Thrill for Alison"). Of course, this time, "pure entertainment" would have been purely white.

38. *Mixing Nia* is not understood by distributors as universal because it belies many common portrayals of black women in Hollywood films that the film scholar Gloria Gibson-Hudson describes: "The black woman, as presented within mainstream cinema, is a one-dimensional depiction. Black women are shown as sex objects, passive victims, and as 'other' in relation to males (black and white) and white females. Worldwide, black women's images are prescribed by narrative texts that reflect patriarchal visions, myths, stereotypes, and/or fantasies of black womanhood. Consequently, these representations limit the probability of an audience seeing black women as figures of resistance or empowerment" (Gibson-Hudson, "The Ties That Bind," 43). While *Mixing Nia* might not unilaterally present black women as "figures of resistance or empowerment," it certainly does not provide a "one-dimensional" image of Nia, for the very basic reason that she is the protagonist. In addition, Nia is indeed a figure of empowerment and resistance when she quits her advertising agency job because of its racist malt liquor campaign. However, complicating the picture, she is also a "passive victim" when she allows her male sexual partners to dictate the confines of her racialized and sexualized identity. Nevertheless, despite this enactment of a "patriarchal vision," studio executives were not interested in distributing this film perhaps because of the moments in which the protagonist moves beyond the easy filmic stereotypes that Gibson describes.

39. J. Palmer, "A Diamond Waiting to Be Discovered," 13. In addition, perhaps the film itself is responsible for some of its marketing woes—the audience could not identify with her struggle because the film posits that only multiracials think about their races.

40. Underlying other compelling Hollywood rationales, the "universal" tag word does not work here because our protagonist embodies a completely foreign subjectivity, mixed-race womanhood. Swan's "dramedy" fusion of forms makes sense with the protagonist's racial fusion.

41. Interview with Swan, March 2, 2001 (emphasis added).

42. Ibid.

43. Without the worry of "appropriate" niche marketing, *Mixing Nia* received popular and critical support by winning the Festival Grand Prize at World Fest Houston, the *Entertainment Weekly* Audience Award at the Bermuda Film Festival, and the Jean Renoir Award at the Huntington Film Festival (from Swan's own biography flier).

44. Gray, *Watching Race*, 67.

45. Zook, *Color by Fox*, 3.

46. In a *Los Angeles Times* article titled "Movie Supplier Finds Success Catering to the Black Market," Marion Flanagan reports that Leight Savidge, the founder and CEO of Xenon Entertainment Group, is a white man who "saw a niche" and proceeded

to become "the leading supplier of low-budget, independent films aimed at black consumers."

47. On the Xenon Entertainment Group website, www.xenonpictures.com, the company lists its catalogue within the categories of "Black Audience," "Black Heritage," "Gospel," "Hong Kong Cinema," and "Art and Foreign."

48. "Xenon Entertainment Group," Xenon Pictures, http://www.xenonpictures.com/xenon.html.

49. Additionally, Swan marks Nia as mixed-race but really African American. In the most obvious example, "Nia," the fifth day of Kwanzaa, is a Swahili word meaning purpose. Also demonstrating its success outside of a theatrical release, in the spring of 2001 Swan was in the process of translating *Mixing Nia* into an hour-long television show. While stereotypical black comedies are an easier sell on networks like the former UPN, when I interviewed her Swan asserted, "It's very hard right now to get a black drama." To make her dramedy more marketable, Swan realized that she must eradicate Nia's racial confusion: "So its latest incarnation, it doesn't really deal with the [mixed-race identity] theme. Because I learned my lesson with *Mixing Nia* so I'm trying to come up with another overall theme for the show . . . [S]he's still dealing with being biracial, but it's not the overall theme of the show. So basically now the show is, young girl moves to New York with her two friends. And they try to, build their dreams. It's all about that first couple of years after college." To a contemporary television viewer, this plot sounds both familiar and formulaic. But while those protagonists are white, Nia is mixed-race. Swan is therefore making Nia's identity fluctuations peripheral and removing supporting black actors from the center of her television show. Nia will live with a white girlfriend, a Jewish man, and a black ex-boyfriend, but instead of having her black girlfriend also close, Swan has chosen to locate her in another apartment, explaining, "I feel like it would work better for television this way." Swan pragmatically erases black and Latino elements and fills in white ones in hopes to successfully market her television show.

CHAPTER 4: RECURSIVE RACIAL TRANSFORMATION

1. *America's Next Top Model*, "The Girl Who Is Contagious," episode no. 38, first broadcast March 30, 2005, by The CW, directed by Luis Barreto, and written by Tyra Banks, Ken Mok, and Kenya Barris.

2. For more on the symbolic roles of cleanliness and dirt, see Douglas, *Purity and Danger*.

3. *America's Next Top Model* and Tyra Banks herself are quickly becoming popular scholarly texts. See, for example, Hasinoff, "Fashioning Race for the Free Market on *America's Next Top Model*"; Ngai, "Competitiveness"; L. Palmer, "Gender as the Next Top Model of Global Consumer-Citizenship"; R. Joseph, "Tyra Banks Is Fat"; and M. Thompson, "Learn Something from This!"

4. Racializing terminology is, of course, fraught with problems. How an individual might identify ethnically or racially does not necessarily correspond to how he or she might be racialized by a person on the street or enumerated by an institution.

That being said, my own subjective application of racializing terms is necessary for my textual analysis. Whenever possible I use the terms used by individuals. Here, when describing a multiply raced group I describe them as "multiracial" (eight white contestants, three African Americans, two mixed-race African Americans, one Latina). When describing what I read as a racially ambiguous phenotype I use the terms "racially ambiguous," "mixed-race," and "multiracial."

5. The Nielsen ratings in the spring of 2005 revealed that *Top Model* was the second most popular reality show for African Americans (after *American Idol*), the second most popular reality show for all women aged eighteen to thirty-four (after *American Idol*), and the third most popular reality show for all households (after *American Idol* and *Survivor*). See "Highest-Rated Primetime Programs—Total U.S. Homes," Nielsen Media Online, http://www.nielsenmedia.com/ethnicmeasure/african-american/programsUS.html (accessed September 25, 2006), and "Primetime Metered Market Ratings," TV Tracker, http://www.tvtracker.com/daily_ratings.php (accessed September 25, 2006).

6. Dyer, *Stars*.

7. Yu, "Tiger Woods Is Not the End of History," 1407.

8. Turner, *Understanding Celebrity*, 26.

9. *America's Next Top Model*, "Let's Go Surfing," episode no. 156, first broadcast October 28, 2009, by The CW, directed by Allison Chase, and written by Tyra Banks, Ken Mok, and Kenya Barris.

10. See Awkward, *Negotiating Difference*; Gubar, *Racechanges*; and Smith, *Enacting Others*.

11. The ideology of post-race is prevalent throughout popular culture in the United States. For example, post-race means that a newspaper article on the spring fashion runway shows in 2007 questioned if the white designer Donna Karan's "urban silhouettes" and models with "deep ebony skin" constituted more "black style" than the African American designer Tracee Ross's "Cuba, Spain, and Mexico" inspired collection. With this description, Karan's designs are celebrated as an essentialized ideal of blackness as "urbanness," whereas Ross's designs are posited as inauthentically black because they draw on Latin influences. See Givham, "Race on the Runway." Another related yet slightly different example of post-race is L'Oréal's HiP (High Intensity Pigment) advertising campaign in 2005–6 where white models were featured alongside African American celebrities (e.g., Beyoncé). The darker color range of the makeup appears to better complement darker skin tones. However, white women and women of color are the faces of this ad campaign, and the tag line is "for women who love color" as opposed to "for women of color."

12. I am borrowing Michel Foucault's term from *Discipline and Punish*. Through tracing the "genealogy of history" of the penal system in the eighteenth century, Foucault reveals the coercive nature of modern society where discipline controls populations, which is the ultimate function of capitalism. Coercion occurs through bodily discipline: "policies of coercions . . . act upon the body, a calculated manipulation of its elements, its gestures, its behavior" (138).

13. V. Smith, "Reading the Intersection of Race and Gender in Narratives of Passing,"

57. For more on racial passing, see Ginsberg, *Passing and the Fictions of Identity*; and Wald, *Crossing the Line*.

14. Mr. Jay is so named to distinguish him from "Miss J.," J. Alexander, who occasionally sits on the judging panel and coaches the contestants on their runway walks and general deportment.

15. The safe appropriation of black gay culture, as seen in Mr. Jay's featured snaps, demonstrates how issues of post-identity have migrated across popular culture in the new millennium. In an identity-superscripted, as opposed to post-identity, moment, fifteen years ago, the scholar and filmmaker Marlon Riggs critiqued the blatantly racist and homophobic parodying of African American gay culture that happened in the late 1980s and early 1990s. In "Black Macho Revisited," Riggs writes that the "rank caricature" of the Snap! Queen creates a "persistent psychosocial impulse towards control, displacement, and marginalization of the Black Gay Other" instead of the Snap! signifying, among other things, a "symbol of communal expression and at times cultural defiance" (392, 393, 392).

16. Mr. Jay is Canadian, and is of Italian, Chech, Malaysian, and Dutch descent. See his website at http://www.jaymanuel.com.

17. L. Smith, "When the Plot Pushes Product."

18. Lovell, "The Message Becomes the Medium."

19. Cited in L. Smith, "When the Plot Pushes Product."

20. Quoted in ibid.

21. Quoted in Bosman, "A Match Made in Product Placement Heaven."

22. "Showtime Taps Penny Reiss in Newly Created Position of Vice President, Product Integration," PR *Newswire*, March 2, 2005; Lovell, "The Message Becomes the Medium."

23. See James, "In-Show Product Pushing Chided"; and Carvajal, "When Brands Join Cast, Plot Can Get Murky." A group from the Writers Guild of America, West, set up a (now defunct) website protesting stealth advertising (http://www.productinvasion.com/index.html). The homepage stated, "Infomercials Gone Mad! Will They Succeed in Turning Our Reality Shows into Infomercials? Stay Tuned!"

24. Schiller, "Newscasts Adopt Product Placement."

25. Kellner, *Television and the Crisis of Democracy*, 76.

26. Ibid.

27. I'm thinking here of the outcry over the fall 2006 season of the reality television show *Survivor*, where the "plot twist" entailed the dividing of teams by race. The racial-division plot prompted well-publicized protests by various forces, including the New York City councilman John Liu and the Hispanic Federation. See *Daily Variety*, "The Torches Are Lit: Protests to Push End of Survivor Race Divide," 7.

28. See Guglielmo and Salerno, *Are Italians White?*; and Roediger, *Working toward Whiteness*.

29. See D. White, *Aren't I a Woman?*; and Collins, *Black Feminist Thought*.

30. Deloria, *Playing Indian*.

31. Lest we think the race-switching theme was a one-off for Banks, in the fall of 2009 she repeated the theme, this time switching all of the contestants to multiracial identities. See *America's Next Top Model*, "Let's Go Surfing," episode no. 156, first

broadcast October 28, 2009, by The CW, directed by Allison Chase, and written by Tyra Banks, Kenya Barris, and Ken Mok.

32. Neither woman looks like popular images of civil rights workers. However, pre–Black Power civil rights workers often dressed up or dressed as middle class (which they were), which white onlookers found unexpected and safer. Middle-class-identity performance helped counter white racist notions of dirty, unappealing black people.

33. Although Gomez might not be first-generation multiracial and might not identify as mixed-race, I include her here with my reading of the two multiracial women because of the manner in which the show racializes her outside the "normal" poles of race and makes her answer the "what are you?" question.

34. Jacobson, *Roots Too*, 315. See also Lipsitz, *The Possessive Investment in Whiteness*; and Roediger, *Wages of Whiteness*.

35. Root, *The Multiracial Experience* and *Racially Mixed People in America*; and Jones, *Bulletproof Diva*.

36. Jordan and Wheedon, "The Celebration of Difference and the Cultural Politics of Racism," 150.

37. Aiello and Thurlow, "Symbolic Capitals," 154.

38. Douglas and Michaels, *The Mommy Myth*, 5.

39. While there is nothing new about commercialism's infiltration into childhood, the scope of marking to children has increased significantly. See Pugh, "Toys, Motherhood, and the Cultural Deal."

40. Lott, *Love and Theft*, 52.

41. I'm leaving out a mention of a number of gender-switch films from the 1980s to 2000s, both comedic and "message," and which bear many similarities and some differences. These include *Just One of the Guys* (1985), *Boys Don't Cry* (1999), *The Hot Chick* (2002), *White Chicks* (2004), and *She's the Man* (2006).

42. Brooks, "Tainted Love," 35.

43. C. Smith, *Enacting Others*, 15–16.

44. Ibid., 17.

45. Hall, "Minimal Selves," 117.

46. Hall, "New Ethnicities," 168.

47. Ibid.

48. Flores and Moon, "Rethinking Race, Revealing Dilemmas," 182.

49. See Crenshaw, "Mapping the Margins."

50. Aiello and Thurlow, "Symbolic Capitals," 149.

51. Stewart, "Tyra Banks."

52. See Sut Jhally, Johanna Hughes, and Stuart Hall, *Race: The Floating Signifier*, video-cassette, 85 minutes (Northhampton: Media Educational Foundation, 1996).

CONCLUSION: RACIST JOKES

1. Lusane, "Obama's Victory and the Myth of Post Raciality," 67.

2. See Connell, *Masculinities*; and Jackson Katz, "Masculinity of the Presidency and Sexism in Politics with Jackson Katz," radio broadcast, *The David Pakman Show*, February 14, 2011.

3. Neal, *New Black Man*, 29.

4. During the election campaign, Obama was affectionately teased for such characteristics by the *New York Times* columnist Maureen Dowd (Dowd, "May We Mock, Barack?").

5. Barack Obama, "Election Night Victory Speech," speech at Grant Park, Illinois, November 4, 2008 (available at http://obamaspeeches.com). It should not be a surprise that the media read his mixed-race into all manner of Obama's politics. For example, in an article in the *New York Times* on how Obama reads issues of race, class, and preference, or on who should benefit from affirmative action, Rachel L. Swarns writes, "Mr. Obama's biracial background in many ways makes him an ideal bridge between racial sensibilities" (Swarns, "If Elected . . . Delicate Obama Path on Race and Class Preferences").

6. Bogel, *Toms, Coons, Mulattoes, Mammies, and Bucks*.

7. I investigated the logical places where he might racialize himself for the public. These include his famous speeches at the 2004 and 2008 Democratic National Conventions, his speech after the Iowa caucus victory, his speech after the New Hampshire primary defeat, his Martin Luther King Day speech, and his speech about race in Philadelphia, as well as the introductions to his books.

8. In this article Obama connects running for president to change things for the better with his desire for change and "unyielding faith in the decency and generosity of the American people." Obama asserts that his ability to reach multiple and diverse interest groups "comes from [his] own American story." He continues, "I was raised with the help of a white grandfather . . . and a white grandmother. . . . I am married to a black American who carries within her the blood of slaves and slaveowners—an inheritance we pass on to our two precious daughters. I have brothers, sisters, nieces, nephews, uncles and cousins, of every race and every hue, scattered across three continents, and for as long as I live, I will never forget that in no other country on Earth is my story even possible (Obama, "Sacrifice for the Common Good," 4). There is such a degree of specificity here.

9. The two exceptions are in his two books: in *Dreams from My Father* he explains that he was given the opportunity to write his memoirs because he was the first "African American" editor of the *Harvard Law Review* (vii). In *The Audacity of Hope* he writes, "I am a prisoner of my own biography: I can't help but view the American experience through the lens of a black man of mixed heritage, forever mindful of how generations of people who looked like me were subjugated and stigmatized, and the subtle and not so subtle ways that race and class continue to shape our lives" (10). While all racialized subjects exhibit such contradictions, the manner in which mixed-race functions in the public sphere shines a light on these issues for multiracial subjects, who are assumed to be able to engage in racialized identity play more than monoracial people.

10. Obama, *Dreams from My Father*, xv.

11. Terrill, "Unity and Duality in Barack Obama's 'A More Perfect Union,'" 381.

12. Obama, *Dreams from My Father*, 100.

13. "Exit Polls: Election Results," *New York Times*, November 5, 2008, http://www.elections.nytimes.com/2008/results/president/exit-polls.html.

14. Squires, *Dispatches from the Color Line*.

15. *The Oprah Winfrey Show*, "Mariah Carey Talks to Biracial Teens," episode no. 126, first broadcast December 27, 1999, syndicated.

16. Chong, "'Look, an Asian!,'" 33.

17. As with "color blindness," when the term "post-race" is applied to Obama it is used to show that he can garner white votes.

18. Civil Rights Project and the Advancement Project, "Opportunities Suspended."

19. University of Michigan Documents Center, "Affirmative Action in College Admissions.

20. Schmidt, "Yale U. Opens an Orientation Program, Formerly for Minority Students Only, to All Freshmen."

21. Eljera, "Berkeley Group Hopes to Put Measure on 1998 Ballot."

22. Briscoe-Smith, "How to Talk with Kids about Race," 19.

23. Brooks, *Bodies in Dissent*, 5.

24. This is not to say that mixed-race Afro-alienation acts do not exist. Nevertheless, they have yet to seep into the mainstream narrative on multiracial blackness.

25. Bhabha, "Signs Taken for Wonders," 172.

26. Ibid., 173.

27. Ibid., 175.

28. Ibid., 177 (emphasis in the original).

29. Rosaldo, "Foreword," xi. Here Rosaldo is discussing the interplay of modernization and democratization, which precisely signify hybridity and colorblindness.

30. Ibid., xv.

31. Nyong'o, *The Amalgamation Waltz*, 175.

32. Sexton, *Amalgamation Schemes*, 156.

33. See the MAVIN Foundation's "About Us" page at http://www.mavinfoundation.org/about/mission.html (accessed March 26, 2011); and Critical Mixed Race Studies Conference, "Emerging Paradigms in Critical Mixed Race Studies," DePaul University, Chicago, Illinois, November 5–6, 2010, http://las.depaul.edu/aas/About/CMRSConference/index.asp.

34. Critical Mixed Race Studies Conference, "Emerging Paradigms in Critical Mixed Race Studies."

35. DaCosta, *Making Multiracials*, 34.

36. Hall, "Subjects in History," 299.

BIBLIOGRAPHY

=

Aiello, Georgia, and Crispin Thurlow. "Symbolic Capitals: Visual Discourse and Intercultural Exchange in the European Capital of Culture Scheme." *Language and Intercultural Communication* 6, no. 2 (2006): 148–62.

Alexander, Michelle. *The New Jim Crow: Mass Incarceration in the Age of Colorblindness.* New York: The New Press, 2010.

Almaguer, Tomás. *Racial Fault Lines: The Historical Origins of White Supremacy in California.* Berkeley: University of California Press, 1994.

Althusser, Louis. "Ideology and the Ideological State Apparatus." In Louis Althusser, *Lenin and Philosophy and Other Essays.* New York: Monthly Review Press, 1971.

Andrews, William L. "Miscegenation in the Late Nineteenth-Century American Novel." *Southern Humanities Review* 13, no. 1 (Winter 1979): 13–24.

Anzaldúa, Gloria. *Borderlands/La Frontera: The New Mestiza.* San Francisco: Spinsters/Aunt Lute Press, 1987.

Arias, Claudia M. Milian. "An Interview with Danzy Senna." *Callaloo* 25, no. 2 (2002): 447–52.

Asante, Molefi. *The Afrocentric Idea.* Philadelphia: Temple University Press, 1987.

Awkward, Michael. *Negotiating Difference: Race, Gender, and the Politics of Positionality.* Chicago: University of Chicago Press, 1994.

Baker, Lee. "Profit, Power, and Privilege: The Racial Politics of Ancestry." *Souls: A Critical Journal of Black Politics, Culture, and Society* 3, no. 4 (Fall 2001): 66–72.

Balibar, Etienne. "Is There a 'Neo-Racism?'" In Etienne Balibar and Immanuel Wallerstein, *Race, Nation, Class: Ambiguous Identities.* London: Verso, 1991.

Banet-Weiser, Sarah. *Kids Rule! Nickelodeon and Consumer Culture.* Durham: Duke University Press, 2007.

———. *The Most Beautiful Girl in the World: Beauty Pageants and National Identity.* Berkeley: University of California Press, 1999.

Barclay, Alex. "Festival's a Reel Thrill for Alison." *Royal Gazette*, May 8, 1998.

Barthes, Roland. "Introduction to the Structural Analysis of Narratives." In Roland Barthes, *Image-Music-Text*, translated by Stephen Heath. New York: Hill and Wang, 1977.

Bean, Frank, and Gillian Stevens. "Interracial Marriage by Racial Group and Race of Partner." In Frank Bean and Gillian Stevens, *America's Newcomers and the Dynamics of Diversity.* New York: Russell Sage Foundation, 2003.

Beech, Hannah. "Eurasian Invasion." *Time Asia*, April 23, 2001, 1.

Beirne, Rebecca. "Fashioning The L Word." *Nebula* 3, no. 4 (2006): 1–37.

Bellafante, Ginia. "Feminism: It's All about Me!" *Time*, June 29, 1998, 54–55.

Berlant, Lauren. "National Brands/National Body: *Imitation of Life*." In *The Phantom Public Sphere*, edited by Bruce Robbins. Minneapolis: University of Minnesota Press, 1993.

———. "The Queen of America Goes to Washington City: Harriet Jacobs, Frances Harper, Anita Hill." *American Literature* 65, no. 3 (September 1993): 549–74.

Berlin, Ira. *Slaves without Masters: The Free Negro in the Antebellum South*. New York: Pantheon Press, 1974.

Bernardi, Daniel. *The Birth of Whiteness: Race and the Emergence of U.S. Cinema*. New Brunswick, N.J.: Rutgers University Press, 1996.

Berzon, Judith R. *Neither White nor Black: The Mulatto Character in American Fiction*. New York: New York University Press, 1978.

Bhabha, Homi. "Signs Taken for Wonders: Questions of Ambivalence and Authority under a Tree Outside Delhi, May 1817." In *"Race," Writing, and Difference*, edited by Henry Louis Gates Jr. Chicago: University of Chicago Press, 1985.

Blassingame, John. *Black New Orleans: 1860–1880*. Chicago: University of Chicago Press, 1973.

Blumner, Robyn. "Here's a Radical Thought: If We Stop Obsessing on Race, People Might Actually Become Colorblind." *Jewish World Review*, December 7, 2000.

Bobo, Jacqueline. *Black Women as Cultural Readers*. New York: Columbia University Press, 1995.

Bogel, Donald. *Toms, Coons, Mulattoes, Mammies, and Bucks: An Interpretive History of Blacks in American Film*. New York: Continuum, 1990.

Bonilla-Silva, Eduardo. *Racism without Racists: Color-Blind Racism and the Persistence of Racial Inequality in the United States*. Lanham, Md.: Rowman and Littlefield Publishers, 2003.

Bosman, Julie. "A Match Made in Product Placement Heaven." *New York Times*, May 31, 2006.

Bost, Suzanne. *Mulattas and Mestizas: Representing Mixed Identities in the Americas, 1850–2000*. Athens: University of Georgia Press, 2003.

Boudreau, Brenda. "Letting the Body Speak: 'Becoming' White in *Caucasia*." *Modern Language Studies* 32, no. 1 (Spring 2003): 59–70.

Bowman, Elizabeth Atkins. "Black Like Who?" *Black Issues Book Review*, January 2001.

Bradford, Judith, and Crispin Sartwell. "Voiced Bodies/Embodies Voices." In *Race/Sex: Their Sameness, Difference, and Interplay*, edited by Naomi Zack. New York: Routledge, 1997.

Briggs, Charles. *Learning How to Ask: A Sociolinguistic Appraisal of the Role of the Interview in Social Science Research*. Cambridge, U.K.: Cambridge University Press, 1986.

Briscoe-Smith, Allison. "How to Talk with Kids about Race." In *Are We Born Racist?*, edited by Jason Marsh, Rodolfo Mendoza-Denton, and Jeremy Adam Smith. Boston: Beacon Press, 2010.

Brody, Jennifer Devere. *Impossible Purities: Blackness, Femininity, and Victorian Culture*. Durham: Duke University Press, 1998.

Brooks, Daphne. *Bodies in Dissent: Spectacular Performances of Race and Freedom, 1950–1910*. Durham: Duke University Press, 2006.

———. "Tainted Love." *The Nation*, September 29, 2008.

Brown, Frank. "Nixon's 'Southern Strategy' and Forces against Brown." *Journal of Negro Education* 73, no. 3 (2004): 191–208.

Brown, Michael, Martin Carnoy, Elliot Curie, Troy Duster, David Oppenheimer, Marjorie Shultz, and David Wellman. *Whitewashing Race: The Myth of a Color-Blind Society*. Berkeley: University of California Press, 2003.

Brunsdon, Charlotte. "Feminism, Postfeminism, Martha, Martha, and Nigella." *Cinema Journal* 44, no. 2 (2005): 110–16.

Brunsma, David L. *Mixed Messages: Multiracial Identites in the "Color-Blind" Era*. Boulder, Colo.: Lynne Rienner Publishers, 2006.

Bullock, Penelope. "The Mulatto in American Fiction." *Phylon* 6 (1945): 78–82.

Butler, Judith. *Gender Trouble: Feminism and the Subversion of Identity*. New York: Routledge, 1999.

———. "Lana's 'Imitation': Melodramatic Repetition and the Gender Performative." *Genders* no. 9 (Fall 1990): 1–18.

Carby, Hazel V. *Reconstructing Womanhood: The Emergence of the Afro-American Woman Novelist*. New York: Oxford University Press, 1987.

Card, Claudia. "The L Word and the F Word." *Hypatia* 21, no. 2 (2006): 223–29.

Cardwell, Diane. "Culture Zone: Crossing the Great Divide." *The New York Times Magazine*, June 21, 1998.

Carmichael, Stokeley, and Charles V. Hamilton. *Black Power: The Politics of Liberation in America*. New York: Vintage Books, 1967.

Carter, D. T. "The 'Southern Strategy.'" In *Civil Rights since 1787: A Reader on the Black Struggle*, edited by Jonathan Birnbaum and Clarence Taylor. New York: New York University Press, 2000.

Carvajal, Doreen. "When Brands Join Cast, Plot Can Get Murky." *International Herald Tribune Paris*, December 26, 2005.

Casey, Bernadette, Neil Casey, Ben Calvert, Liam French, and Justin Lewis. *Television Studies: The Key Concepts*. London: Routledge, 2002.

Cashman, Sean Dennis. *African-Americans and the Quest for Civil Rights, 1900–1990*. New York: New York University Press, 1991.

Ceccerelli, Leah. "Polysemy: Multiple Meanings in Rhetorical Criticism." *Quarterly Journal of Speech* 84, no. 4 (November 1998): 395–415.

Chambers, Jason. *Madison Avenue and the Color Line: African Americans in the Ad Industry*. Philadelphia: University of Pennsylvania Press, 2009.

Chaplin, Julia. "Rounding Up the L Girls." *New York Times*, January 11, 2004.

Chong, Sylvia. "'Look, an Asian!' The Politics of Racial Interpellation in the Wake of the Virginia Tech Shootings." *Journal of Asian American Studies* 11, no. 1 (February 2008): 33.

Christian, Barbara. *Black Women Novelists: The Development of a Tradition 1892–1976*. Westport, Conn.: Greenwood Press, 1980.

———. "The Race for Theory." *Feminist Studies* 14, no. 1 (1988): 67–80.

———. "What Celie Knows That You Should Know." In *Anatomy of Racism*, edited by David Theo Goldberg. Minneapolis: University of Minnesota Press, 1990.

Civil Rights Project and the Advancement Project. "Opportunities Suspended: The Devastating Consequences of Zero Tolerance and School Discipline Policies." Report from a National Summit on Zero Tolerance, June 1, 2000.

Clark, William Bedford. "The Serpent of Lust in the Southern Garden." *The Southern Review* 10, no. 4 (October 1974).

Clifford, James. *The Predicament of Culture: Twentieth-Century Ethnography, Literature, and Art*. Cambridge: Harvard University Press, 1988.

Collier, Peter, and David Horowitz. *The Race Card: White Guilt, Black Resentment, and the Assault on Truth and Justice*. Rocklin, Calif.: Prima Publications, 1997.

Collins, Patricia Hill. *Black Feminist Thought: Knowledge, Consciousness, and the Politics of Empowerment*. Boston: Unwin Hyman, 1990.

———. "Learning from the Outsider Within: The Sociological Significance of Black Feminist Thought." *Social Problems* 33, no. 6 (1986): s14–s32.

Connell, R. W. *Masculinities*. 2nd ed. Cambridge, U.K.: Polity Press, 2005.

Cooper, Anna Julia. "The Negro as Presented in American Literature." In *The Voice of Anna Julia Cooper*, edited by Charles Lemert and Esme Bhan. Lanham, Md.: Rowman and Littlefield Publishers, 1998.

Crenshaw, Kimberlé. *Critical Race Theory: The Key Writings That Formed the Movement*. New York: The New Press, 1995.

———. "Mapping the Margins: Intersectionality, Identity Politics, and Violence against Women of Color." *Stanford Law Review* 43, no. 6 (1991): 1241–99.

Cripps, Thomas. *Making Movies Black: The Hollywood Message Movie from World War II to the Civil Rights Era*. New York: Oxford University Press, 1993.

———. "The Reaction of the Negro to the Motion Picture *Birth of a Nation*." In *Focus on The Birth of a Nation*, edited by Fred Silva. Englewood Cliffs, N.J.: Prentice-Hall, 1971.

Cruse, Harold. *The Crisis of the Negro Intellectual: A Historical Analysis of the Failure of Black Leadership*. New York: Quill, 1967.

DaCosta, Kimberly McClain. *Making Multiracials: State, Family, and Market in the Redrawing of the Color Line*. Stanford: Stanford University Press, 2007.

Dagbovie, Sika Alaine. "Star-Light, Star-Bright, Star Damn Near White: Mixed-Race Superstars." *Journal of Popular Culture* 40, no. 2 (April 2007): 217–37.

Daily Variety. "The Torches Are Lit: Protests to Push End of Survivor Race Divide." August 28, 2006.

Daniel, G. Reginald. "Passers and Pluralists: Subverting the Racial Divide." *Racially Mixed People in America*, edited by Maria P. P. Root. Newbury Park, Calif.: Sage Publications, 1992.

Danquah, Meri Nana-Ama, ed. *Shaking the Tree: A Collection of New Fiction and Memoir by Black Women*. New York: W. W. Norton and Co., 2003.

Davis, F. James. *Who Is Black?* University Park: Pennsylvania State University Press, 1991.

Dei, George J. Sefa, Leeno Luke Karumanchery, and Nisha Karumanchery-Luik. *Playing the Race Card: Exposing White Power and Privilege*. New York: P. Lang, 2004.

De Klerk, Vivian. "Expletives: Men Only?" *Communication Monographs* 58, no. 2 (1991): 156–69.

Deloria, Philip J. *Playing Indian.* New Haven: Yale University Press, 1998.

Derricotte, Toi. *The Black Notebooks: An Interior Journey.* New York: W. W. Norton and Co., 1997.

Douglas, Mary. *Purity and Danger: An Analysis of the Concepts of Pollution and Taboo.* London: Routledge, 1966.

Douglas, Susan J. "Manufacturing Postfeminism." *AlterNet,* May 13, 2002.

Douglas, Susan J., and Meredith Michaels. *The Mommy Myth: The Idealization of Motherhood and How It Has Undermined All Women.* New York: Free Press, 2005.

Dowd, Maureen. "May We Mock, Barack?" *New York Times,* July 16, 2008.

Drake, St. Clair, and Horace R. Cayton. *Black Metropolis: A Study of Negro Life in a Northern City.* Chicago: University of Chicago Press, 1945.

D'Souza, Dinesh. *The End of Racism: Principles for a Multiracial Society.* New York: Free Press, 1995.

Du Bois, W. E. B., ed. *The Health and Physique of the Negro American.* Atlanta: Atlanta University Press, 1906.

———. *The Souls of Black Folk.* New York: Penguin Books, 1996.

duCille, Ann. *The Coupling Convention: Sex, Text, and Tradition in Black Women's Fiction.* Oxford: Oxford University Press, 1993.

Dunn, Stephane. *"Baad Bitches" and Sassy Supermamas: Black Power Action Films.* Urbana: University of Illinois Press, 2008.

Dyer, Richard. *Stars.* 2nd ed. London: British Film Institute, 1998.

———. *White.* London: Routledge, 1997.

Edwards, Kathryn. "Powell's 'River of Blood' Legacy." *BBC News,* April 18, 2008.

Eljera, Bert. "Berkeley Group Hopes to Put Measure on 1998 Ballot." *Asianweek,* December 4, 1997.

Ellis, Trey. "The New Black Aesthetic." *Callaloo* 12, no. 1 (Winter 1989).

Erndst, James. "'The L Word' Here Is Limelight: Private 'Flashdance' Star Returns with a Racy Showtime Series." *USA Today,* January 15, 2004.

Espiritu, Yen Le. *Asian American Women and Men: Labor, Laws, and Love.* Thousand Oaks, Calif.: Sage Publications, 1997.

Fanon, Franz. *Black Skin, White Masks.* New York: Grove Press, 2008.

Favor, J. Martin. *Authentic Blackness: The Folk in the New Negro Renaissance.* Durham: Duke University Press, 1999.

Featherstone, Mike. "Postmodernism and the Aestheticization of Everyday Life." In *Modernity and Identity,* edited by Scott Lash and Jonathan Friedman. Oxford, U.K.: Blackwell, 1992.

Fischer, Lucy, ed. *Imitation of Life.* New Brunswick, N.J.: Rutgers University Press, 1991.

Flanagan, Marion. "Movie Supplier Finds Success Catering to the Black Market." *Los Angeles Times,* June 4, 1998.

Flitterman-Lewis, Sandy. "Imitation(s) of Life: The Black Woman's Double Determination as 'Troubling Other.'" In *Imitation of life: Douglas Sirk, director,* edited by Lucy Fischer. New Brunswick, N.J.: Rutgers University Press, 1991.

Flores, Lisa, and Dreama Moon. "Rethinking Race, Revealing Dilemmas: Imagining a New Racial Subject in Race Traitor." *Western Journal of Communication* 66, no. 2 (Spring 2002): 181–207.

Ford, Richard T. *The Race Card: How Bluffing about Bias Makes Race Relations Worse*. New York: Farrar, Straus and Giroux, 2008.

Foreman, P. Gabrielle. "Who's Your Mama? 'White' Mulatta Genealogies, Early Photography, and Anti-Passing Narratives of Slavery and Freedom." *American Literary History* 14, no. 3 (2002): 505–39.

Foucault, Michel. *Discipline and Punish: The Birth of the Prison*. Translated by Alan Sheridan. New York: Vintage, 1977.

———. "Two Lectures." In Michel Foucault, *Power, Knowledge: Selected Interviews and Other Writings*, edited by Colin Gordon. New York: Pantheon, 1980.

Frankenberg, Ruth. *White Women, Race Matters: The Social Construction of Whiteness*. Minneapolis: University of Minnesota Press, 1993.

Funderburg, Lise. *Black, White, Other: Biracial Americans Talk about Race and Identity*. New York: William Morrow and Company, 1994.

Garber, Marjorie B. *Vested Interests: Cross Dressing and Cultural Anxiety*. New York: Routledge, 1997.

Genovese, Eugene D. *Roll, Jordan, Roll: The World the Slaves Made*. New York: Vintage Books, 1972.

Gerbner, George, and Larry Gross. "Living with Television: The Violence Profile." *Journal of Communication* 26, no. 2 (1976): 172–99.

Gibbs, Jewelle Taylor, and Alice M. Hines. "Negotiating Ethnic Identity: Issues for Black-White Biracial Adolescents" In *Racially Mixed People in America*, edited by Maria P. P. Root. Newbury Park, Calif.: Sage Publications, 1992.

Gibson-Hudson, Gloria. "The Ties That Bind: Cinematic Representations by Black Women Filmmakers." In *Black Women Film and Video Artists*, edited by Jacqueline Bobo. New York: Routledge, 1998.

Gilroy, Paul. *Against Race: Imagining Political Culture beyond the Color Line*. Cambridge: The Belknap Press of Harvard University Press, 2000.

Ginsberg, Elaine K. *Passing and the Fictions of Identity*. Durham: Duke University Press, 1996.

Gish, Lillian. "The Making of The Birth of a Nation." *Focus on The Birth of a Nation*, edited by Fred Silva. Englewood Cliffs: Prentice-Hall, Inc., 1971.

Givham, Robin. "Race on the Runway." *Seattle Times*, September 17, 2006.

Gladwell, Malcolm. "Lost in the Middle." In *Half and Half: Writers on Growing Up Biracial and Bicultural*, edited by Claudine Chiawei O'Hearn. New York: Pantheon Books, 1998.

Glazer, Nathan. "Reflections on Race, Hispanicity, and Ancestry in the U.S. Census." In *The New Race Question: How the Census Counts Multiracial Individuals*, edited by Joel Perlmann and Mary C. Waters. New York: Russell Sage Foundation, 2002.

Goodale, Gloria. "'House Divided' Breaks Down Realities of Race." *Christian Science Monitor*, July 28, 2000, 20.

Gordon, Avery F., and Christopher Newfield. "Introduction." In *Mapping Multiculturalism*, edited by Avery F. Gordon and Christopher Newfield. Minnesota: University of Minnesota Press, 1996.

Gossett, Thomas F. *Race: The History of an Idea in America*. New York: Oxford University Press, 1963.

Gotanda, Neil. "A Critique of 'Our Constitution Is Colorblind.'" In *Critical Race Theory: The Key Writings That Formed the Movement*, edited by Kimberlé Crenshaw, Neil Gotanda, Gary Peller, and Kendall Thomas. New York: The New Press, 1995.

Gray, Herman. "Black Masculinity and Visual Culture." *Callaloo* 18, no. 2 (1995): 401–5.

———. *Cultural Moves: African Americans and the Politics of Representation*. Berkeley: University of California Press, 2005.

———. *Watching Race: Television and the Struggle for "Blackness."* Minneapolis: University of Minnesota Press, 1995.

Grayson, Deborah. "Is It Fake? Black Women's Hair as Spectacle and Spec(tac)ular." *Camera Obscura: Feminism, Culture, and Media Studies* 12, no. 3 (September 1995): 12–31.

Gross, Larry. "The Ethics of Misrepresentation." In *Image Ethics: The Moral Rights of Subjects in Photograph, Film and Television*, edited by Larry Gross, John Stuart Katz, and Jay Ruby. Oxford: Oxford University Press.

Grossman, James R. "A Chance to Make Good, 1900–1929." In *To Make Our World Anew: A History of African Americans*, edited by Robin D. G. Kelley and Earl Lewis. Oxford: Oxford University Press, 2000.

Gubar, Susan. *Racechanges: White Skin, Black Face in American Culture*. Oxford: Oxford University Press, 2000.

Guerrero, Ed. *Framing Blackness: The African American Image in Film*. Philadelphia: Temple University Press, 1993.

Guglielmo, Jennifer, and Salvatore Salerno. *Are Italians White? How Race Is Made in America*. New York: Routledge, 2003.

Guinier, Lani, and Gerald Torres. *The Miner's Canary: Enlisting Race, Resisting Power, and Transforming Democracy*. Cambridge: Harvard University Press, 2003.

Hall, Stuart. "Cultural Identity and Cinematic Representation." In *Black British Cultural Studies: A Reader*, edited by Houston A. Baker Jr., Manthia Diawara, and Ruth H. Lindeborg. Chicago: University of Chicago Press, 1996.

———. "Cultural Identity and Diaspora." In *Theorizing Diaspora: A Reader*, edited by Jana Evans Braziel and Anita Mannur. Malden, Mass.: Blackwell Publishing, 2003.

———. "Encoding, Decoding." In *Cultural Studies Reader*, edited by Simon During. London: Routledge, 1993.

———. "Minimal Selves." In *Black British Cultural Studies: A Reader*, edited by Houston A. Baker Jr., Manthia Diawara, and Ruth H. Lindeborg. Chicago: University of Chicago Press, 1996.

———. "New Ethnicities." In *Black British Cultural Studies: A Reader*, edited by Houston A. Baker Jr., Manthia Diawara, and Ruth H. Lindeborg. Chicago: University of Chicago Press, 1996.

———. "Signification, Representation, Ideology: Althusser and the Post-Structuralist Debates." In *Critical Perspectives on Media and Society*, edited by R. Avery and D. Eason. New York: Guilford Press.

———. "Subjects in History: Making Diasporic Identities." In *The House That Race Built*, edited by Waheema Lubiano. New York: Vintage Books, 1998.

————. "What Is This 'Black' in Black Popular Culture?" In *Stuart Hall: Critical Dialogues in Cultural Studies*, edited by David Morley and Kuan-Hsing Chen. New York: Routledge, 1996.

————. "The Whites of Their Eyes." In *The Media Reader*, edited by Manuel Alvarado and John O. Thompson. London: British Film Institute, 1990.

————. "The Work of Representation." In *Representation: Cultural Representations and Signifying Practices*, edited by Stuart Hall. London: Sage Publications, 1997.

Hammonds, Evelynne M. "New Technologies of Race." *Processed Lives: Gender and Technology in Everyday Life*, edited by Jennifer Terry and Melody Calvert. New York: Routledge, 1997.

Harding, Vincent, Robin D. G. Kelly, and Earl Lewis. "We Changed the World, 1945–1970." In *To Make Our World Anew: A History of African Americans*, edited by Robin D. G. Kelly and Earl Lewis. Oxford: Oxford University Press, 2000.

Hardy, Ernest. "I, Too, Sing Hollywood: Four Women on Race, Art, and Making Movies." *LA Weekly*, October 20–26, 2000.

Harris, Cheryl. "Whiteness as Property." In *Critical Race Theory: The Key Writings That Formed the Movement*, edited by Kimberlé Crenshaw, Neil Gotanda, Gary Peller, and Kendall Thomas. New York: The New Press, 1995.

Harris, David R., and Jeremiah Joseph Sim. "Who Is Multiracial? Assessing the Complexity of Lived Race." *American Sociological Review* 67, no. 4 (2002): 614–27.

Hartman, Saidiya. *Scenes of Subjection: Terror, Slavery, and Self-Making in Nineteenth-Century America*. New York: Oxford University Press, 1997.

Hasinoff, Amy Adele. "Fashioning Race for the Free Market on *America's Next Top Model*." *Critical Studies in Media Communication* 25, no. 3 (2008): 324–43.

Henderson, Lisa. "How to Recognize a Lesbian: The Cultural Politics of Looking Like What You Are." *Signs: A Journal of Women in Culture and Society* 18, no. 4 (1993): 869.

————. "Simple Pleasures: Lesbian Community and *Go Fish*." *Signs: A Journal of Women in Culture and Society* 25, no. 1 (Autumn 1999), 37–64.

Heung, Marina. "'What's the Matter with Sarah Jane?' Daughters and Mothers in Douglas Sirk's *Imitation of Life*." In *Imitation of Life*, edited by Lucy Fischer. New Brunswick: Rutgers University Press, 1991.

Heyman, Kathryn. "Novel of the Week." *New Statesman*, December 18, 2000.

Hickman, Christine B. "The Devil and the One Drop Rule: Racial Categories, African Americans, and the U.S. Census." *Michigan Law Review* 95 (March 1997): 1161–265.

Hodes, Martha. *White Women, Black Men: Illicit Sex in the Nineteenth Century South*. New Haven: Yale University Press, 1997.

Hollinger, David. *Postethnic America: Beyond Multiculturalism*. New York: BasicBooks, 1995.

hooks, bell. *Black Looks: Race and Representation*. Boston: South End Press, 1992.

Horowitz, David. "American Apartheid." *Salon*, July 18, 1997.

Hudson, Lynn M. *The Making of "Mammy Pleasant": A Black Entrepreneur in Nineteenth-Century San Francisco*. Urbana: University of Illinois Press, 2003.

Hunt, Robert. "*Mixing Nia*, Written and Directed by Alison Swan." *Riverfront Times*, March 17–23, 1999.

Ibrahim, Habiba. "Toward Black and Multiracial 'Kinship' after 1997, or How a Race Man Became Cablinasian." Special issue, "The Politics of Biracialism," *The Black Scholar* 39, no. 3 (2009): 23–31.

Ifekwunigwe, Jayne O. *Scattered Belongings: Cultural Paradoxes of "Race," Nation and Gender*. London: Routledge, 1999.

Jacobs, Harriet A. *Incidents in the Life of a Slave Girl*, with an introduction by Valerie Smith. New York: Oxford University Press, 1990.

Jacobson, Matthew Frey. *Roots Too*. Cambridge: Harvard University Press, 2006.

James, Meg. "In-Show Product Pushing Chided: Writers Guild and SAG Say the Growing Practice of Placing Goods in TV Scripts Hurts Stories." *Los Angeles Times*, November 14, 2005.

Janusonis, Michael. "A Life without FLASH: Unpretentious Beals Is Just a Yalie." *Providence Journal*, August 18, 1985.

Jefferson, Margo. "Seeing Race as a Costume That Everyone Wears." *New York Times*, May 4, 1998.

Johnson, E. Patrick. *Appropriating Blackness: Performance and the Politics of Authenticity*. Durham: Duke University Press, 2003.

Johnson, Kevin R. *How Did You Get to Be Mexican? A White/Brown Man's Search for Identity*. Philadelphia: Temple University Press, 1999.

Johnson, Sally, and Ulrike Hanna Meinhof, eds. *Language and Masculinity*. Oxford: Blackwell Publishers, 1997.

Jones, Lisa. *Bulletproof Diva: Tales of Race, Sex, and Hair*. New York: Doubleday, 1994.

Jordan, Glenn, and Chris Wheedon. "The Celebration of Difference and the Cultural Politics of Racism." In *Theorizing Culture: An Interdisciplinary Critique after Postmodernism*, edited by Barbara Adam and Stuart Allan. London: UCL Press, 1995.

Jordan, Winthrop D. *White over Black: American Attitudes towards the Negro, 1550–1812*. Baltimore: Penguin Books, 1968.

Joseph, May. *Nomadic Identities: The Performance of Citizenship*. Minneapolis: University of Minnesota Press, 1999.

Joseph, Ralina L. "Tyra Banks Is Fat: Reading (Post-)Racism and (Post-)Feminism in the New Millennium." *Critical Studies in Media Communication* 26, no. 3 (2009): 237–54.

Kauanui, J. J. Kehaulani. *Hawaiian Blood: Colonialism and the Politics of Sovereignty and Indigeneity*. Durham: Duke University Press, 2008.

Kawai, Yuko. "Stereotyping Asian Americans: The Dialectic of the Model Minority and the Yellow Peril." *The Howard Journal of Communications* 16, no. 2 (2005): 109–30.

Kawash, Samira. "The Autobiography of an Ex-Colored Man: (Passing for) Black Passing for White." In *Passing and the Fictions of Identity*, edited by Elaine K. Ginsberg. Durham: Duke University Press, 1996.

Kelley, Robin. *Race Rebels: Culture, Politics, and the Black Working Class*. New York: The Free Press, 1994.

Kellner, Douglas. *Television and the Crisis of Democracy*. Boulder, Colo.: Westview Press, 1990.

Kennedy, Randall. *Interracial Intimacies: Sex, Marriage, Identity, and Adoption*. New York: Pantheon Books, 2003.

Kiesling, Scott Fabius. "From the 'Margins' to the 'Mainstream': Gender Identity and Fraternity Men's Discourse." *Women and Language* 20 (1997): 13–17.

Korgen, Kathleen Odell. *From Black to Biracial: Transforming Racial Identity among Americans*. Westport: Praeger, 1998.

Kort, Michele. "Power Lesbian." *Advocate*, July 18, 2006, 38–45.

Koshy, Susan. "Race in the Future Perfect Tense: The Age of Obama." Paper presented at the "Mixed Race in the Age of Obama" conference, Center for the Study of Race, Politics and Culture at the University of Chicago, Ill., March 5, 2010.

Larkin, Alile Sharon. "Black Women Film-Makers Defining Ourselves: Feminism in Our Own Voice." In *Female Spectators: Looking at Film and Television*, edited by E. Deidre Pribram. London: Verso, 1988.

Lee, Don. *Country of Origin*. New York: W. W. Norton and Co., 2004.

Lévi-Strauss, Claude. *Introduction to Marcel Mauss*. London: Routledge, 1987.

Lipsitz, George. *The Possessive Investment in Whiteness: How White People Profit from Identity Politics*. Philadelphia: Temple University Press, 1998.

———. *Time Passages: Collective Memory and American Popular Culture*. Minneapolis: University of Minnesota Press, 1990.

Locke, Alain. "American Literary Tradition and the Negro." *Modern Quarterly* 3, no. 3 (May–June 1916): 215–22.

Lott, Eric. *Love and Theft: Blackface Minstrelsy and the American Working Class*. New York: Oxford University Press, 1993.

Lovell, Glen. "The Message Becomes the Medium." *Ottawa Citizen*, May 28, 2005.

Lowe, Lisa. *Immigrant Acts: On Asian American Cultural Politics*. Durham: Duke University Press, 1996.

Lusane, Clarence. "Obama's Victory and the Myth of Post Raciality." In *Changing the Race: Racial Politics and the Election of Barack Obama*, edited by Lisa Burnham. Oakland, Calif.: Applied Research Center, 2009.

Mahtani, Minelle. "What's in a Name? Exploring the Employment of 'Mixed Race' as an Identification." *Ethnicities* 2, no. 4 (2002): 469–90.

Makalani, Minkah. "A Biracial Identity or a New Race? The Historical Limitations and Political Implications of a Biracial Identity." *Souls: A Critical Journal of Black Politics, Culture, and Society* 3, no. 4 (Fall 2001): 83–112.

Marable, Manning. *Race, Reform, and Rebellion: The Second Reconstruction in Black America, 1945–1990*. 2nd ed. Jackson: University of Mississippi Press, 1991.

Marcus, Erica. "A Role She Can Relate To." *Newsday*, July 30, 2000.

McCabe, Janet, and Kim Akass, "Prologue." In *Reading the L Word: Outing Contemporary Television*, edited by Janet McCabe, Kim Akass, and Sarah Warn. New York: I.B. Taurus and Company, 2006.

McRobbie, Angela. "Postfeminism and Popular Culture." *Feminist Media Studies* 4, no. 3 (2004): 255–64.

———. *The Uses of Cultural Studies*. Thousand Oaks, Calif.: Sage Publications, 2005.

Meehan, Eileen, Vincent Mosco, and Janet Wasko. "Rethinking Political Economy: Change and Continuity." *Journal of Communication* 43, no. 4 (Autumn 1993): 105–16.

Mencke, John G. *Mulattoes and Race Mixture: American Attitudes and Images, 1865–1918*. Washington, D.C.: UMI Research Press, 1976.

Mercer, Kobena. "Black Hair/Style Politics." In Kobena Mercer, *Welcome to the Jungle: New Positions in Black Cultural Studies*. New York: Routledge, 1994.

Merritt, Greg. *Celluloid Mavericks: The History of American Independent Film*. New York: Thunder's Mouth Press, 2000.

Miller, Toby. *Cultural Citizenship: Cosmopolitanism, Consumerism, and Television in a Golden Age*. Philadelphia: Temple University Press, 2006.

Millner, Michael. "Post Post-Identity." *American Quarterly* 57, no. 2 (June 2005): 541–54.

Mirza, Heidi Safia. "Transcendence over Diversity: Black Women in the Academy." *Policy Futures in Education* 4, no. 2 (2006): 101–13.

Moore, Candace. "Having It All Ways: The Tourist, the Traveler, and the Local in *The L Word*." *Cinema Journal* 46, no. 4 (Summer 2007): 3–23.

Moore, Frazier. "Jennifer Beals Returns for a New Season of 'The L Word.'" *Associated Press*, February 20, 2005.

Moran, Rachel F. *Interracial Intimacy: The Regulation of Race and Romance*. Chicago: University of Chicago Press, 2001.

Morning, Ann. "Multiracial Classification on the United States Census: Myth, Reality, and Future Impact." *Revue Européenne des Migrations Internationales* 21, no. 2 (2005): 111–34.

———. "New Faces, Old Faces: Counting the Multiracial Population Past and Present." In *New Faces in a Changing America: Multiracial Identity in the 21st Century*, edited by Loretta I. Winters and Herman L. DeBose. Thousand Oaks, Calif.: Sage Publications, 2003.

Morris, Charles E., III. "Pink Herring and the Fourth Persona: J. Edgar Hoover's Sex Crime Panic." *Quarterly Journal of Speech* 88, no. 2 (May 2002): 228–44.

Morrison, Toni. *Playing in the Dark: Whiteness and the Literary Imagination*. Cambridge: Harvard University Press, 1992.

Morse, Rob. "Kiss Me — I'm White." *San Francisco Chronicle*, March 13, 2001.

Mukherjee, Roopali. *The Racial Order of Things: Cultural Imaginaries of the Post-Soul Era*. Minneapolis: University of Minnesota Press, 2006.

Mulvey, Laura, and Jon Halliday, eds. *Douglas Sirk*. Edinburgh: Edinburgh Film Festival '72 in association with The National Film Theatre and John Player and Sons, 1972.

Muñoz, José Esteban. "Queer Minstrels for the Straight Eye: Race as Surplus in Gay TV." *GLQ: A Journal of Lesbian and Gay Studies* 11, no. 1 (2005): 101–2.

Naficy, Hamid. *The Making of Exile Cultures: Iranian Television in Los Angeles*. Minneapolis: University of Minnesota Press, 1993.

Nagle, Joane. *American Indian Ethnic Renewal: Red Power and the Resurgence of Identity and Culture*. New York: Oxford University Press, 1996.

Neal, Mark Anthony. *New Black Man*. New York: Routledge, 2005.

Negra, Diane, and Yvonne Tasker, eds. *Interrogating Postfeminism: Gender and the Politics of Popular Culture*. Durham: Duke University Press, 2007.

Neubeck, Kenneth J., and Noel A. Cazenave. *Welfare Racism: Playing the Race Card Against America's Poor*. New York: Routledge, 2001.

———. "Television and the Present Climate of Criticism." In *Television: A Critical View*, edited by Horace Newcomb. New York: Oxford University Press, 2007.

Ngai, Sianne. "Competitiveness: From 'Sula to Tyra.'" *Women's Studies Quarterly* 34, nos. 3–4 (2006): 107–39.

Nishime, LeiLani. "Guilty Pleasures: Keanu Reeves, Superman, and Racial Outing." In *East Main Street: Asian American Popular Culture*, edited by Shilpa Dave, LeiLani Nishime, and Tasha G. Oren. New York: New York University Press, 2005.

———. "The Mulatto Cyborg: Imagining a Multiracial Future." *Cinema Journal* 44, no. 2 (Winter 2005): 34–49.

Nyong'o, Tavia. *The Amalgamation Waltz: Race, Performance, and the Ruses of Memory*. Minneapolis: University of Minnesota Press, 2009.

———. "Queer TV: A Comment." *GLQ: A Journal of Lesbian and Gay Studies* 11, no. 1 (2005): 103–5.

Obama, Barack. *The Audacity of Hope: Thoughts on Reclaiming the American Dream*. New York: Crown Publishers, 2006.

———. *Dreams from My Father: A Story of Race and Inheritance*. New York: Three Rivers Press, 2004.

———. "Sacrifice for the Common Good." *Parade Magazine*, July 6, 2008.

———. "What Is Patriotism? Faith in One Another as Americans." *Parade Magazine*, July 1, 2008.

Odenwald, Dan. "Girls on Film: Showtime's L Word Is an Intriguing Lesbian Soap Opera." *Metro Weekly*, January 24, 2004.

Olumide, Jill. *Raiding the Gene Pool: The Social Construction of Mixed Race*. London: Pluto Press, 2002.

Omi, Michael. "Racialization in the Post–Civil Rights Era." In *Mapping Multiculturalism*, edited by Avery F. Gordon and Christopher Newfield. Minneapolis: University of Minnesota Press, 1996.

Omi, Michael, and Howard Winant. *Racial Formation in the United States: From the 1960s to the 1980s*. New York: Routledge, 1986.

Ono, Kent, and Derek Buescher. "Deciphering Pocahontas: Unpacking the Commodification of a Native American Woman." *Critical Studies in Media Communication* 18, no. 1 (2001): 23–43.

Oyewumi, Oyeronke. *The Invention of Women: Making an African Sense of Western Gender Discourses*. Minneapolis: University of Minnesota Press, 1997.

Packer, ZZ. *Drinking Coffee Elsewhere*. New York: Riverhead Books, 2003.

Paglia, Camille. *Sexual Personae. Art and Decadence from Nefertiti to Emily Dickinson*. New Haven: Yale University Press, 1990.

Palmer, J. Coyden. "A Diamond Waiting to Be Discovered." *Chicago State University Tempo*, September 9, 1998.

Palmer, Lindsay. "Gender as the Next Top Model of Global Consumer-Citizenship." *Genders*, no. 51 (2010).

Parker, David, and Miri Song, eds. *Rethinking Mixed Race*. London: Pluto Press, 2001.

Pascoe, Peggy. "Race, Gender, and the Privileges of Property: On the Significance of Miscegenation Law in the U.S. West." In *Over the Edge: Remapping the American West*, edited by Valerie Matsumoto and Blake Allmendinger. Berkeley: University of California Press, 1999.

Peck, Renee. "Daughter of Master and Slave: Biracial Actress Identifies with Role." *Plain Dealer* (Cleveland), July 30, 2000.

Perlmann, Joel, and Mary Waters, eds. *The New Race Question: How the Census Counts Multiracial Individuals*. New York: Russell Sage Foundation, 2002.

Piper, Adrian, "Passing for White, Passing for Black." In *Passing and the Fictions of Identity*, edited by Elaine K. Ginsberg. Durham: Duke University Press, 1996.

Post, Deborah W. "Cultural Inversion and the One-Drop Rule: An Essay on Biology, Racial Classification, and the Rhetoric of Racial Transcendence." *Albany Law Review* 72, no. 4 (2009): 909–28.

Postel, Danny. "Invisible Sister: Interview with Author Danzy Senna." *LiP Magazine*, August 1998.

PR *Newswire*. "Showtime Taps Penny Reiss in Newly Created Position of Vice President, Product Integration." March 2, 2005.

Pugh, Allison. "Toys, Motherhood, and the Cultural Deal." *Gender and Society* 19, no. 6 (December 2005): 729–49.

Raimon, Eve Allegra. *The "Tragic Mulatta" Revisited: Race and Nationalism in Nineteenth-Century Antislavery Fiction*. New Brunswick, N.J.: Rutgers University Press, 2004.

Reddy, Maureen T. *Crossing the Color Line: Race, Parenting, and Culture*. New Brunswick, N.J.: Rutgers University Press, 1994.

Reid, Mark. *Redefining Black Film*. Berkeley: University of California Press, 1993.

Remnick, David. *The Bridge: The Life and Rise of Barack Obama*. New York: Knopf, 2010.

Reuter, Edward. *The Mulatto in the United States*. New York: Negro Universities Press, 1918.

Rhodes, Jane. "Fanning the Flames of Racial Discord: The National Press and the Black Party." *The Harvard International Journal of Press Politics* 4, no. 4 (1999): 95–118.

————. *Framing the Black Panthers: The Spectacular Rise of Black Power Icon*. New York: The New Press, 2006.

Richardson, Marilyn. "Caucasia." *The Women's Review of Books*, July 1998.

Riggs, Marlon T. "Black Macho Revisited: Reflections of a Snap! Queen." *Black American Literature Forum* 25, no. 2 (1991): 389–94.

Roberts, Tara. "Independents' Day: Black Women behind the Camera Are Fighting to Tell Our Stories. A Few You Should Know—And How You Can Help." *Essence*, September 1998.

Robinson, Amy. "It Takes One to Know One: Passing and Communities of Common Interest." *Critical Inquiry* 20, no. 4 (Summer 1994): 715–36.

Rodriguez, Richard. *Brown: The Last Discovery of America*. New York: Viking, 2002.

————. *Days of Obligation: An Argument with My Mexican Father*. New York: Viking, 2002.

————. *Hunger of Memory: The Education of Richard Rodriguez; An Autobiography*. Boston: D. R. Godine, 1982.

Roediger, David R. *The Wages of Whiteness: Race and the Making of the American Working Class*. London: Verso, 1991.

————. *Working towards Whiteness: How America's Immigrants Became White; The Strange Journey from Ellis Island to the Suburbs*. New York: Basic Books, 2005.

Roiphe, Katie. *The Morning After: Sex, Fear, and Feminism on Campus*. Boston: Little, Brown, 1993.

Root, Maria. "The Biracial Baby Boom: Understanding Ecological Constructions of Racial Identity in the 21st Century." In *Racial and Ethnic Identity in School Practices: Aspects of Development*, edited by Rosa Hernández-Sheets and Etta R. Hollins. Mahwah, N.J.: Lawrence Erlbaum Associates Publishers, 1999.

————. "Mixed-Race Women." In *Race/Sex: Their Sameness, Difference, and Interplay*, edited by Naomi Zack. New York: Routledge, 1997.

————, ed. *The Multiracial Experience*. Thousand Oaks, Calif.: Sage Publications, 1996.

————, ed. *Racially Mixed People in America*. Newbury Park, Calif.: Sage Publications, 1992.

Rosaldo, Renato. "Forward." In Nestor Garcia Canclini, *Hybrid Cultures: Strategies for Entering and Leaving Modernity*. Minneapolis: University of Minnesota Press, 1995.

Rose, Tricia. *Black Noise: Rap Music and Black Culture in Contemporary America*. Hanover, N.H.: University Press of New England, 1994.

Saks, Eva. "Representing Miscegenation Law." *Raritan* 8, no. 2 (Fall 1988): 39–69.

Salamon, Julie. "Big House on the Plantation Has a Family Secret." *New York Times*, July 28, 2000.

Saulny, Susan. "Black? White? Asian? More Young Americans Choose All of the Above." *New York Times*, January 30, 2011, A1.

Schiller, Gail. "Newscasts Adopt Product Placement." *National Post*, March 17, 2006.

Schmidt, Peter. "Yale U. Opens an Orientation Program, Formerly for Minority Students Only, to All Freshmen." *The Chronicle of Higher Education*, February 25, 2004.

Schmitt, Eric. "Multiracial Identification Might Affect Programs." *New York Times*, March 14, 2001.

Scott, Joan Wallach. *Gender and the Politics of History*. New York: Columbia University Press, 1988.

Seaman, Donna. "*Caucasia*." *Booklist*, February 15, 1998.

Sedgwick, Eve Kosofsky. "Foreword: The Letter L." In *Reading the L Word: Outing Contemporary Television*, edited by Kim Akass and Janet McCabe. New York: I.B. Taurus and Company, 2006.

Sender, Katherine. "Selling Sexual Subjectivities: Audience Response to Gay Window Advertising." *Critical Studies in Mass Communication* 16, no. 2 (1999): 172–96.

Senna, Danzy. "Are You Experienced?" In *Gumbo: An Anthology of African American Writing*, edited by Marita Golden and E. Lynn Harris. New York: Harlem Moon, 2002.

————. "The Body of Luce Rivera." In *Shaking the Tree: A Collection of New Fiction and Memoir by Black Women*, edited by Meri Nana-Ama Danquah. New York: W. W. Norton and Co., 2003.

————. *Caucasia*. New York: Riverhead Books, 1998.

————. "The Mulatto Millennium." In *Half and Half: Writers on Growing Up Biracial and Bicultural*, edited by Claudine Chiawei O'Hearn. New York: Pantheon Books, 1998.

————. *Where Did You Sleep Last Night?* New York: Farrar, Strauss, and Giroux, 2009.

Sexton, Jared. *Amalgamation Schemes: Antiblackness and the Critique of Multiracialism*. Minneapolis: University of Minnesota Press, 2008.

Shapiro, Laura. "*Caucasia.*" *Newsweek*, February 16, 1998.

Shohat, Ella, and Robert Stam, eds. *Multiculturalism, Postcoloniality, and Transnational Media*. New Brunswick, N.J.: Rutgers University Press, 2003.

Shrage, Laurie. "Passing beyond the Other Race or Sex." In *Race/Sex: Their Sameness, Difference, and Interplay*, edited by Naomi Zack. New York: Routledge, 1997.

Silva, Fred. *Focus on* The Birth of a Nation. Englewood Cliffs, N.J.: Prentice Hall, 1971.

Singh, Nikhil Pal. *Black Is a Country: Race and the Unfinished Struggle for Democracy*. Cambridge: Harvard University Press, 2004.

Sirk, Douglas, and Jon Halliday. *Sirk on Sirk: Interviews with Jon Halliday*. New York: Viking Press, 1972.

Small, Stephen. "Discursive Terrains and Institutional Domains: Engaging the 'Mixed Race Movement' in the United States." Unpublished manuscript, University of California, Berkeley.

Smith, Cherise. *Enacting Others: Politics of Identity in Eleanor Antin, Nikki S. Lee, Adrian Piper, and Anna Deavere Smith*. Durham: Duke University Press, 2011.

Smith, Lynn. "When the Plot Pushes Product." *Los Angeles Times*, February 12, 2006.

Smith, Sidonie, and Julia Watson, eds. "Introduction." In *Women, Autobiography, Theory: A Reader*. Madison: University of Wisconsin Press, 1998.

Smith, Valerie. "From 'Race' to Race Transcendence: 'Race,' Writing, and Difference Twenty Years Later." PMLA: *Publications of the Modern Language Association of America* 123, no. 5 (2008): 1528–33.

———. "Introduction." In Harriet A. Jacobs, *Incidents in the Life of a Slave Girl*. New York: Oxford University Press, 1990.

———. *Not Just Race, Not Just Gender: Black Feminist Readings*. New York: Routledge, 1998.

———. "Reading the Intersection of Race and Gender in Narratives of Passing." *Diacritics* 24, no. 2–3 (1994): 43–57.

Sollors, Werner. *Neither Black nor White yet Both: Thematic Explorations of Interracial Literature*. New York: Oxford University Press, 1997.

Somerville, Siobham B. *Queering the Color Line: Race and the Invention of Homosexuality in American Culture*. Durham: Duke University Press, 2000.

Spencer, Jon Michael. *The New Colored People: The Mixed-Race Movement in America*. New York: New York University Press, 1997.

Spencer, Rainier. *Spurious Issues: Race and Multiracial Identity Politics in the United States*. Boulder, Colo.: Westview Press, 1999.

Spickard, Paul R. *Mixed Blood: Intermarriage and Ethnic Identity in Twentieth-Century America*. Wisconsin: University of Wisconsin Press, 1989.

———. "Obama Nation? Race, Multiraciality and American Identity." Paper presented at the Mixed Race in the Age of Obama conference, Center for the Study of Race, Politics and Culture at the University of Chicago, Ill., March 5, 2010.

———. "The Subject Is Mixed Race: The Boom in Biracial Biography." In *Rethinking 'Mixed Race,'* edited by David Parker and Miri Song. London: Pluto Press, 2001.

Spillers, Hortense. "Mama's Baby, Papa's Maybe: An American Grammar Book." *Diacritics* 17, no. 2 (1987): 64–81.

———. "Notes on an Alternative Model—Neither/Nor." In *The Difference Within: Feminism and Critical Theory*, edited by Elizabeth Meese and Alice Parker. Amsterdam: J. Benjamins Publishing Company, 1989.

Springer, Kimberly. "Divas, Evil Black Bitches, and Bitter Black Women." In *Interrogating Postfeminism*, edited by Yvonne Tasker and Dionne Negra. Durham: Duke University Press, 2007.

———. "Third Wave Black Feminism?" *Signs: Journal of Women in Culture and Society* 27, no. 4 (2002): 1059–82.

Squires, Catherine R. *African Americans and the Media*. Cambridge, U.K.: Polity, 2009.

———. *Dispatches from the Color Line: The Press and Multiracial America*. Albany, N.Y.: suny Press, 2007.

Steinberg, Stephen. *The Ethnic Myth: Race, Ethnicity and Class in America*. New York: W. W. Norton and Co., 1999.

Stern, Michael. "*Imitation of Life*." In *Imitation of Life*, edited by Lucy Fischer. New Brunswick, N.J.: Rutgers University Press, 1991.

Sternbergh, Adam. "Back in a Flash." *New York Magazine*, February 21, 2005: 63–64.

Stewart, Pearl. "Tyra Banks: It All Began Right Here." *Black Collegian Online*, February 2010.

Stonequist, Everett V. *The Marginal Man: A Study in Personality and Culture Conflict*. New York: Charles Scribner's Sons, 1937.

Streeter, Caroline. "The Hazards of Visibility: 'Biracial' Women, Media Images, and Narratives of Identity." In *New Faces in a Changing America*, edited by Loretta I. Winters and Herman L. DeBose. Thousand Oaks, Calif.: Sage Publications, 2003.

Swarns, Rachel L. "If Elected . . . Delicate Obama Path on Race and Class Preferences." *New York Times*, August 3, 2008.

Talty, Steven. *Mulatto America at the Crossroads of Black and White Culture: A Social History*. New York: HarperCollins Publishers, 2003.

Terrill, Robert E. "Unity and Duality in Barack Obama's 'A More Perfect Union.'" *Quarterly Journal of Speech* 95, no. 4 (2009): 363–86.

Tesler, Michael, and David O. Sears. *The 2008 Election and the Dream of a Post-Racial America*. Chicago: University of Chicago Press, 2010.

Thomas, Cal. "America Doesn't Need Racial Labels." *Holland Sentinel*, December 9, 1997.

Thomas, June. "Women's Work: The L Word Locates America's G Spot." *Slate*, March 22, 2007.

Thompson, Beverly Yuen. "Fence Sitters, Switch Hitters, and Bi-Bi Girls: An Exploration of *Hapa* and Bisexual Identities." *Frontiers* 21 nos. 1/2 (2000): 171–80.

Thompson, Mary. "Learn Something from This!" *Feminist Media Studies* 10, no. 3 (2010): 335–52.

Thurman, Judith. *Secrets of the Flesh: A Life of Colette*. New York: Ballentine Books, 1999.

Trotter, Joe William, Jr. "From a Raw Deal to a New Deal? 1929–1945." In *To Make Our World Anew: A History of African Americans*, edited by Robin D. G. Kelley and Earl Lewis. Oxford: Oxford University Press, 2000.

Tucker, Neely. "Loving Day Recalls a Time When the Union of a Man and a Woman Was Banned." *Washington Post*, June 13, 2006, c01.

Turner, Graeme. *Understanding Celebrity*. London: Sage Publications, 2004.

University of Michigan Documents Center. "Affirmative Action in College Admissions: *Gratch and Hamacher/Grutter v. The Regents of the University of Michigan (1999)*."

Vaucher, Andrea. "Showtime's 'House' of a Different Color; for Cast Members, Tale of Mulatto's Plight Hit Close to Home." *Washington Post*, July 30, 2000.

Voss, Karen. "Replacing L.A.: Mi Familia, Devil in a Blue Dress, and Screening the Other Los Angeles." *Wide Angle: A Film Quarterly of Theory, Criticism, and Practice* 20, no. 3 (1998): 156–81.

Wald, Gayle. *Crossing the Line: Racial Passing in Twentieth-Century U.S. Literature and Culture*. Durham: Duke University Press, 2000.

Walker, Rebecca. *Black, White, and Jewish: Autobiography of a Shifting Self*. New York: Riverhead Books, 2001.

———, ed. *To Be Real: Telling the Truth and Changing the Face of Feminism*. New York: Anchor Books, 1995.

Wallace, Michele. *Black Macho and the Myth of the Superwoman*. London: Verso, 1978.

Wardel, Francis. "Helping Multiracial and Multiethnic Children Escape No Man's Land." *National PTA* 25, no. 5 (2000).

Warn, Sarah. "Introduction." In *Reading the L Word: Outing Contemporary Television*, edited by Janet McCabe, Kim Akass, and Sarah Warn. New York: I.B. Taurus and Company, 2006.

———. "Radical Acts: Biracial Visibility and The L Word." In *Reading the L Word: Outing Contemporary Television*, edited by Janet McCabe, Kim Akass, and Sarah Warn. New York: I.B. Taurus and Company, 2006.

Waters, Mary. *Ethnic Options: Choosing Identities in America*. Berkeley: University of California Press, 1990.

———. "Optional Ethnicities: For Whites Only?" In *Origins and Destinies: Immigration, Race, and Ethnicity in America*, edited by Sylvia Pedraza and Ruben G. Rumbaut. Belmont: Wadsworth, 1996.

White, Deborah Gray. *Aren't I a Woman? Female Slaves in the Plantation South*. New York: W. W. Norton and Co., 1999.

White, E. Frances. *Dark Continent of Our Bodies: Black Feminism and the Politics of Respectability*. Philadelphia: Temple University Press, 2001.

———. *Mark One or More: Civil Rights in Multiracial America*. Ann Arbor: University of Michigan Press, 2006.

Williams, Linda. *Hard Core: Power, Pleasure, and the "Frenzy of the Visible."* Berkeley: University of California Press, 1989.

———. *Playing the Race Card: Melodramas of Black and White from Uncle Tom to O.J. Simpson*. Princeton: Princeton University Press, 2001.

Williamson, Joel. *New People: Miscegenation and Mulattoes in the United States*. New York: The Free Press, 1980.

Winters, Lisa Ze. "'More Desultory and Unconnected Than Any Other': Geography, Desire, and Freedom in Eliza Potter's *A Hairdresser's Experience in High Life*." *American Quarterly* 63, no. 3 (2009): 455–75.

Wolf, Naomi. *Fire with Fire: The New Female Power and How It Will Change the 21st Century*. New York: Random House, 1993.

————. *Promiscuities: The Secret Struggle for Womanhood*. New York: Random House, 1997.

Wolfe, Susan, and Lee Ann Roripaugh. "The (In)Visible Lesbian: Anxieties of Representation on The L Word." In *Reading the L Word: Outing Contemporary Television*, edited by Janet McCabe, Kim Akass, and Sarah Warn. New York: I.B. Taurus and Company, 2006.

Wyatt, Edward. "Wanda Sykes Has a Show (or So They Tell Her)." *New York Times*, November 7, 2009, C1.

Yu, Henry. "Tiger Woods Is Not the End of History: Or, Why Sex across the Color Line Won't Save Us All." *The American Historical Review* 108, no. 5 (December 2003): 1406–14.

Zack, Naomi, ed. *American Mixed Race: The Culture of Microdiversity*. Lantham, Md.: Rowman and Littlefield Publishers, 1995.

————. "Introduction." In *Race/Sex: Their Sameness, Difference, and Interplay*, edited by Naomi Zack. New York: Routledge, 1997.

Zanger, Jules. "The 'Tragic Octoroon' in Pre-Civil War Fiction." *American Quarterly* 19 (1966): 63–70.

Zook, Krystal Brent. *Color by Fox: The Fox Network and the Revolution in Black Television*. New York: Oxford University Press, 1999.

128, 137, 141, 143, 145, 152; color-blind racism and, 26; critique of post-race/feminism and, 27; Danzy Senna as, 82, 89; in dialectic with new millennium multiracial, 4; dismissing of the black voice by, 22; essentialism and, 21; as floating signifiers, 26; Jennifer Beals's as, 65; *Loving vs. Virginia* and, 22; mixed-raced blackness and, 5; in *Mixing Nia*, 96, 98, 100, 104, 117, 123; neo-racism and, 27; Obama as, 157–63, 165; racial transcendence and, 126; representational ubiquity of as cause of racist jokes, 157; selling of, 129; texts and media exploring, 6; transcending blackness and, 20, 104; Tyra Banks as, 125–28, 147; via makeup, 131; white liberal racism and, 155–57

Femininity, 69, 81–82
Feminism: black feminism, 68, 71; victim versus power, 28. *See also* Postfeminism
Film, universal, 120–21
Floating signifiers, 26

Gender, 20–21, 148–49; masculinity of Barack Obama and, 121, 158–60; mixed-race African American women characters and, 169; race and, 4–5, 27–28, 34, 69, 71, 74–75, 79; representations and, 3; stereotypes of, 98. *See also* Postfeminism
Gendered performance: of Barack and Michelle Obama, 158–59; by Birdie in *Caucasia*, 28, 69–71, 79, 83–85, 88–89; on *Oprah Winfrey Show*, 164; transcending blackness and, 4
Gingrich, Newt, 24–25
Got Milk? ad on *America's Next Top Model*, 129, 133, 135, 137, 144
Grier, Pam, 37

Hair, 74–75, 97, 104–13, 123; race switching on *America's Next Top Model* and, 135, 137
Hall, Stuart, 22, 33, 65, 110–11, 171; defini-

tion of representation by, 3; on identity, 90–91, 149
History, 5, 150, 157, 170–71; passing and, 72
Hopeful representations of multiraciality, 22–23
Horowitz, David, 43–44, 119
Hybrid constructions of blackness, 4, 31, 114, 167, 169–70; degenerate constructions, 13, 22–24
Hypodescent, 2, 31, 90

Identity, 90–91; versus identifications, 34; identity masquerades, 149–50. *See also* Racialized identity
Imitation of Life (film), 17–19, 97–100
Interracial relationships, 47–48, 55–57, 81, 99, 165; marriage, 19–20; in *Mixing Nia*, 104, 112–14, 120
Invisibility, 72, 77–80
Italians: Birdie as, 76–78, 134; as unexceptional multiracials in *America's Next Top Model*, 134

Jim Crow racism, 2
Judaism, 96, 115

Kohner, Susan, 17–18

Liberal racism, 155–57
Lott, Eric, 148, 150
Loving v. Virginia (1967), 20, 22–23
The L Word (TV show), 31, 37, 40, 47–48, 60, 169; actors of color on, 45, 58; intra–African American dynamics of race on, 59; lesbian representation on, 60–61; "mulatta gal" episode, 38–39; race card on, 40, 42, 44–45, 50–54, 57, 60–61; race and gender as disturbing forces in, 169; scenes of race, reproduction, and multiraciality in, 50–54; still from, 39. *See also* Beals, Jennifer; Porter, Bette
Lydia (film character from *Birth of a Nation*), 14–17, 99–100, 103

Make-up, 130–33, 133, 152, 154
Marginal man constructions, 24

representations of as symbol of post-race and feminism, 167; resonance with non-black public and, 158; sexuality and, 33, 98–99; Tyra Banks as, 125. *See also America's Next Top Model*; Beals, Jennifer; Carey, Mariah; *Caucasia*; *The L Word*; *Mixing Nia*; Porter, Bette; Senna, Danzy; Tragic mulatta

Muñoz, José Esteban, 45

Names, racialization of, 79–80

Negro, as terminology, 9

Neoconservatism, 22–25, 45, 167

Neoliberal citizenship, 5, 24; on *The L Word*, 45, 50

Neo-racism, 27

New Black Aesthetic, 31

New millennium mulatta, 6–7, 11, 22, 31, 72; Bette Porter as, 40, 47, 57, 62–63, 67; Birdie in *Caucasia* and, 32, 67, 71–72, 76, 91; black transcendence and, 31, 57; genealogy of, 20–28; isolation of, 4; Mariah Carey as, 163–65; *Mixing Nia* and, 96, 98, 119, 123; versus mulattaroons, 90–91; Obama's divergence from rules of, 165; punishing of, 62–63; race card as mark of, 41–45, 50; stereotype of, 4–5; tragic mulatta and, 20, 40; volitional engagement with race and, 57, 123. *See also* Bad race girl; Sad race girl; Tragic mulatta

New Momism, 147

New People: Miscegenation and Mulattoes in the United States (Williamson), 23

Obama, Barack, 1–2, 8–9, 31, 83, 157–60; *Dreams from My Father: A Story of Race and Inheritance* and, 1, 160–63; maleness of, 121, 158–60; versus Mariah Carey, 163, 165; new racialized terminology and, 165; post-racialism of, 5, 158, 163, 166

Obama, Michelle, 159

Omi, Michael, 46–47

One-drop rule, 2, 10, 72

The Oprah Winfrey Show, 163–64

Optional ethnicity, 27, 83

Parsons, Karyn, 96, 117

Passing. *See* Racial passing

Performance of race. *See* Racialized performance

Plessy v. Ferguson (1896), 13–14

Popular culture, 3, 28; blackface minstrelsy and racial masquerade in, 148–49; maternity in, 147

Porter, Bette (TV character played by Jennifer Beals), 38–39, 45–46, 50, 59, 65–66; as "bad" race girl, 31, 39, 67; lesbian representation of, 60–61; as new millennium mulatta, 40, 47, 57, 62–63, 67; politics of opacity and, 46; as a privileged superwoman, 40, 46–49, 66; punishment of, 38, 40, 49, 55, 62–63, 66, 68; relationship with Tina and, 47–48, 55–57; reproduction and race and, 49–54, 58; sexual passing of, 60; stills of, 37, 56; whiteness and, 55–57. *See also* Beals, Jennifer; *The L Word*

Post-feminism, 26–28, 33–34, 167; as commodity on *America's Next Top Model*, 132; defined, 28; maternity in popular culture and, 147; in *Mixing Nia*, 110–11, 116; new momism and, 147; sexuality and, 27

Post-modernism, 144

Post-racialism, 26–28, 33–34, 167–69; in *America's Next Top Model*, 128–29, 132, 135, 137, 141, 143, 147–49; anti-affirmative action measures and, 168; author's personal experience of, 156; in *Caucasia*, 70, 83, 85–86; celebrating of mixed-race and, 86; cognitive dissonance of for children, 168; as commodity, 132; erasing the mixed-race of multiracial backgrounds, 168; exceptional multiracials and, 4, 26; as imagined, 168; in *The L Word*, 40, 45; in *Mixing Nia*, 96–97, 110, 114; as neoliberal/conservative fantasy, 167; Obama and, 5, 158, 163, 166; terminology and definition of, 165–66; transcending blackness trope and, 6

Product placement, 131–32

Proposition 209, 25, 166, 168

Punishment, 18, 31, 66, 68, 75; of Bette
Porter on *The L Word*, 38, 40, 49, 55,
62–63

Race, 6, 24–25, 170; additive race model,
24; on *America's Next Top Model*, 128–
29, 143–44, 149–50, 154; appropriate
iterations of for mixed-race African
American women characters, 169;
cognitive dissonance of not discussing for children, 168; commodification
of, 33, 126, 128–29, 135, 137, 143, 145;
culture and, 3, 144; empty diversity
practices in popular culture and, 166;
versus ethnicity, 134; fluid and flexible, 10, 26, 30, 33, 106, 149, 151, 153,
161–63; gender and, 4, 34, 121; intra–
African American dynamics of, 59; on
The L Word, 39–40, 44–47, 60; as material reality and social construction,
10; in *Mixing Nia*, 95–96; new millennium mulatta and, 57, 123; Obama and,
157–63; power dynamics and, 23; race
baiting, 41–42; race-based measures,
24–25, 27, 123; racial chameleonism,
77–78; racialized terminology and, 3,
7–10, 165–66; racial paradox, 151; representations and, 3; U.S. census and,
13; What are you? question on, 143. *See
also* Post-racialism

Race card, 66; contextualized, 41; in *The
L Word*, 40, 42, 44–45, 50–54, 57,
59–61; as mark of new millennium
mulatta, 41–45, 50; in trial of O. J.
Simpson, 42–43

Race girl, 6, 11, 20, 31–32; bad race girl in
The L Word, 6, 38–39, 67; sad race girl
in *Caucasia*, 6, 67, 69–71, 82, 89–91

Race switching and racial masquerade, 26,
126–28, 130, 133–36, 145, 153; biracial,
137, 140; blackface minstrelsy, 133,
148–49; black to Korean and Native
American, 135, 137–39; children and,
144–47; CoverGirl makeup and, 152;
gender and sexual identity and, 133,
151, 169; as identity masquerades,
149–50; mixed-race African Ameri-

can to white Scandinavian, 142–43;
post-racialism and feminism as commodity on, 132; racial ambiguity and,
140; racialized performance on, 129;
racial paradox on, 151; regressive and
transgressive nature of, 148–49, 151; as
trend in popular culture, 149; whiteness and, 140; white to African American, 135–36

Racial inequalities, 21, 24–25, 44;
America's Next Top Model failure to
convey, 144, 148, 151–54; in *Mixing
Nia*, 103, 117, 123, 148–49; white/black
divide in, 28–30

Racialized beauty, 21–22, 34, 75, 152; in reviews of *Caucasia*, 85

Racialized identity, 20, 31–33; on *America's
Next Top Model*, 141, 143, 149; of Bette
in *The L Word*, 38–40, 46–47, 50,
55–59, 61; of Birdie in *Caucasia*, 69,
79, 90–91; in *Mixing Nia*, 95–97, 99,
102–4, 111, 113–15

Racialized performance, 4, 32–33, 152;
in *America's Next Top Model*, 128–30,
135, 137, 148, 152, 168–69; in *Caucasia*,
69–74, 89–91; in *Mixing Nia*, 168–69;
on *Oprah Winfrey Show*, 164; transcending blackness and, 4

Racialized transformations, 20, 128, 130,
133–34; in *Caucasia*, 72–73. *See also*
Race switching and racial masquerade

Racially Mixed People in America (ed. Root),
9, 24, 63

Racial passing, 26, 58, 60–62, 70, 72–74,
76–78; on *America's Next Top Model*,
141; of Birdie in *Caucasia*, 32, 67–81,
89–90; historic passing of Jim Crow
era, 72; on *The L Word*, 58–61; novels
of, 70–71; "triangular theater" of, 59

Racial transcendence, 126, 128, 145, 148.
See also Transcending blackness

Racism, 6, 14–15, 27, 155–56, 170–71; anti-
black, 6–7, 27, 30, 158; in *Caucasia*, 70;
color-blind, 25; growth and strength
of multiracial African Americans and,
2; Jim Crow, 2; neo-racism, 27; white
racism, 20, 41–43, 51, 155–57

Racist laws: antimiscegenation laws, 11,

19–20; blackness and, 2–3; *Loving v. Virginia*, 20; *Plessy vs. Ferguson*, 13–14

Representations of blackness and mixed-race/multiraciality, 1–2, 5–6, 31, 157; antimiscegenation law and, 11, 19–20; in *The Birth of a Nation*, 14–17; burden of, 62; chronological genealogy of, 10; conservative backlash of 1980s and, 23; defined, 3; Du Bois's critique of racist, 14; in film, 100; as floating signifiers of flexible race, 26; forms of, 3; gendering of as female, 20–21; historic image of, 11–13, 20–28; hopeful representations of during era of civil rights legislation, 23; Jennifer Beals in the popular press and, 63–65; lived experience of true diversity of multiraciality versus, 3–4, 30–31, 61, 157; *Loving vs. Virginia* and, 22; mixed race women as signifiers of mixed-race blackness, 5; overview of, 6; popular culture and, 3; positive, 66, 169; post-racial and post-feminism and, 167–69; as racialized expression, 3; racial tensions and, 170; searching for "racial truths" and, 32; sexuality and, 3, 12; transcending blackness and, 4, 7, 20, 34, 167–69; U.S. census as, 29–30; visual, 3; works examined in book, 31, 34, 168–69. *See also America's Next Top Model*; *Caucasia*; Exceptional multiracial; *The L Word*; *Mixing Nia*; New millennium mulatta; New millennium multiracial; Race girl; Televisual representation; Tragic mulattas

Reproduction, 12, 164–65; Bette Porter and, 49–55, 58

Reuter, Edward, 17

Sad race girl: in *Caucasia*, 67, 69–72, 76, 82, 89–91; tragic mulatta and, 20

Scrubs, use of mulatto on, 8

Senna, Danzy, 32, 67, 70, 85–86, 111; on Elemeno (secret language), 77–78; as exceptional multiracial, 82, 89; "The Mulatto Millennium" essay, 4, 82–83; photo of, 88. *See also Caucasia*

Sex and sexuality, 14–19, 71; of Birdie, 71, 81–82, 89–90; in *The Birth of a Nation*,

14–15; interracial, 11–13; lesbian representation on *The L Word*, 60–61; of Mariah Carey, 163; mixed-race African Americans and, 33, 169; mixed-race African American women and, 98–99; in *Mixing Nia*, 98–100, 106, 111–12, 123, 164; passing and, 60; post-feminism and, 27; representations of multiraciality and mulattoes and, 2–3, 12–14, 31; sexual passing of Bette Porter, 60; tragic mulattas and, 5, 31, 40, 47, 89; transcending blackness and, 4. *See also* Gendered performance

Simpson, O. J., 41–42

Slavery, 11–13, 21

Smith, Cherise, 149–50

Smith, Valerie, 2–3

Stereotypes: in *America's Next Top Model*, 135, 137, 140, 148; of angry black woman, 60; dialectical exceptional and new millennium multiracial, 4; in *Mixing Nia*, 98, 101–3, 107–8, 110, 119; of new millennium mulatto, 4–5; of threatening black masculinity, 159; of tragic mulatta, 2, 5, 119

Stonequist, Everett, 17

Structural racial inequalities. *See* Racial inequalities

Swan, Alison, 96, 99–100, 117–18, 119. *See also Mixing Nia*

Sykes, Wanda, 8–9

Televisual representation, 31–32, 45, 60, 129, 131, 137, 144, 169. *See also by* film; show

Terminology. *See under* Race; Racialized terminology

Tina (TV character from *The L Word*), 47–48, 50–54, 56

Tragic mulatta, 11, 20–21, 102–3, 161; Bette Porter as, 6, 31, 40, 46, 48, 55–56, 66; Birdie in *Caucasia* and, 32, 89, 91; filmic past of, 98–100; in *Imitation of Life*, 17–19, 99–100; Jennifer Beals as, 65; Mariah Carey as, 164; in *The Mulatto in the United States*, 17; new millennium mulattas and, 31, 57; punishment of, 40; sad race girl and,

Ralina L. Joseph is associate professor of communication
at the University of Washington.

Library of Congress Cataloging-in-Publication Data
Joseph, Ralina L. (Ralina Landwehr), 1974–
Transcending Blackness : from the new millennium
mulatta to the exceptional multiracial / Ralina L. Joseph.
p. cm.
Includes bibliographical references and index.
ISBN 978-0-8223-5277-8 (cloth : alk. paper)
ISBN 978-0-8223-5292-1 (pbk. : alk. paper)
1. Racially mixed people—Race identity—United States.
2. African American women—Race identity.
3. Racism in mass media. 4. Minorities in mass media.
I. Title.
P94.5.M552U6475 2013
305.8'0500973—dc23 2012011639